AMERICAN
HISTORY

A.S.A.P.*

*As Soon As Possible,
As Simple As Possible

AMERICAN HISTORY

A.S.A.P.*

*As Soon As Possible,
As Simple As Possible

Alan Axelrod, Ph.D.

PRENTICE HALL PRESS

Prentice Hall Press
Published by The Berkley Publishing Group
A division of Penguin Group (USA) Inc.
375 Hudson Street
New York, New York 10014

Prentice Hall Press edition: August 2003

Library of Congress Cataloging-in-Publication Data

Axelrod, Alan, 1952–
American history A.S.A.P : as soon as possible,
as simple as possible / Alan Axelrod.
p.   cm.
ISBN 0-7352-0305-9
1. United States—History—Miscellanea.
2. United States—History—Chronology.   I. Title.

E179.A95 2003
973—dc21
2003043611

Printed in the United States of America

For Anita
All I really need

Contents

What This Is and What This Isn't

The best way to explain the purpose of this book is to examine the tail end of its title: *A.S.A.P.*—"As Soon as Possible," and "As Simple as Possible." The "soon" and the "simple" parts are key, of course, but so is the "as possible." For the goal is to deliver, in an informal, enjoyable, and highly efficient one-stop source, all the American history the general reader needs to stake a legitimate claim to cultural literacy. This much and no more, but no less, either—which is what is meant by "as simple as possible."

American History A.S.A.P. is not a compact narrative history of the United States, nor is it a brief encyclopedia. Instead, it selects 200 events that everyone needs to know about American history and uses them as sturdy springboards to related events and, even more important, to the ideas, concepts, and themes that underlie and inform American history. There are just 200 events here, but they are leveraged into a full-scale appreciation of American history from the Ice Age to September 11, 2001, and beyond.

40,000 B.C.
(approximately)

The First Immigrants

A glance at a map of Alaska shows that North America and Asia are separated by a mere fifty-five miles of the Bering Sea. Now, fifty-five miles in some of the coldest water on the planet is a long swim, but it's not much of an ocean voyage, and if the geologists and paleontologists are right, there was a time when you didn't even need a boat. During the Quaternary Period (that is, the last two million years), a "land bridge" emerged in the Bering and Chukchi Seas as the sea level dropped because of the expansion of the ice cap surrounding the North Pole. It is believed that anywhere from 45,000 to 10,000 years ago, people used the Bering land bridge to enter the New World, emigrating from what is now northeast Asia to northwestern North America. Beringia, as the land bridge is sometimes called, disappeared when the major continental ice sheets and other glaciers melted, causing the sea level to rise again and thereby separate Asia from North America.

It is not that, 45,000 years ago or so, a group of Asians decided to take an evening's stroll. The trek across Beringia must have spanned thousands of years of settlement and re-

> **What was the** population of "Native America" some 10,000 years ago? In the area that is the present-day United States, it is generally estimated that the Native American population reached 11 million—although estimates vary from about 8.4 million to 112 million. For comparison, in 1990, 1,959,234 Indians, including Eskimos and Aleuts, lived in the United States, and the Native American population is growing at a rate of 3.8 percent per year.

settlement. Presumably, the land mass supported such Arctic vegetation as dry grasslands and boreal forests, which supplied adequate food for grazing animals, including the horse and the reindeer, as well as such Ice Age species as the mastodon and the woolly rhinoceros. As the animal herds ate their way southward, the hunting-and-gathering migrants followed, across Beringia, then fanned out onto what we now call North America. By approximately 9000 B.C., it is likely that some of these former Asians reached Patagonia, at the southern tip of South America. The human population of the New World was complete.

5500 B.C.

The Anasazi ("Ancient Ones")

No written records exist of the vast American history that preceded October 12, 1492, the day Christopher Columbus landed in the Caribbean. Assuming a prehistoric population of about 11 million, it is most likely that early Native Americans were very thinly distributed over a vast area in bands of a hundred or even fewer individuals living on the ragged edge of subsistence. About 9,000 years ago, perhaps, some bands began to domesticate plants, and by the end of the fifteenth century—when the Europeans first arrived—Indians were cultivating maize, beans, squash, manioc, potatoes, and grains. Farming created a more stable and settled lifestyle than subsistence hunting and gathering. With stability came the time and resources to create *things*.

In the American Southwest, the Anasazi (from a Navajo word meaning "the ancient ones") appeared as early as 5500 B.C. Today, they are sometimes called the Basket Makers, because of the many beautifully woven baskets that have been discovered in sites associated with their culture. The Anasazi built communal dwellings, some of them of wood and thatch, and some no more than shallow caves closed off with rocks. By A.D. 400 to 700, the Anasazi settlements were becoming genuine communities, collections of pit houses, built over shallow excavations. From about 700 to 1100, the Anasazi started building what the Spanish invaders would later call pueblos (Spanish for "town" or "village" and also "people"). The Hopi and the Navajo today revere the Anasazi as the ancestors of the native people of the West.

Works of the Mound Builders

From the Appalachian Mountains to the eastern edge of the midwestern prairies, and from the Great Lakes to the Gulf of Mexico, from roughly 1000 B.C. until sometime after A.D. 1500, various Indian societies constructed great earthworks. These ranged from relatively simple burial mounds to elaborate temple mounds (which served as the foundations for important public and private buildings), as well as circular and geometric ceremonial earthworks.

What archaeologists call the Woodland Mounds were built in eastern North America from about 1000 B.C. to the beginning of the eighteenth century. The most impressive surviving examples are the mounds of the Hopewell people, so-called because the structures they raised were discovered at Hopewell, Ohio. Another type of mound was built by people of the "Mississippian" culture. These structures were actually villages consisting of palisades and flat-topped, rectangular mounds that served not for burial but as the foundations of temples and other important structures. The Cahokia Mounds in Illinois, just across the Mississippi River from present-day St. Louis, must have once contained as many as fifty platform mounds and probably supported a population numbering in the thousands.

The Norse Landings

n 986, a Norse navigator, Bjarni Herjulfsson—blown off course on his way to Greenland—sighted the North American continent. He made note of it, which may or may not have influenced another Norseman, Leif Ericson, who landed on the continent in the year 1000. Ericson established a settlement he called Vinland on Newfoundland, probably at the place now known as L'Anse aux Meadows.

During 1004–1008, Leif's brothers, Thorvald and Thorstein, explored more of the continent, and they may even have reached modern New England. Then, between 1010 and 1013, an Icelandic trader named Thorfinn Karlsefni visited the North American coast, and it is quite possible that Freydis, Leif Ericson's sister, sailed with Thorfinn to the New World in 1014–1015.

And then . . . ?

Well, apparently not very much. North America made so little impression on the people of Europe that no one thought of bothering with it for another 500 years, making the Norse explorations of the New World perhaps the most important *non*events in American history.

1492

Columbus Sails to America

C hristopher Columbus, though born to a Genoa weaver in 1451, had no interest in his father's trade and, early in life, took to the sea. Unlike most seafarers of his day, he learned to read, and he devoured all he could find concerning westward sea voyages. His reading persuaded him that the world was round—something most well-educated people believed in the fifteenth century, but, then again, the vast majority of fifteenth-century Europeans were not well educated. Although Columbus neither "discovered" nor "proved" the roundness of the Earth, he came up with the boldly original idea of using that roundness to go east by sailing west. The East—Asia—presented many trading opportunities, but, most important, it was the land of spice, which, in an era before refrigeration, was the sovereign element of food preservation and palatability. As such, spice was more precious than gold. Fifteenth-century trade routes from Europe to Asia lay mostly overland and were slow, dangerous, and costly. The nation that could find a sea route to the lands of spice would become a mighty nation indeed.

Yet Columbus had a monumentally hard time selling his idea to those who could authorize and finance a voyage. King John II of Portugal turned him down, in part because he thought Columbus had underestimated the circumference of the Earth—which, in fact, he had. Columbus misused data from Marco Polo's travels in China, fudged them with the gross miscalculations of the Greek astronomer Ptolemy (ca. 100–170), then bolstered all of this with the bad guesswork of the Florentine cosmographer Paolo dal

Pozzo Toscanelli. He concluded that Japan—his proposed destination—was just 5,000 miles *west* of Portugal.

Booted by the Portuguese monarch, Columbus moved on to Don Enrique de Guzmán, duke of Medina Sidonia, who likewise turned him down. He next approached Don Luis de la Cerda, Count of Medina Celi, who was sufficiently impressed to arrange an audience, on or about May 1, 1486, with Queen Isabella I of Castile. But it was not until 1492, and only thanks to the influence of a courtier named Luis de Santangel, that Isabella and her royal consort Ferdinand finally agreed to sponsor the voyage.

On August 3, 1492, Columbus sailed from Palos on ships that were small even by the standards of the day, the *Niña* (Vincente Yáñez Pinzón, captain), the *Pinta* (skippered by Vincente's brother, Martin Alonso Pinzón), and his own flagship, the *Santa Maria*. For about a month and a half, it was smooth sailing, driven by highly favorable winds. Then, between September 20 and September 30, the winds died, progress all but halted, crews grumbled. Columbus began to keep two logbooks. One, intended for the crew, brimmed with fictitious computations of distances; the other, kept secret, consisted of accurate figures. This trip was taking *much* longer than Columbus had expected, and, to the crew, each day without sight of land seemed to prove their captain was very, very wrong. The men spoke of sailing off the edge of a flat Earth and of being swallowed up by demons. Even those who believed no such thing rightly feared endless drift and eventual starvation.

By the time land was sighted on October 12, 1492, it is doubtful Columbus could have held his crew off a day longer. Landfall came at a place the natives called Guanahani and Columbus named San Salvador.

> **Most modern historians** believe Columbus touched land at present-day Watling Island, although, in 1986, a group of scholars suggested that the true landfall was another Bahamian island, Samana Cay, 65 miles south of Watling.

Columbus and his crew were greeted by Arawak tribespeople, who welcomed them in a most friendly fashion. Now, Columbus had sailed about 3,900 miles, and he believed Japan was 5,000 miles from Spain. Yet he persuaded himself that he had reached Asia, known as the "Indies," so he called the people he met *Indians*, and, from San Salvador, he sailed to Cuba, believing that he would find there the court of the Mongol emperor of China (for he at least understood that he had not reached Japan) and, with the emperor, he intended to negotiate an agreement for trade in spices and gold.

In Cuba, of course, he found no emperor, so he set off for Hispaniola (modern Santo Domingo, Dominican Republic), where, in a Christmas Day storm, the *Santa Maria* was wrecked near Cap Haitien. Columbus deposited his crew onto the shore, determined that here, too, the "Indians" were friendly, and, leaving a garrison of thirty-nine at the place he decided to call La Navidad in honor of the holiday, set off on his return to Spain on January 16, 1493, sailing on the *Niña*.

1493

The Letter of Columbus

Returning from what would be the first of four voyages to the New World, Columbus paused on February 15, 1493, at the Spanish-controlled Canary Islands to replenish supplies and to send a letter to Luis de Santangel announcing nothing less than the discovery of a New World.

When the precious letter reached him, Santangel instantly recognized its importance and wasted no time publishing it to the world, and it is this letter as much as the deed itself that made Columbus's voyage of 1492 so important in American history. After all, he wasn't the first European to visit the New World. What about those Norsemen 500 years earlier? But none of them had written home about it, and nobody much cared about what they had found. It was Columbus's letter of February 15, 1493, that brought the New World to the Old, and set into motion American history as we know it.

1493

The First Euro–Indian War

In countless poems, plays, histories, textbooks, and movies, Columbus is portrayed as the "discoverer" of America. Discounting the Norse voyages of half a millennium earlier, this is true enough—from the point of view of Euro-America. But from the perspective of the *Americans*—that is, the people Columbus misnamed "Indians"—Columbus was not a discoverer, but an invader, in whose wake violence and oppression were quick to follow.

When he departed La Navidad to return to Spain, Columbus left on the island a Spanish garrison of thirty-nine men. No sooner had he departed than the members of the garrison began stealing the natives' things and molesting the local women. The Indians, whose friendliness Columbus had misjudged as timidity, retaliated by night, murdering ten Spaniards as they slept. Then they hunted down the rest of the garrison. When Columbus returned in November 1493, on his second voyage to the New World, no Spaniard was left alive. It was the beginning of 400 years of almost continuous warfare between Europeans (and, later, Americans) and Native Americans. For while Columbus had "discovered" a *new* world, he also set into motion a very *old* process, the ancient engine of history itself, a hard-grinding machine that turns contact into conquest.

1540

Coronado's Quest for
the Seven Cities of Gold

The conquistador Hernan Cortés conquered the Aztec empire of Mexico in 1521 and became a man of unimaginable wealth and power. His exploits ignited the hope that somewhere else in the New World another golden Aztec empire would be found. This hope was fostered by something the Indians had told Columbus years earlier: tales of villages that held vast treasuries of gold. Alvar Nuñez Cabeza de Vaca, a member of an ill-fated expedition led by Cortés's rival, Panfilo de Narvaez, wandered throughout the American Southwest for eight years beginning in 1520 and brought back to Spain accounts of fabulously rich pueblos, the "Seven Cities of Cibola," although he himself had not seen them. One survivor of the Narvaez expedition, a black slave named Estevan, joined an expedition led by Marcos de Niza in 1539 to locate the Seven Cities. Zuni Indians killed the unfortunate Estevan in a battle outside the Hawikuh pueblo, but Marcos returned to Mexico City and there rendered a vivid account of the pueblo and its treasures. It was true that Marcos had not himself entered Hawikuh, but Estevan had. Of course, he was dead.

Driven by these rumors, Francisco Vasquez de Coronado traveled throughout the Southwest, as far as present-day Kansas, during 1540–1542. In July 1540, he and his troops rode into Hawikuh and, in conquistador fashion, demanded the surrender of the pueblo. In response, the traditionally peaceful Zuni showered Coronado with stones, one of which knocked him unconscious. Within an hour, however, Hawikuh fell to the Spaniards, who, with great anticipation, rode into the village, and there they found—very little indeed. Hawikuh had no gold.

So Coronado continued his quest for the Seven Cities of Cibola. He traveled through the pueblo region along the Rio Grande, capturing one town after another, forcing the inhabitants into slavery and taking from them whatever food and shelter he required. His experience in the Southwest was typical of the early Spanish period of exploration, driven by dreams of wealth, guided by a ruthless disregard for the natives of the country. But with Coronado's disappointment, the legend of the Seven Cities of Cibola dimmed, as did Spain's interest in the American Southwest. More than a half century passed before the ambitious newly appointed governor of New Spain, Don Juan de Oñate, led an expedition in 1598 from Mexico City into the American Southwest. He reached the site of present-day El Paso, Texas, and claimed for Spain—as well as for his own governance and (he hoped) enrichment—all of "New Mexico," a region extending from Texas to California. Spain's North American empire was born.

The "Lost Colony" of Roanoke

With the blessing of Queen Elizabeth I, Sir Humphrey Gilbert became the first Englishman to set sail for America in 1579. Forced to return when his fleet broke up in a storm, he embarked again in June 1583 and reached St. John's Bay, Newfoundland, in August, claiming that territory for the queen. On the return voyage, Gilbert's overloaded ship sank, and his royal charter passed to his half brother, Sir Walter Raleigh, age 31, and already a favorite of the queen.

In 1584, Raleigh sent a small reconnaissance fleet to America, which probed a place that would later be called Croatan Sound in the Outer Banks of North Carolina. The expedition returned with enthusiastic reports of a land inhabited by "most gentle, loving and faithful" Indians, who lived "after the manner of the Golden Age." Raleigh asked his queen's permission to name the new land for her. She suggested calling it "Virginia," to memorialize her status as the "Virgin Queen."

In 1585–1586, Raleigh dispatched Sir Richard Grenville with a small group of settlers to colonize Virginia. The great British sailor-adventurer Sir Francis Drake encountered this group a year later, starving and wanting nothing so much as passage back to England. Not one to be discouraged, Raleigh launched a larger expedition of three ships carrying 117 men, women, and children. They landed at what is now Roanoke Island, off the coast of North Carolina, in 1587. Their leader, John White, chose a particularly dismal spot on this swampy island to establish his colonists, then, after a time, decided to return to England to fetch the tardy supplies Raleigh had promised to send. (Unknown to White, the supply ships were stalled because of the attack of the Spanish Armada against England.) When White returned to the colony in 1590, he found no settlers and only the barest trace of there ever having been a settlement—a few rusted implements and what he took to be the name of a neighboring island carved into the trunk of a tree: CROATOAN.

What had happened? Did the colonists all sicken and die on this pestilential island? Did they starve? Or did not so "gentle, loving and faithful" Indians kill them or take them captive to a place called "Croatoan"? White didn't know, and he never found out. No one has. And thus, with a disaster as miserable as it was mysterious, began the most important phase of the European colonization of what would become the United States.

1607

Founding of Jamestown

The first English attempts to settle in America were not part of some titanic government effort to colonize the New World. They were business ventures, and fairly modest ones at that. In 1605, two groups of merchants—the Virginia Company of London (also called the London Company) and the Plymouth Company—petitioned King James I for a charter to establish a colony in Virginia. Such matters were handled pretty loosely back then, and, as far as anyone knew, Raleigh's Virginia patent took in whatever parts of North America Spain had not already claimed. The Virginia Company was granted a charter to colonize southern Virginia, while the Plymouth Company was given rights to northern Virginia.

The Virginia Company quickly recruited 144 settlers, among them the families of moneyed gentlemen as well as poor people. Since passage to America wasn't free, the poor folk purchased their places on the ship and in the colony by binding themselves to serve the Virginia Company as indentured servants for a period of seven years, working the land and creating a settlement.

In December 1606, this small band of men, women, and children boarded the *Susan Constant*, the *Discovery*, and the *Goodspeed*. Travel in the tiny, filthy ships of the day was a terrible ordeal, and that 39 of the colonists died en route was hardly remarkable. The 105 survivors arrived at the mouth of a river—they called it the James, to honor their king—on May 24, 1607. No sooner had they landed than they began to scratch out Jamestown.

As history would see it, Jamestown was "the first permanent English colony" in the New World. "Permanent," however, may be too strong a word. For Jamestown was staked out in a malaria-infested swamp, and the colonists had landed in late spring, well past the season for planting. Moreover, not all of the colonists—the "gentlemen," those who had paid cash to come to America and were indentured to no one—were willing or even able to do the hard work needed to start a farm, let alone with bare hands to hack a colony out of a wilderness. While many colonists worked tirelessly, just as many did not, and many died or disappeared. Within a few months of the landing, half of the settlers were dead or had run off into the woods, to meet whatever fate the local Indians might offer. Then things got worse. By 1609, famine drove some to cannibalism, even to looting fresh graves for food.

Jamestown would probably have met the fate of the "lost colony" of Roanoke had it not been for the soldier of fortune the Virginia Company had hired to look after the military defense of the colony. Captain John Smith ingratiated himself with the local Indians, people the English called the Powhatans, after the name they also applied to their aged but powerful chief. Smith was able to obtain enough corn and yams from the Powhatans to keep the surviving colonists from starving. Smith also assumed dictatorial powers over the colony, ruling it by martial law: Those who worked, he decreed, would eat. Those who did not work would starve. This dictum, combined with the charity of the Powhatans, saved Jamestown and established the English in America.

Champlain Stakes France's Claim

Europe made its first significant contact with the New World in 1492, but it took many years before the Europeans began to see America for what it was and what it had to offer. When the search for cities of gold failed, some began looking for a "Northwest Passage" to Asia, a way to cut through the unknown continent to the known riches of the East. En route, many wanderers ended up farming. The French were even more immediately attracted by another resource: fur. By the early seventeenth century, fashion dictated the use of fur not only to line warm coats, but as trim on collars, cuffs, and fancy hats. People were willing to pay, and fur became an increasingly valuable commodity. Who needed gold? Who needed a passage to India?

Cardinal Richelieu (1585–1642), the strategist behind the throne of the weak-willed King Louis XIII, needed cash to finance his ongoing campaign to make France the dominant power in Europe. Seeing opportunity in America, Richelieu hired Samuel de Champlain (ca. 1570–1635) to probe the waters of North America and to explore inland. During the seven voyages he made between 1603 and 1616, Champlain mapped the northern reaches of the continent, accurately charting the Atlantic coast from the Bay of Fundy to Cape Cod. He also established settlements and got the French fur trade off to a most promising start. In July 1608, Champlain directed the digging of a ditch and the erection of a stockade. He called this Quebec, and it was the nucleus of French settlement in North America.

Hudson Sails for the Dutch

Henry Hudson was a British master mariner—such men proudly called themselves "sea dogs"—who sold his services to the Dutch and, in their employ, sailed his *Half Moon* out of Amsterdam, bound for the New World. Like so many other explorers before and after him, Hudson's primary mission was to find a "Northwest Passage," a watercourse through America and directly to the Pacific and the spice-rich Asian trade.

Hudson explored the Chesapeake Bay, then sailed north, encountering a great palisaded river that would be named for him. He sailed the Hudson as far as the location of present-day Albany, but, finding that the river was not subject to tides, he concluded that it was a dead end. He returned to Holland, then came back to the New World two years later to press on with the search for the Northwest Passage. His discouraged crew mutinied and cast him adrift in an open boat on what would be called Hudson Bay. He disappeared—without knowing that he had explored the site of what would become one of the great cities of the world, richer and more fantastic than any in Asia: New York.

The Pocahontas Story

Once they were on their feet, the settlers of Jamestown proved remarkably ungrateful to the Indians who had been their salvation. In 1613, Captain Samuel Argall kidnapped the chief's daughter, presumably in a move intended to intimidate Chief Powhatan and his people. Her given name was Matoaka, but Powhatan and others called her Pocahontas, which the English translated as "Little Wanton," a description of her playful ways. Argall took her as a hostage to Jamestown and, later, to a new village, Henrico. Yet, unafraid, she never behaved like a hostage. Instead, fascinated by the English, she quickly learned their language and customs. Soon, she was no hostage, but an ambassador or, rather, a mediator between the English and her own people. Among Europeans, it was customary for the families of rival nations to marry in order to bring peace. In 1614, with the blessing of Powhatan, Pocahontas married John Rolfe, a tobacco planter. This brought eight years of uninterrupted peace between the colonists and the Powhatans, a period crucial to the growth of the colony, which became a thriving exporter of the New World's first cash crop, tobacco.

As for Pocahontas, Rolfe took his bride back to England, where she was an instant hit with London society and became a favorite of the royal court. She and Rolfe were genuinely in love, though, sadly, their bliss did not last long. Pocahontas, one of the most remarkable women in American history, succumbed to an illness and died in England on March 21, 1617, at the age of twenty-two.

Very little is known about Pocahontas, who has nevertheless fascinated generations of Americans. Most famous of the tantalizing stories concerning her is the tale of how she saved the life of Captain John Smith. The original version was related in *A History of the Settlement of Virginia,* by the early seventeenth-century Virginia merchant Thomas Studley and Smith himself:

At last they brought Captain Smith to Powhatan, their emperor. Here more than two hundred of those grim courtiers stood wondering at Smith as if he had been a monster. . . . Before a fire, and upon a seat like a bedstead, Powhatan sat covered with a great robe made of raccoon skins with all the tails hanging. . . .

At Captain Smith's entrance before the king all the people gave a great shout. The queen was appointed to bring him water to wash his hands, and another brought him a bunch of feathers, instead of a towel, on which to dry them. Having feasted him after the best barbarous manner they could, a long consultation was held. At last two great stones were brought before Powhatan. Then as many as could lay hands on Captain Smith dragged him to the stones, and laid his head on them, and were ready with their clubs to beat out his brains. At this instant, Pocahontas, the king's dearest daughter, when no entreaty could prevail, got his head in her arms, and laid her own head upon his to save him from death. . . .

1619

Slavery Comes to America

Almost immediately after Columbus "discovered" America in 1492, Europeans immersed themselves in the mythology of a *new* world, the notion that they had found a pristine place, a place for humanity to get a fresh start, a place that represented the future and yet also recalled Eden as it must have been before the fall. What those early mythologists failed to comprehend, however, is that simply traveling to a new world does not create new minds and new morality. In 1607, English men and women planted Jamestown, the first permanent English colony in America, and just twelve years later, in August 1619, Virginia tobacco farmers bought their first consignment of twenty slaves from Dutch traders.

While the twenty slaves brought to Virginia were the first introduced into what would become the United States, they were not the first brought to the New World. By 1619, Spanish and Portuguese slave traders had already transported more than a million Africans to their Caribbean and South American colonies.

> **During the 1600s,** a slave could be purchased in Africa for about $25 and sold in America for $125.

The planters who came to the New World from Spain and Portugal were typically wealthy and could afford many slaves. In contrast, most of the English farmers who settled in Virginia and New England lacked the means to buy many African slaves. At first, indentured servitude, whereby English men and women bound themselves to a *limited* period of service in return for passage to the New World, was a far more common source of cheap labor than African slaves. By the end of the seventeenth century, however, the price of slaves began to fall, even as the wealth of American planters increased. It now made economic sense to invest in a slave who, though he or she cost twice as much as an indentured servant, would yield not seven years of labor, but more than a lifetime; for the children of slaves were born slaves, and their children likewise.

1620

Voyage of the "Pilgrims"

The Spanish came to America in search of gold, empire, and souls to recruit for the Catholic Church. The English who settled Jamestown and the rest of Virginia were moved by commercial enthusiasm, but, farther north, in New England, English settlement was motivated mostly by a desire for religious freedom.

Not many years after Henry VIII, during 1536–1540, created a Church of England separate from the Roman Catholic Church, a growing minority of English Protestants began to criticize what they considered immoral compromises made with Catholic practice. These people felt that the mainstream Anglican church had not gone far enough in reforming worship, and when King James I ascended the throne in 1603, these religious reformers—called Puritans because they advocated a new purity of religious practice—clamored for major changes in the Anglican Church. James refused, and the Anglican archbishop, William Laud, initiated a campaign of persecution against the Puritans. Some Puritans chose to remain in England, where they formed an increasingly powerful political bloc and would ultimately fight a successful civil war against the crown. Others left England for Holland, celebrated for its religious toleration. These, called Separatists, were mostly farmers, poorly educated and of lowly social status; Puritanism appealed to few aristocrats.

The Separatist congregation of Scrooby, Nottinghamshire, was led by William Brewster and the Reverend Richard Clifton. They brought their flock from Scrooby to Amsterdam in 1608, then, the following year, moved to another Dutch town, Leyden, where they lived for a dozen years. Although treated with tolerance by the Dutch, these groups were beset by economic hardship and were disturbed by the prospect of their children growing up Dutch rather than English. Therefore, in 1617, some of them voted to strike out for America.

The Scrooby–Leyden congregation secured a pair of royal patents authorizing them to settle in the northern part of the American territory belonging to the Virginia Company. Somewhat less than half of the congregation finally decided to embark. One hundred two souls piled into a single vessel, the *Mayflower*, on September 16, 1620. Fewer than half of these passengers were Separatists. The rest, whom the Separatists referred to as Strangers, belonged to no particular religious group and simply sought new opportunity in the New World. After a sixty-five-day voyage, the Pilgrims (for so their first historian and early leader, William Bradford, would later label them) sighted land on November 19.

Here, the story gets a bit cloudy. The Pilgrims themselves claimed that rough seas off Nantucket forced the *Mayflower*'s skipper, Captain Christopher Jones, to steer away from the mouth of the Hudson River, where, according to the terms of their patent, the Pilgrims were supposed to establish their "plantation." He landed instead at Cape Cod, in present-day Massachusetts, *beyond* the Virginia Company's jurisdiction. This fact has led many modern historians to conclude that the "wrong turn" was no accident, but, rather, the result of a Pilgrim bribe. The Separatists *wanted* to ensure independence from the external authority of the Virginia Company. Whether by accident or design, then, the *Mayflower* dropped anchor off present-day Provincetown, Massachusetts, on November 21.

The "*Mayflower* Compact"— The First American Constitution

Small as it was, the band that rode at anchor off the Massachusetts coast was not united. There were the Separatists— the Pilgrims—but there were also the so-called "Strangers," who were not beholden to the Separatists and who were united

The *Mayflower* Compact, 1620

IN THE NAME OF GOD, AMEN. We, whose names are underwritten, the Loyal Subjects of our dread Sovereign Lord King James, by the Grace of God, of Great Britain, France, and Ireland, King, Defender of the Faith, &c. Having undertaken for the Glory of God, and Advancement of the Christian Faith, and the Honour of our King and Country, a Voyage to plant the first Colony in the northern Parts of Virginia; Do by these Presents, solemnly and mutually, in the Presence of God and one another, covenant and combine ourselves together into a civil Body Politick, for our better Ordering and Preservation, and Furtherance of the Ends aforesaid: And by Virtue hereof do enact, constitute, and frame, such just and equal Laws, Ordinances, Acts, Constitutions, and Officers, from time to time, as shall be thought most meet and convenient for the general Good of the Colony; unto which we promise all due Submission and Obedience. IN WITNESS whereof we have hereunto subscribed our names at Cape-Cod the eleventh of November, in the Reign of our Sovereign Lord King James, of England, France, and Ireland, the eighteenth, and of Scotland the fifty-fourth, Anno Domini; 1620.

among themselves by nothing more than a desire for economic opportunity. Moreover, neither the Pilgrims nor the Strangers had a *legal* right to settle here, beyond the boundary of their charter.

The two groups decided to resolve the first problem and, by declaring allegiance to King James I, clear the way to a resolution of the second problem. They gathered below decks and drew up the "*Mayflower* Compact," the first constitution written in North America. Very brief, its purpose was to create a "Civil Body Politic" and a set of laws for the good of the colony.

1620

Plymouth Rock Landing

After the "*Mayflower* Compact" was signed, Captain Jones probed for a likely landing and found Plymouth Harbor, on the western side of Cape Cod Bay. An advance party set foot on shore—supposedly on a rock now carved with the year 1620 and enshrined in a modest tabernacle—on December 21. The main body of settlers disembarked on December 26.

Religiously inspired, they saw themselves as guided to this spot by God's providence. Yet whether Plymouth had been chosen by God, by accident, or by the Pilgrims themselves, the wayfarers could hardly have found a less favorable place or time for their landing. There were no ample harbors here—so trade would always be limited—and the flinty, ungenerous soil promised little fertility. As for the time of the landing, a characteristically bitter New England winter already had the land in its iron grip. During the first winter at Plymouth, more than half of the tiny colony would die.

1621

The First Thanksgiving

In contrast to the settlers of Jamestown, many of whom were "gentlemen" unaccustomed and unwilling to work, most of the Plymouth colonists were yeoman farmers, led by tough, able men. But hard work, a passion for liberty, and able leadership would not alone have brought the colony through its first dreadful winter. It was the charity of the neighboring Wampanoag Indians that saved the Pilgrims. Two Indians in particular, Squanto (a Pawtuxet living among the Wampanoags) and Samoset (an Abnaki), gave the newcomers hands-on help in planting crops and building shelters. Samoset also introduced the settlers to Massasoit, principal leader of the Wampanoags (with whom Edward Winslow negotiated an important treaty), and Squanto served as interpreter between the chief and the Pilgrim leaders.

In the fall of 1621, the Pil-

To this day, some Virginians lay claim to the first Thanksgiving, citing a collective prayer of thanksgiving offered on December 4, 1619, by members of the Berkeley plantation near modern Charles City, Virginia. George Washington proclaimed the first national Thanksgiving Day on November 26, 1789, but it wasn't until 1863 that Abraham Lincoln made Thanksgiving an official annual holiday, to be commemorated on the last Thursday in November. Between 1939 and 1941, by proclamation of Franklin D. Roosevelt, the day was celebrated on the third Thursday in November, but then was returned by act of Congress to the date set by Lincoln.

grims invited their Indian neighbors—and saviors—to a feast in celebration of the first harvest, the bounty of which was in no small measure due to Indian aid and expertise. It is this event that we usually identify as the first Thanksgiving.

Dutch Settlement Begins

Of all the peoples of Europe, the Dutch of the seventeenth century were perhaps the greatest traders. Their activities had made Amsterdam the busiest and wealthiest city in Europe, and in 1621 Dutch merchants incorporated the Dutch West India Company with the intention of dominating trade in the New World.

Holland soon displaced Portugal as the leading trader in sugar and slaves, and, in 1624, the Dutch penetrated the fur market by opening up a trading post, Fort Orange, at the site of present-day Albany, New York. Two years after this, Peter Minuit became governor-general of New Netherland, as the Dutch colony was called. He purchased from the Manhattan Indians, a local subtribe of the Delawares, the Hudson River island named for them, paying in trade goods valued at sixty guilders. The Dutch founded a village at the mouth of the Hudson, calling it New Amsterdam. This town would become not only a center of trade, but of immigration. Whereas the English Puritans of New England were loath to welcome strangers, the cosmopolitan Dutch of New Amsterdam threw open the settlement to all comers. Manhattan (such was the Indian name of the island on whose southern tip New Amsterdam had been settled) became home to a polyglot assortment of residents, even as New York City is today.

At the prevailing exchange rate, 60 Dutch guilders was the equivalent of 2,400 English pennies, and so it is traditionally said that Manhattan was purchased for the sum of $24. Even factoring in almost 400 years of inflation, it was a bargain.

1638

Individual Liberty—
Anne Hutchinson Takes a Stand

B orn in Alford, Lincolnshire, England, in 1591, Anne Marbury married a merchant, William Hutchinson, in 1612. She sailed with him to Boston in 1634, eager to follow the Puritan minister she most respected, the Reverend John Cotton, who had recently left for New England.

Expecting religious enlightenment in the Massachusetts Bay Colony, what Hutchinson found were ministers devoted far less to affairs of the spirit than to the dry duty of prayer, fasting, and iron self-discipline. Hungry for something more, and noting that the male members of Boston's church met regularly after sermons to discuss the Bible, Hutchinson started to hold similar meetings for women in her own home. Although fully versed in the Bible and theology, Hutchinson espoused the radical point of view that mere conformity to religious laws was no proof of godliness. True spirituality derived not from ministers' sermons, from books, or even from the Bible itself, but came instead from an inner experience of the Holy Spirit. This gospel of inner revelation and total freedom of conscience began to draw a following, among men as well as women.

Perhaps inevitably, Hutchinson's growing popularity brought criticism from the church establishment. In time, what started as a difference in religious point of view became a gaping schism, one which threatened the political stability of the Massachusetts Bay Colony by challenging basic assumptions of religion and governance. As Hutchinson's opponents saw it, to question the church was to challenge the state. She was condemned as an "Antinomian," an adherent to the heretical doctrine that Christians are not bound by moral law. When the conservative John Winthrop became Bay Colony governor in 1637, he barred more "Antinomians" from settling in the colony, and he banned all private religious meetings. Hutchinson continued to hold her meetings and was charged with heresy. Winthrop described Hutchinson's meetings as "a thing not tolerable nor comely in the sight of God, nor fitting for your sex," and he accused her of breaking the Fifth Commandment by not honoring her father and mother—by which he meant, metaphorically, the magistrates of the colony.

At trial, Hutchinson proved more than the intellectual equal of Winthrop; however, she let her emotions get in the way. The Lord, she said, had revealed Himself to her, "upon a Throne of Justice." Take heed, she warned Winthrop, "God will ruin you and your posterity, and this whole State." With that, the governor pounced: "I am persuaded that the revelation she brings forth is delusion." The court voted to banish her from the colony, "as being a woman not fit for our society."

After another trial in the early spring of 1638, Hutchinson was excommunicated. Anne replied calmly: "The Lord judgeth not as man judgeth. Better to be cast out of the church than to deny Christ."

Fortunately for Anne Hutchinson, she was not the only spiritual outcast in New England. In 1636, Roger Williams, minister of the Puritan congregation in Salem, Massachusetts, was banished from the Bay Colony for having preached the ultimate authority of individual conscience—what he called "soul liberty"—for advocating toleration of all faiths, for seeking respect and fair treatment of the Indians, and for preaching the separation of church and state. "Forced religion," he said, "stinks in God's nostrils." Williams and his followers settled near Narragansett Bay, where they established the town of Providence in 1636, and then established the colony of Rhode Island, a haven of religious liberty.

Anne Hutchinson, with her husband, children, and sixty followers, moved to Rhode Island and purchased from the Narragansett chief Miantonomah the island of Aquidneck, which she called Peaceable Island. When her husband died in 1642, she took her children, except for the five eldest, to the Dutch colony in New Amsterdam, where she built a home on Pelham Bay (now in the Bronx, New York). Tragically, in August 1643, a band of Mahican Indians raided the house and slaughtered Anne Hutchinson and five of her youngest children, taking a sixth, Susanna, captive.

The murder of women like Anne Hutchinson was not an uncommon fate across the colonial frontier. Nevertheless, it was a sad end for the woman many credit as being among the first to lead the public fight for religious freedom, the sanctity of conscience, and women's rights.

1664

New Netherland Becomes New York

So much of the European settlement of the New World was wrapped in violence that the peacefulness with which Dutch New Netherland became British New York is rather astonishing. Toward the Indians, New Netherlanders had vacillated between friendly trade, barbaric cruelty (in the "Pavonia Massacre" of 1641, slaughtering Indian men, women, and children, then playing football in the streets of Manhattan with the severed heads of executed prisoners), and timid defensiveness. Relations with other colonies were similarly inconsistent, but relations between New Netherland and New England steadily deteriorated as the colonies competed for Indian loyalty and trade.

The Dutch military position was inferior to the English, but, even more important, the Dutch settlers were victims of the settlement scheme originally established by the Dutch West India Company. Dutch settlement was hampered by the patroon system, a policy that gave land ownership to absentee landlords who installed tenant farmers. Thus, New Netherland became mainly a colony of tenants, a fact that discouraged settlement and compromised patriotism, so that, by the 1660s, New Netherland was weak and torn by dissension. The irascible Dutch governor, Peter Stuyvesant, tried in vain to rally his countrymen when, on September 8, 1664, a fleet of British warships sailed up the Hudson. The Dutch colonists declined to offer resistance, and the frustrated Stuyvesant had no choice but to surrender.

The British renamed both the colony and its chief town New York to honor the Duke of York (the future King James II), and Stuyvesant retired peacefully to his farm, the Bouwerie.

1673

Discovery of the Mississippi

For about two-thirds of the seventeenth century, New France, as the French territory in America was called, was practically the exclusive province of the explorer Samuel de Champlain. In 1642, on the death of his father, four-year-old Louis XIV ascended the throne under the regency of Cardinal Mazarin. When Mazarin died in 1661, Louis XIV began to rule in his own right. No longer content to let the fate of his North American possessions rest in the hands of a single individual, the king promoted not exploration, but the establishment of farms and cities in areas that had already been explored. However, in 1673, the French *intendant* (chief administrator) in Canada, Jean Baptiste Talon, couldn't resist going against this royal policy by hiring a fur trader named Louis Joliet to strike out into the unknown, following up on Indian tales concerning a "father" of all the rivers. This water source, Talon reasoned, might well prove to be the passage to the Pacific. The Indians called it the "Mesippi."

In company with a Jesuit priest, Jacques Marquette, Joliet went west and reported on many wonders, including herds of great buffalo and fish big enough to wreck a canoe. They also found the Mississippi, and while it was apparent that this was not a shortcut to the Pacific, it was grand enough. More important, its discovery established France's claim to a vast portion of what would one day be the United States. Joliet and Marquette named the realm Louisiana, in honor of their monarch, and figured that it encompassed everything between the Appalachian Mountains and the Rockies, which, they vaguely knew, lay far to the west. Neither the explorers nor Louis XIV had an inkling of the great commercial artery the Mississippi would become, and how it would one day demarcate East and West, the West becoming an immense magnet that drew millions. Indeed, by the end of Louis's long reign, New France remained nothing more than a few precarious settlements through Nova Scotia and along the St. Lawrence, with one or two isolated outposts huddled in "Louisiana."

King Philip's War

While today it is a conflict that mostly interests professional historians, in proportion to the region's population at the time, King Philip's War was the costliest war ever fought on American soil. Among New England colonists, one in sixteen males of military age was killed, and many others—old men, women, children—were also killed, starved, or captured. As for the Indians, at least 3,000 perished, and many who did not die were sold into slavery.

King Philip's War began on June 11, 1675, when a Massachusetts settler killed an Indian who was stealing his cattle. Led by the Wampanoag chief, Metacomet, known to the English as King Philip, a delegation of Indians demanded justice for the slain Indian. Rebuffed, they sought out the farmer and killed him, along with six others. This triggered reprisals, which, in turn, set off an uprising among the Wampanoags, Narragansetts, Nipmucks, and allied tribes. Murder, arson, and looting by Indians in the frontier regions of settlement became so widespread by the late spring of 1675 that colonists began retreating from the wilderness.

The colonists, poorly organized and more competitive than cooperative, fared very badly during the first months of the conflict. Only after they banded together as the United Colonies were they able to muster a substantial intercolonial army to counter King Philip and his allies. During the remainder of 1675 and well into 1676, the colonists fought a war of attrition against the Indians. In the course of the conflict, half the towns of New England were destroyed or severely damaged. It would require the work of a full generation to restore them. Disruption of the fur trade, of fishing, and of the West Indies trade devastated the fledgling colonial economy. Farm labor was greatly diminished, first by the absence of farmers gone to war, then by the fact that many never returned.

The cost to the Indians was even greater. The Wampanoag, Narragansett, and Nipmuck tribes were rendered forever subject to the English will. Many died. Many were sold into West Indian slavery, the profits of the sales used to help defray the direct costs of the war. If there is anything at all positive to be found in this war, it is that for the first time an effective (if temporary) union among the colonies was formed.

The Pennsylvania Experiment

The New World appeared to the people of the Old as many things: a place of potentially vast wealth, a place of trade, a place for religious freedom, a place to conquer. To William Penn, prominent member of the then-radical Christian sect popularly called the Quakers, Pennsylvania appeared the perfect place to conduct an experiment in peace and toleration during an age of war and intolerance.

On March 14, 1681, King Charles II of England granted Penn a proprietary charter for the region encompassing present-day Pennsylvania and present-day Delaware as well. Here, Penn welcomed not only Quakers (victims of persecution elsewhere), but people of all creeds and nationalities. Upon this heterogeneous population, Penn imposed a mild government, which quickly fostered the development of something closely resembling our contemporary democracy: representative government. Pennsylvania and the great city that became its capital, Philadelphia, emerged as early models of free government, long before there was the slightest whiff of independence or softest whisper of revolution.

1692

Salem Punishes the Witches

On January 20, 1692, nine-year-old Elizabeth Parris (daughter of the Reverend Samuel Parris) and eleven-year-old Abigail Williams began to behave strangely, screaming out blasphemies, going into convulsions, slipping into trancelike states. Soon, other girls in the strongly Puritan settlement of Salem, Massachusetts, began to exhibit similar behavior. By mid-February, baffled Salem physicians, unable to find a physical cause for the girls' symptoms, concluded that they were possessed by Satan. In late February, after prayer services and community fasting failed to dispel the force of evil, and after a special "witch cake" (baked with rye meal and urine from the afflicted girls) failed to reveal the identity of Satan's agents, the girls themselves, under ceaseless interrogation, finally named three women, including Tituba, Parris's Caribbean slave, as witches. On February 29, warrants were issued for the arrest of Tituba, Sarah Good, and Sarah Osborne. Under examination, Osborne and Good maintained their innocence, but Tituba confessed to having seen the devil, and she went on to testify to a conspiracy of witches at work in Salem.

Over the next few weeks, townspeople came forward to testify that they had been harmed by certain people or had seen strange apparitions of those people. Soon, accusations were made against many Salem residents. Most frequently denounced were those typically accused of witchcraft in other communities: poor, elderly women or men who owned no property, the quarrelsome and disruptive, the social outcasts. But also accused were a number of upstanding members of the churchgoing community.

On May 27, after more than twenty persons were arrested and

interrogated, Governor Phips set up a special seven-judge Court of Oyer and Terminer. The judges weighed all manner of "evidence," ranging from direct confessions, stories of supernatural attributes, and the state and reactions of the afflicted girls themselves. Most controversial was "spectral evidence," which was based on the assumption that the devil could assume the "specter" of any person, no matter how innocent.

In 1692, more than 140 people were accused, 107 of them women. The first to be found guilty and condemned to death, on June 2, 1692, was Bridget Bishop, who was hanged on June 10. Through the summer and into the fall, fifty of the accused confessed to practicing witchcraft, twenty-six were convicted, and twenty, including Bishop, were executed. All were hanged, except for Giles Corey, who, on September 19, was pressed to death under heavy stones because he refused to stand trial.

A colonial merchant and voice of reason, Thomas Brattle, appalled at the pace of conviction and execution, wrote a letter on October 8 criticizing the trials. Governor Phips took heed and declared that reliance on spectral evidence and intangible evidence would no longer be allowed. Deprived of these legal weapons, the Court of Oyer and Terminer was dissolved, and Phips decreed that the Superior Court of Judicature would hear the remaining cases. From October until the end of the year, this court indicted twenty-one of the more than fifty remaining individuals accused. Subsequent trials resulted in only three convictions, which were overturned the following year. In 1693, individuals whose cases were still pending were given a pardon by the governor. Before 1693 was over, witchcraft was no longer regarded as a criminal offense.

The Salem witch trials have entered American history as well as American folklore, and they endure as cautionary tales about the dangers of superstition and guilt by suspicion. In 1953, when the nation was in the grip of the anticommunist hysteria orchestrated by the opportunistic Republican senator from Wisconsin, Joseph McCarthy, the playwright Arthur Miller used the Salem experience as the basis of a powerful play, *The Crucible,* which served as an allegory of the "witch hunt" over which McCarthy presided. By dramatizing the Salem trials, Miller reminded the nation of how political bullying and ideological hysteria could ruin lives and destroy democratic institutions.

1732

Georgia Is Chartered

The colony of Georgia began as a social experiment even more radical than Penn's Pennsylvania. In 1732, a high-minded entrepreneur named James Oglethorpe was granted a royal charter to found Georgia, last of the original thirteen colonies. Oglethorpe had leagued with other London-based philanthropists to create a colony that was to be populated by select inmates from English debtors' prisons. Not only would Georgia give these individuals new lives, the colony would serve the British empire by creating a buffer zone between England's Carolina colonies and Spain's colonial territory. But Oglethorpe's vision extended even beyond this. For Oglethorpe planned to install his colonists on fifty-acre farms, which they could neither sell nor transfer. Thus, they had no motives for greedy acquisition and envy. Both liquor and slavery—two great social evils—were to be banned from the colony.

Unfortunately for Oglethorpe's vision of utopia, only a few of the original colonists who came with the founder in 1733 were debtors. Most were speculators and land-hungry settlers. They quickly found loopholes that allowed them to amass great plantations far in excess of the stipulated fifty acres, and, with vast lands to work, slaves were soon imported as well. In 1752, Georgia was proclaimed a royal colony—no different from any of the others.

The Case of John Peter Zenger

Lewis Morris, chief justice of New York's provincial court, ruled against Governor William Cosby in a 1733 salary dispute. Cosby promptly responded by suspending Justice Morris, who appealed to the colony's only newspaper, the *New York Gazette,* to tell his story. Because the *Gazette* was wholly dependent on Governor Cosby's patronage, its editor declined to print anything Morris had to say. The justice joined several other lawyers and merchants in hiring a local printer, John Peter Zenger, to start up a new paper, the *New-York Weekly Journal,* which began publication on November 5, 1733.

As soon as Zenger published articles critical of Cosby, the governor had Zenger arrested on charges of "seditious libel." For ten months he was imprisoned without trial while his wife, Anna, kept publishing the paper. The case finally came to bench in 1735, and Zenger's attorney, Andrew Hamilton of Philadelphia, argued that Zenger was innocent of seditious libel because all that he had printed was true. The judge in the case did his best to block evidence to prove the truth of Zenger's articles, but the argument itself persuaded the jury, who acquitted the printer.

The Zenger case stands as a foundation of the freedom of the American press and established the sovereign defense against charges of libel: The truth cannot be defined as libelous and cannot, therefore, be stifled by legal prosecution.

1754

The French and Indian War Begins

Since the late seventeenth century, French and English colonists had been fighting one another over control of North America, often enlisting into the conflict the alliance of Indians. When, in 1749, England's King George II granted great tracts of the American wilderness to a cartel of entrepreneurs calling itself the Ohio Company, the governor of New France, the marquis de La Galissonière, responded by sending an expedition to lay claim to as much of the "Ohio country" (roughly, present-day western Pennsylvania, Ohio, Indiana, and Illinois) as could be encompassed in a round-trip of 3,000 miles. Over the next several years, a succession of French governors built a chain of forts from Montreal down to New Orleans and cultivated more and more Indian allies and trading partners. By the early 1750s, war fever had spread through the British American colonies. Virginia governor Robert Dinwiddie commissioned a twenty-one-year-old Virginia militia captain named George Washington to deliver to the French "invaders" an eviction notice. Washington confronted the commandant of Fort LeBoeuf (Waterford, Pennsylvania) on December 12, 1753. Captain Legardeur politely but firmly declined to depart, and Dinwiddie ordered the construction of a fort at the junction of the Monongahela, Allegheny, and Ohio rivers, site of present-day Pittsburgh. The French patiently watched construction, then, in April 1754, suddenly overran and took over the completed fort, christening it Fort Duquesne.

On the very day that the fort fell, Dinwiddie, quite unaware of what had occurred, sent Washington (now promoted to lieutenant colonel) with 150 men to reinforce it. En route, on May 28, Washington surprised a 33-man French reconnaissance party, attacked, and killed ten of the Frenchmen, including Ensign Joseph Coulon de Villiers de Jumonville, a French "ambassador." Thus, the English won the first battle of the French and Indian War.

But Washington did not let his victory go to his head. Realizing that the French would counterattack in force, he hurriedly built a makeshift stockade, aptly named Fort Necessity, at Great Meadows, Pennsylvania. On July 3, Major Coulon de Villiers, brother of the man Washington's detachment had killed, led a large force against Fort Necessity. After half his men had fallen, Washington, on the fourth of July, surrendered. He and the other survivors were permitted to leave, save for two hostages, who were taken back to Fort Duquesne. It was the English, not the French, who had been evicted from the Ohio country, and the French and Indian War began in earnest.

1755

Exile of the Acadians

While war between the French and English began in western Pennsylvania at the gateway to the Ohio country, up in Nova Scotia, British authorities demanded that the Acadians, French-speaking Roman Catholic farmers and fishermen who freely intermarried with the local Micmac and Abnaki Indians, swear loyalty to the British crown. French authorities countered not by threatening the English, but by warning the Acadians that the Indians would be turned loose against them if they caved in to British demands.

At last, during July 1755, the Acadians of Nova Scotia announced their refusal to submit to the loyalty oath, and, on July 28, 1755, Nova Scotia's newly appointed British governor, Charles Lawrence, ordered their deportation. On October 13, 1,100 Acadians were sent into exile. Many others followed—six to seven thousand in all—resettling throughout the colonies. But the Acadians made the best of it, and the many who settled in Louisiana immeasurably enriched the culture of the region. Through a contraction of the word *Acadians,* they became known as *Cajuns.*

1755

British Defeat at the Battle of the Wilderness

D uring 1754–1755, the French and Indian War escalated with the arrival of troops from the mother countries. From England, Major General Edward Braddock arrived with an army and sat down with the colonial commanders to lay out a grand strategy for the war. He proposed to send Brigadier General Robert Monckton against Nova Scotia, while he himself set about capturing Forts Duquesne and Niagara. Massachusetts governor William Shirley's army was assigned to reinforce Fort Oswego, in New York, and then to proceed to Fort Niagara. Another colonial commander, William Johnson, was detailed to capture Fort Saint Frédéric at Crown Point, on Lake Champlain.

Monckton and John Winslow (a colonial commander) successfully took Nova Scotia, but Braddock encountered great delay in starting his expedition to Fort Duquesne. Finally, two regiments of British regulars and a provincial detachment (under George Washington) marched out of Fort Cumberland, Maryland, 2,500 men in all, loaded down with heavy equipment. As French-allied Indians sniped at the slow-moving column, Washington advised Braddock to detach a "flying column" of 1,500 men to move swiftly for the initial attack on Fort Duquesne. By July 7, the flying column set up a camp ten miles from its objective. Two days later, French and Indian forces fell on the camp in a surprise attack that sent panic through the ranks of the British regulars. Some troops fired wildly at each other. Some simply huddled together like sheep. Braddock, dull but brave, had five horses shot from under him as he vainly tried to rally his men. He finally fell, mortally wounded. Of 1,459 officers and men who had engaged in the Battle of the Wilderness, only 462 survived. (George Washington, though unhurt, had two horses shot from under him, and his coat had been pierced by four bullets.) As he lay dying, Braddock remarked incredulously: "Who would have thought it?"

The disaster at the Battle of the Wilderness drove many more Indians into the camp of the French and laid open to attack English settlements all along the frontier. By June 1756, British settlers in Virginia had withdrawn 150 miles from the prewar frontier.

Chief Scarouady of the English-allied Oneida Indians said of Braddock: "He was a bad man when he was alive; he looked upon us as dogs, and would never hear anything that was said to him. We often endeavoured to advise him of the danger he was in with his Soldiers; but he never appeared pleased with us and that was the reason that a great many of our Warriors left him and would not be under his Command."

The First "World" War

For its first three years, the French and Indian War was a North American conflict. In 1756, it became truly a *world* war as Prussia invaded Saxony. The following year, the Holy Roman Empire (principally Austria) declared war on Prussia, which then invaded Bohemia. Through a complex of interests, intrigues, and alliances, the French, the British, the Spanish, and the Russians also joined the war, which eventually encompassed major fronts in Europe, India, Cuba, the Philippines, and North America. The world conflict was given the generic title of the Seven Years' War.

Committed now to an expanded war, France, on May 11, 1756, sent the dashing marquis de Montcalm to take charge of Canadian forces. The British still muddled along with mediocre commanders, who persisted in their haughty refusal to cooperate effectively with provincial forces. Montcalm easily took Fort Oswego, which yielded Lake Ontario to the French and made it impossible for the English to attack Fort Niagara. Even worse, Montcalm's victory brought the Iroquois into an alliance with the French. In all, 1756 was a very bad year for the British, but, at the end of it, in December, William Pitt became British secretary of state for the southern department, a post that put him in charge of American colonial affairs. He replaced incompetent commanders with more able ones, and he adopted a far more cooperative attitude toward colonial commanders. Although Fort William Henry fell to the French on August 9, 1757 (followed by the slaughter of the fort's garrison by Montcalm's Indian warriors), the tide began to turn in favor of the British.

Brigadier General John Forbes, one of Britain's best field commanders, prepared a new assault on the main French headquarters at Fort Duquesne. Despite many delays, Forbes attacked on November 24, 1757. The French abandoned Fort Duquesne and blew it up. No matter, the English had at last seized control of the gateway to the West.

1759

The Fall of Quebec and the Triumph of the English

I f 1758 marked the turning of the tide in favor of the British, 1759 was appropriately dubbed "the year of French disaster." It culminated in the siege, battle, and loss of Quebec on September 18, 1759, which effectively brought to an end French power in North America. The British capture of Quebec was the long, arduous, frustrating work of British general James Wolfe, who made his first attack on the city on July 31, 1759. It wasn't until September 12, however, that Wolfe was able to deploy troops stealthily along the Plains of Abraham, which lay before Quebec, then mount a brilliantly executed attack, which took the city after a mere quarter-hour of fighting. Grievously wounded in the engagement, Wolfe lived just long enough to see the battle through to victory. By that time, Montcalm also lay dead. Quebec formally surrendered on September 18, 1759.

For all practical purposes, the Battle of Quebec effectively decided the French and Indian War, yet the fighting continued as the British steadily contracted the circle around French Canada. Combat between the English and the French diminished, while fighting between the English and Indians, who justifiably feared dispossession at the hands of the victors, intensified. Indian-held Detroit rapidly fell to English forces under Robert Rogers and his famed Rangers, but fighting along the southern frontier took two armies and two years to bring to an end. In the waning months of the war, Spain entered the picture on the side of France. England declared war on the new belligerent on January 2, 1762, and crushed it with sea power alone. On February 10, 1763, the Treaty of Paris ended both the French and Indian War in America and the Seven Years' War in Europe. Having given all of Louisiana to its ally Spain in compensation for what it had lost in the war, France ceded the rest of its North American holdings to Great Britain. England was now the supreme American power east of the Mississippi and throughout Canada.

1763

King George's Proclamation Line

F or the British crown, the French and Indian War was a glorious victory, but an expensive one, and King George III was eager to prevent further costly conflict with the Indians. Therefore, at the close of the war, on October 7, 1763, he issued a royal proclamation forbidding white settlement west of the Appalachian Mountains. He trusted that this would effectively prevent settlers from encroaching on Indian territory.

In fact, the Proclamation Line did conciliate the Indians, but it proved impossible to enforce. Settlers generally ignored it and persisted in pushing settlement westward. This provoked Indian raids, which, in turn, sent settlers appealing to royal governors for aid. As often as not, colonial officials turned a deaf ear to the pleas of frontiersmen who had violated the Proclamation Line. This contributed to growing alienation between the frontier regions and the Tidewater—the thickly settled coast. Increasingly, over the years, officials in these coastal areas were forced to choose allegiance to the policies of the mother country or the demands of those who lived on the western fringes of the colonies. By the 1770s, the trans-Appalachian bonds between east coast and interior were growing stronger than the trans-Atlantic bonds between the colonies and England.

1765

The Stamp Act

Following the French and Indian War, at the behest of King George III, Parliament—for the first time in history—imposed a series of taxes on the colonies in an effort to defray some of the costs of the war. Each new tax was met with colonial protest, grounded in a concept articulated by Boston lawyer James Otis in 1761. "Taxation without representation," he declared, "is tyranny." And since the colonies were not represented in Parliament, Parliament had no right to tax them.

The passage of the Stamp Act, put into force on March 22, 1765, galvanized colonial opposition, unified the colonies to an unprecedented degree, and pushed them closer to rebellion. The Stamp Act taxed all sorts of printed matter, including newspapers, legal documents, and paper itself, all of which required a government stamp as proof that the tax had been paid.

Opposition took three principal forms. First, colonists simply refused to buy the stamps. Second, militant organizations, such as one led by a Boston agitator named Samuel Adams, formed to intimidate the stamp agents (those responsible for selling the stamps and enforcing their use) into resigning. These groups, known collectively as the Sons of Liberty, proved highly effective. Finally, on October 7, 1765, a Stamp Act Congress convened in New York City and brought together representatives from South Carolina, Rhode Island, Connecticut, Pennsylvania, Maryland, New Jersey, Delaware, and New York. The congress drafted a Declaration of Rights and Grievances and masterminded a boycott of English goods. Not only did the boycott result in the repeal of the Stamp Act, but the congress also proved a major step in unifying the colonies, which began to develop a national identity separate from that imposed by the mother country.

1769

Daniel Boone Traverses the Cumberland Gap

Where the borders of the present-day states of Tennessee, Kentucky, and Virginia meet, millennia of wind and water carved a major break in the great Appalachian Mountain barrier that divides the Atlantic seaboard from the vast lands to the west. Like many other Americans of the mid- to late eighteenth century, Daniel Boone hankered after those lands, but, unlike most of his contemporaries, he was not only a frontiersman, but a natural-born leader. He didn't discover the Cumberland Gap—white hunters had been using it for years, Indians for untold centuries, and, doubtless, herds of migratory animals before both of these groups—but, on June 7, 1769, the Cumberland Gap took Boone to Kentucky, changed his life, and changed the course of American history.

"We found every where abundance of wild beasts of all sorts, through this vast forest," Boone—or, rather, a ghostwriting land promoter, John Filson—wrote in 1784. Boone saw Kentucky as a new Garden of Eden. Financed by a colorful and influential North Carolina entrepreneur, Judge Richard Henderson, Boone would hew out the first readily passable road through the Gap, the Wilderness Road, and in 1775 led the first substantial group of settlers into Kentucky, where he founded Boonesborough.

The settlement suffered mightily through the American Revolution (Boone himself was captured by the Shawnee and lived among them for several months before making a break for it), but it stuck, and by the end of the Revolution, 12,000 persons had migrated to Kentucky. In 1792, when the territory's population hit 100,000, it was admitted to the Union. The trans-Appalachian West was on its way to being settled.

The Boston Massacre

In 1770, times were hard for American colonists as well as for the British troops sent to police them. The British were paid so poorly that many looked for off-duty work just to make ends meet. Hard-pressed colonists resented this, and when an off-duty soldier sought employment at Grey's Ropewalk (a Boston wharf-side rope maker) on the evening of March 5, 1770, he was mobbed. By nine o'clock that night, the situation had escalated into a near riot as Bostonians confronted Redcoats.

The mob threw insults, then ice balls, and, finally, a wooden club. This elicited a musket shot from a soldier, then another. A Bostonian named Samuel Gray lay mortally wounded, and Crispus Attucks, a runaway slave, was killed instantly. Crispus Attucks is traditionally counted as the first American to die in the struggle for independence.

More shots were fired, two more citizens fell dead, and a third, wounded, would die later. But at this point, the British commander regained control of his men, and the melee ended.

Samuel Adams and others did their best to propagandize the "Boston Massacre" and elevate it to an immediate cause for revolution. However, two brilliant colonial attorneys, Josiah Quincy and future president John Adams, intervened to defend the British captain and six Redcoats who had been indicted for murder. Although both Quincy and Adams were partisans of independence, they believed that mob rule was fatal to a people who craved democracy. Thanks to their skill, Captain Preston and four men were acquitted, and two others were found guilty of the lesser charge of manslaughter.

Sam Adams and other Sons of Liberty were frustrated that the Boston Massacre did not produce an instant revolution. However, the fair trial and the verdict that followed demonstrated that the people of Boston were both worthy of and ready for liberty.

The Boston Tea Party

By 1773, the colonists had succeeded in forcing the crown to repeal most of the taxes levied on them. However, King George insisted on keeping a tax on tea, primarily because he believed that "there must always be one tax" in order to preserve Parliament's right to tax the colonies. Colonists evaded the tax by smuggling Dutch tea, which worked a hardship on the financially ailing British East India Company. If the company couldn't soon ship to America some of the 17 million pounds of Indian tea lying in its London warehouses, the whole lot would go rotten. The company asked prime minister Lord North for help. He understood that the East India Company paid two taxes: one when it landed tea in Britain, whether for sale or shipment elsewhere, and another tax when it landed a shipment in America. The Tea Act of May 10, 1773, forgave the first tax and retained the lesser three-penny-a-pound duty due on landing in America. This would price East India tea below the smuggled tea.

But instead of prompting American consumers to buy British tea, the Tea Act was seen as a government-enforced monopoly and yet another affront to colonial rights. Throughout the colonies, Sons of Liberty and other activists intimidated into resignation East India Company consignees in Philadelphia, New York, and Charleston, and American captains and harbor pilots refused to handle the East India Company cargo. Tea ships were turned back to London from Philadelphia and New York. In Boston, when three Tea Act ships landed at Boston Harbor, the Sons of Liberty prevented their being unloaded—even as the royal governor refused to allow the ships to leave the harbor and return to London.

At the height of this standoff, on the night of December 16, a group of protestors dressed as Mohawk Indians boarded the ships and dumped 90,000 pounds of tea overboard.

Parliament's response to this outrage was to punish Massachusetts by passing the Port Act, which blocked trade in and out of Boston until the tea had been paid for; the Administration of Justice Act, which allowed crown officials to be tried outside of the colony; and the Massachusetts Government Act, which increased the power of the royal governor at the expense of the colonial assembly. In addition, the Quartering Act allowed royal governors throughout the colonies to seize privately owned buildings as barracks and billets for British troops.

> "The flame is kindled, and like lightning it catches from soul to soul."
> —letter from Abigail Adams to her husband, John, as the tea ships stood in Boston harbor

The colonists branded these laws the "Intolerable Acts," and the colonies united in solidarity with Massachusetts. In its effort to break the colonial will and force obedience to the crown, the British government pushed the colonies ever closer to union. Leaders of rebellion called for a "Continental Congress" to convene.

1774

The First Continental Congress

Spurred by the Boston Tea Party and the "Intolerable Acts" that followed, delegates from every colony except Georgia converged on Philadelphia in September 1774 for the First Continental Congress. Whereas the concept of taxation without representation had been the focus of most colonial protest, the delegates now held that Parliament had no right to make *any* laws for the colonies. Some delegates believed that reform of the colonial system was still possible, but the majority were radicals who would settle for nothing short of independence. What moderates and radicals did agree on was the creation of a Continental Association to conduct boycotts of British goods and to enforce an embargo on exports to England. Beyond this, the Congress endorsed a call by Massachusetts delegates for citizens to recognize their right to take up arms in defense of their liberties.

> **"The revolution was complete, in the minds of the people, and the Union of the colonies, before the war commenced." —John Adams, recalling the significance of the First Continental Congress**

Although opinion in the First Continental Congress was by no means unanimous, colonial solidarity and identity had reached an unprecedented level of intensity.

Patrick Henry Demands Liberty— or Death

By 1775, acts of disorder and rebellion were breaking out all over New England. At midnight on February 25, 1775, General Thomas Gage, British commander in chief and military governor of the American colonies, sent 240 men of the 64th Foot Regiment from Boston to Salem, Massachusetts, where, he had heard, the rebels stored cannon and munitions stolen from the royal arsenal. But the well-developed colonial network of spies and informers warned the people of Salem, who managed to move to safety the nineteen cannon and other munitions that had, indeed, been stored there.

The following month, when Virginia's House of Burgesses, barred by royal order from their official place of assembly, met at Raleigh Tavern on March 23, 1775, Patrick Henry made an electrifying speech alluding to the outbreaks in New England:

> There is no retreat but in submission and slavery! Our chains are forged. Their clanking may be heard on the plains of Boston! The war is inevitable—and let it come! I repeat it, sir, let it come!
>
> It is in vain, sir, to extenuate the matter. Gentlemen may cry, "Peace! Peace!"—but there is no peace. The war is actually begun! The next gale that sweeps down from the north will bring to our ears the clash of resounding arms! Our brethren are already in the field! Why stand we here idle? What is it that gentlemen wish? What would they have? Is life so dear, or peace so sweet, as to be purchased at the price of chains and slavery? For-

bid it, Almighty God! I know not what course others may take, but as for me, give me liberty or give me death!

His speech instantly united South and North, providing just enough momentum to ensure that a great American revolution would begin to roll, then rush forward.

1775

The Midnight Ride of Paul Revere

U nlike Virginia's Patrick Henry, Paul Revere of Charlestown, Massachusetts, was no politician. He was a silversmith by trade, the son of a silversmith, Apollos Rivoire, who had come to America as one of thousands of Huguenots (French Protestants) fleeing the deadly religious persecution they suffered at home. Paul Revere prospered in his profession and fathered a large family—eight children by his first wife and eight more by his second. With many mouths to feed, it was a good thing that Revere did so well, but he was not content merely to earn money. The son of a man who had known persecution firsthand, Revere was drawn to the political movers and shakers of Boston, members of the Sons of Liberty, including Sam Adams and his distant cousin John Adams, John Hancock, James Otis, and Dr. Joseph Warren. Revere served the Sons of Liberty as a courier, and on April 16, 1775, it was Revere who rode to Lexington, Massachusetts, to warn Sam Adams and John Hancock that they were in imminent danger of arrest. Shortly after this mission, on April 18, 1775, Revere was one of three riders who alerted the citizen militia of the Massachusetts countryside to the approach of the British, who were determined to capture an important cache of Patriot arms at Concord.

The British troops stepped off at 10:30 P.M. Revere had stationed a friend, John Pulling, in the steeple of Charlestown's North Church, his task to signal whether the British were marching out by land or using whaleboats to cut across the Back Bay. A one-lantern signal meant they were coming overland; two, via the Back Bay.

As soon as Revere saw two lanterns in the steeple, he and another Sons of Liberty courier, William Dawes, raced ahead of the advancing British column. Thanks to Revere, Dawes, and a third courier, Samuel Prescott, the British lost the element of surprise, and the Minutemen—the citizen militia so-called because they claimed combat readiness on a minute's notice—were prepared to fight.

Battle of Lexington

A t Lexington, Massachusetts, which lay squarely in the line of march between Boston and Concord, militia captain Jonas Parker formed up the ranks of seventy or so citizen-soldiers on Lexington's green, which fronted the Concord road.

"Stand your ground," Captain Parker ordered. "Don't fire unless fired upon. But if they want to have a war, let it begin here!"

Such brave words, tailor-made for history, were probably concocted long after the fact by some historian. No one knows what Parker actually said. Whatever it was, though, it failed to inspire all of the militiamen. Some, staring at the unbroken line of advancing Redcoats, shook their heads, shrugged, and walked away.

> "So many of them, so few of us. It is folly to stand here." —one of the Minutemen, at the approach of battle, Lexington, Massachusetts

For his part, the British second in command, John Pitcairn, restrained his own men while calling out to the Americans, "Lay down your arms, you rebels, and disperse!"

Parker ordered his men to disband—but he told them to take their weapons with them. After Pitcairn repeated his demand that they lay down their weapons, shots rang out. A Redcoat was wounded slightly in the leg, and two balls grazed Pitcairn's horse.

Were the shots American or British? No one knows. But they were enough to prompt a British officer to command, "Fire, by God, fire!"

AMERICAN HISTORY A.S.A.P.

When the Battle of Lexington was over, eight militiamen, including Captain Parker, lay dead on Lexington green. Ten more were wounded. A single British soldier was slightly hurt. Then the British resumed their march on Concord.

1775

Battle of Concord

No one knows just how many Americans were ultimately involved in the Battle of Concord. Wild guesses have run as high as 20,000, but, most likely, a total of 3,763 Americans fought—though never more than half this number at any one time. However, at the moment of the British arrival in Concord—which was unopposed—only about 400 militiamen, under the command of local resident "Colonel" James Barrett, had assembled on a ridge overlooking the town.

Not one to be hurried, British Lieutenant Colonel Francis Smith dined at a local tavern while his grenadiers searched the town for hidden munitions. When the grenadiers set fire to some gun carriages they found, one of Barrett's officers turned to him: "Will you let them burn the town down?" At this, Barrett ordered the militia to march to the defense of Concord.

And so the battle began. The captain of the British light infantry ordered his men to form two ranks for firing. It was the standard maneuver, drilled countless times, but, this time, something went wrong. The volleys of the first British rank fell short—hitting only two marks, militia captain Isaac Davis and Abner Hosmer, a little drummer boy who marched bravely at the head of the American column.

"Fire, fellow soldiers!" an unidentified American officer called to his men. "For God's sake, fire!"

Years later, the poet-philosopher Ralph Waldo Emerson would call this the "shot heard 'round the world": Three British soldiers were killed, nine more wounded, and the Redcoats retreated into the town. The American Revolution had truly begun.

Had the Americans been more disciplined soldiers, they would have pursued the retreating British. Instead, Colonel Smith was permitted to withdraw from Concord, although his troops were sniped at all the way back to Boston. In the twin engagements at Lexington and Concord, which opened the American Revolution, seventy-three Redcoats were confirmed dead and twenty-six were reported missing and presumed dead. One hundred seventy-four British solders were wounded. The Americans suffered forty-nine deaths, as well as five missing and thirty-nine to forty-one wounded.

Battle of Bunker Hill

The British military chief and governor of Massachusetts, General Thomas Gage, received reinforcements from England on May 25 and was also joined by three additional generals, John Burgoyne, William Howe, and Henry Clinton. Thus fortified, he believed he could now intimidate the colonists into giving up the revolution. He offered amnesty to all, save Sam Adams and John Hancock, the two chief troublemakers. In response, the Massachusetts Committee of Public Safety, the body that was now running the war, ordered General Artemus Ward to fortify Bunker Hill on Charlestown Heights, overlooking Boston harbor.

It was a good defensive plan, but Ward chose instead to send Colonel William Prescott with 1,200 men to occupy nearby Breed's Hill, which was lower and more vulnerable than Bunker. Seeing that the colonists intended to fight, Gage directed a naval bombardment against Breed's Hill at dawn on June 17. He followed this with an amphibious attack by 2,500 men under General Howe. Twice, this superior British force attempted to take Breed's Hill. Twice they were repulsed with heavy losses. A third assault—this one with bayonets—succeeded chiefly because the defenders were exhausted and out of ammunition.

Misnamed for Bunker Hill—the position that *should* have been defended—the battle was certainly a tactical defeat for the colonists, but it was also a psychological victory for them. As they saw it, a shortage of ammunition, not the British army, had defeated them. Besides, although the Americans were pushed off Breed's Hill and Bunker Hill, of the 2,500 British troops engaged,

1,000 had died—a devastating casualty rate of 42 percent and the heaviest loss the British were to suffer during the long war. Inspired, the Americans would fight on, would lay siege to Boston, and would drive the British army out.

1775–1776

Early Victories, Early Defeats

The first year of the American Revolution was marked by great success in Boston. The American army, pushed out of the city by the loss of the Battle of Bunker Hill, regrouped and laid siege to the British in Boston. By March 1776, the British had had enough. Evacuating by sea, they moved their headquarters all the way to Halifax, Nova Scotia. Boston was in Patriot hands.

In the South, the Americans also successfully repulsed a British invasion under Sir Henry Clinton. Clinton bombarded the harbor fortifications of the South's chief city, Charleston, South Carolina, but was driven off by June 28, 1776. This effectively neutralized the British in the South for the next two years.

While the Patriot cause fared far better in the first year of the war than anybody could have expected, an American attempt to persuade British Canada to join the revolution was rebuffed, and an American attempt to invade Canada proved a costly failure. Worse, by the summer of 1776, the British began to wrest the initiative from the Americans. The Continental Army led by George Washington was defeated on Long Island on August 27, 1776, but fought a brilliant rearguard action in Manhattan from August through November. Although the Americans relinquished this key city to the British, it cost the Redcoats time, money, energy, and men.

General William Howe pushed Washington into and across New Jersey. Had he been more determined and Washington less skillful, Howe could have destroyed the Continental Army and ended the Revolution. Instead, Washington and his forces escaped across the Delaware River and into Pennsylvania on December 7, 1776.

1776

Thomas Paine's *Common Sense*

The "shot heard 'round the world" was fired on April 19, 1775, and the misnamed Battle of Bunker Hill and the successful siege of Boston followed. Although a revolution had begun, many Americans were still not certain that outright independence from the mother country was a good idea. Even as the war was fought during 1775, individuals and entire colonies wavered. What finally crystallized popular opinion in favor of complete and immediate independence was a modest forty-seven-page pamphlet published on January 9, 1776, and written, according to the title page, "by an Englishman." It was *Common Sense* by Thomas Paine, a newly arrived immigrant from England. After a clear and eloquent argument advocating not merely the desirability of independence, but its very necessity, Paine concluded:

> Ye that dare oppose not only the tyranny but the tyrant, stand forth! Every spot of the old world is overrun with oppression. Freedom hath been hunted round the globe. Asia and Africa have long expelled her. Europe regards her like a stranger, and England hath given her warning to depart. O receive the fugitive, and prepare in time an asylum for mankind!

In less than three months, 120,000 copies of *Common Sense* were sold. Before the end of the Revolution, more than half a million copies had been distributed. As John Adams wrote on May 20, 1776, following the publication of *Common Sense* and George Washington's victory in the siege of Boston: "Every post and every day rolls in upon us Independence like a torrent." One after the other, the colonies now voted for independence.

1776

The Declaration of Independence

The final debate over independence got under way in the Continental Congress on July 1, 1776, with Pennsylvania's John Dickinson counseling delay, while John Adams and others passionately urged immediate action. By July 2, eleven of the twelve colonies represented at the Second Continental Congress—Georgia sent no delegate, and the New York delegation abstained—voted for independence. Earlier, in anticipation of this moment, the Congress had appointed a committee to draft a declaration of independence, naming to it John Adams, Benjamin Franklin, Robert Livingston, Roger Sherman, and Thomas Jefferson.

In 1825, writing to his fellow Virginian and revolutionary colleague Henry Lee, Jefferson explained what he had intended to accomplish in writing the Declaration. He was not trying to be particularly original, to "find out new principles, or new arguments, never before thought of," but, rather, "to justify ourselves in the independent stand we are compelled to take" and to "appeal to the tribunal of the world . . . for our justification."

The choice of committee members was logical. Adams was a prime mover of revolutionary activity in the cradle of the Revolution, Massachusetts. Franklin was a figure of international reputation, renowned as a scientist, inventor, writer, editor, politician, and now emerging as a brilliant statesman. Livingston, son of an old New York family, represented the more conservative wing of the Congress. Sherman, from Connecticut, was a self-educated legislator and economic theorist, as well as a skilled writer. Jefferson, the junior member of the committee, had already written in 1774 *A Summary View of the Rights of British America*. It was to Jefferson that the committee turned for the first draft.

Jefferson drew from the philosophy of the seventeenth-century British philosopher John Locke, who had enumerated the basic rights of human beings as life, liberty, and property. Jefferson borrowed the rights to life and liberty, but for Locke's *property* he substituted the "pursuit of happiness," as if to declare that America offered an opportunity to aspire to a level of satisfaction and self-fulfillment unavailable elsewhere in the world and at any other time in history.

After editing by the Second Continental Congress—antislavery passages were cut so as not to alienate the South—the document was signed by the members of the Congress on July 4, 1776. A nation was born, and the American Revolution now had a unified direction, an international standing, and a bold inspiration.

The Articles of Confederation

N o sooner did the United States declare its independence in 1776 than Pennsylvania's John Dickinson (1732–1808) set to work drafting a constitution for the new republic, the Articles of Confederation. Dickinson favored a strong national government, but the states demanded more rights—especially the power of taxation—and, between 1777 and its ratification in 1781, Dickinson's original was watered down to create not a nation, but a "firm league of friendship" among thirteen essentially sovereign states. There was no president, no federal judiciary, and Congress had no real power, because, while it could enact laws, it could not enforce them. The states chose either to comply—or not. Most important, Congress had no authority to impose taxes.

The Articles went into effect even before the Revolution ended, but their fatal weakness was demonstrated almost daily. Congress, for example, was powerless to aid Massachusetts in 1786 when a farmer named Daniel Shays led a popular "rebellion" against the lawful authority of the state judicial system. Nor could Congress intervene when Rhode Island printed a ruinous torrent of entirely worthless paper money. These crises motivated a 1786 convention at Annapolis, Maryland, which, in turn, called for a constitutional convention to revise the crumbling Articles.

1776

Triumph at Trenton

From the historical perspective of more than 200 years, Washington's long retreat looks less like a defeat than a strategic withdrawal. But, at the time, Washington understood that wars are not won in retreat, and he also understood that Howe viewed his army as defeated and the Revolution all but over. Washington decided on a bold move.

In the dead of a very bitter winter, a season in which armies traditionally avoided battle, Washington collected his scattered militia and regular forces, rallied them, and led them back across the half-frozen Delaware on Christmas night. Back on the New Jersey bank, he stealthily marched his men to confront in battle a force not of Redcoats, but of Hessians, German mercenary troops in the employ of the British. These soldiers, perhaps the finest in Europe, were justly feared for their discipline and cruelty. To oppose them, Washington had an inferior number of ill-equipped, ill-clothed amateurs. But, he knew, he also had the element of surprise. The Hessians and their commander, Colonel Johann Rall, would be groggy from Christmas feasting, and a ragtag American army was certainly the last thing they expected to encounter on December 26.

The battle was short and sharp. Washington's army suffered no casualties, whereas the Hessians lost 106 men killed or wounded. More than 900 became prisoners of war. Colonel Rall was mortally wounded.

This victory, followed by another at Princeton on January 3, 1777, moved the Continental Congress to reject the latest British peace terms and to press ahead with the fight for independence.

1777

Victory at Saratoga, Defeat in Philadelphia

The defeat the Hessians suffered at Trenton was a profound shock to the British. Even more shattering were the results of two battles near Saratoga, New York. American commanders Horatio Gates, Benedict Arnold, and the quasi-guerrilla leader Daniel Morgan twice inflicted heavy losses on the army of British general John Burgoyne, at Bemis Heights on September 19, 1777, and at Frayer's Farm on October 7. Cut off after these defeats, Burgoyne found himself in the unenviable position of surrendering an entire British army—6,000 regulars plus various auxiliary forces—to the Patriots on October 17.

Simultaneously with this great American victory, however, came a dispiriting defeat. General William Howe made an amphibious landing on the upper Chesapeake Bay, then advanced on the capital of the Revolution, Philadelphia, the seat of the Continental Congress and the very place where the Declaration of Independence had been signed.

Washington led an inept defense at the Battle of Brandywine on September 11, 1777, but the British overran Philadelphia, and the Continental Congress fled to York, Pennsylvania.

The British had a right to gloat over the capture of the rebel capital. But what, exactly, had they gained? Congress, in exile, continued to function, and the war went on. Washington made an unsuccessful attempt to retake Philadelphia by attacking the British in the Battle of Germantown on October 4. Yet even this Patriot defeat gained something for the Americans. The French, who had been pondering whether or not to aid the Americans in their fight against the British, were thrilled by the Patriot victory at Saratoga, but even more impressed by the American gallantry displayed at Germantown—despite defeat there. A Franco–American alliance was formally concluded on February 6, 1778, and France became the first foreign power to recognize the United States of America.

1781

Yorktown

After initial frustration in the South, the British returned to the region in 1778 and racked up one victory after another along the coast, only to suffer some notable defeats inland. Lord Charles Cornwallis led British triumphs along the seaboard, but then found himself pinned down by frontier guerrillas. Although he broke free, Cornwallis made the tactical blunder of withdrawing into Virginia, where he established a headquarters at the port of Yorktown. His idea in settling his army on this peninsula was to have ready access to an evacuation by sea; however, the fleet of French admiral François de Grasse blocked the British fleet and thereby cut off any supply or escape by water. Cornwallis had penned himself into the tip of the peninsula.

In collaboration with the French army of the comte de Rochambeau, George Washington laid siege to Cornwallis at Yorktown on October 6, 1781. On October 19, the British commander surrendered to the allies with 17,000 men. Although peace would not formally come until the conclusion of the Treaty of Paris, ratified on April 15, 1783, the American Revolution was suddenly ended. The United States emerged an independent nation, and Cornwallis's regimental band, at the surrender ceremony, played a popular tune of the time: "The World Turned Upside Down."

The Writing of a Constitution

The Annapolis convention, convened in 1786 to revise the Articles of Confederation, instead called for a full-scale constitutional convention to meet in Philadelphia. The fifty-five delegates who convened in May 1787 began to fashion a document that would create a genuine national government rather than a merely hopeful confederation of states. The delegates unanimously elected George Washington president of the convention. Soon, the proposals boiled down to two rival plans: The "Virginia Plan" proposed the creation of a central federal government consisting of a bicameral legislature (House and Senate), an executive branch, and a judicial branch. The chief executive was to be elected by the members of the legislature, who, in turn, would be elected by the citizens. Representation in the two-chambered legislature would be proportionate to state population—a provision that greatly worried and even enraged representatives of the smaller states. The "New Jersey Plan" retained most of the Articles of Confederation, but gave all of the states equal representation in the legislature. There would be no executive branch, but there would be a Supreme Court, separate and independent from the legislature.

It was Roger Sherman, delegate from Connecticut, who formulated the "Great Compromise" between the two plans. It called for a bicameral legislature; however, the Senate would provide each state with equal representation, whereas the House of Representatives would provide representation proportionate to each state's population. There would be a chief executive, the president, who would be elected not directly by the people, but by an electoral college, the members of which were voted into office by the state legislatures.

William Johnson (secretary of the Convention), Alexander Hamilton, James Madison, Rufus King, and Gouverneur Morris wrote the actual Constitution document, the product of three and a half months of debate. When thirty-eight of the fifty-five Convention delegates approved the Constitution, it was sent to Congress, which submitted it to the states for ratification. Now the real battle would begin.

1787

The Three-Fifths Compromise

Unlike many political compromises, the "Great Compromise" between the rival plans for the Constitution was genuinely satisfying. However, it did not resolve the most complex and rancorous outstanding issue, the matter of slavery.

There was no serious movement to abolish slavery outright in this new land dedicated to liberty, but there was serious dispute over how slaves should figure in the calculation of each state's representation in the federal government. The more representatives a state could claim, the more influential it would be in that government. Therefore, the South wanted its slaves counted as population—even though slaves were property rather than people. Northerners objected, arguing that the slaves should be excluded entirely from the calculation. After much debate, Article I, Section 2 of the Constitution was hammered out, a compromise calling for "Representation and direct taxes [to be] apportioned among the several states according to respective numbers determined by adding to the whole number of free persons including those bound to service for a set number of years and excluding Indians not taxed three-fifths of all other persons." In other words, for purposes of levying taxes and apportioning representatives, each slave was counted as three-fifths of a person.

The notorious "Three-Fifths Compromise" was the first of many jury-rigged stopgaps that would be cobbled together in an increasingly desperate effort to keep the fact of slavery from blowing the nation apart.

The Struggle for Ratification

Those who supported the Constitution that Congress approved and submitted for ratification by the states were called Federalists. Those who opposed it—who feared the creation of a strong, perhaps tyrannical federal government—were called Anti-Federalists.

Delaware, Pennsylvania, and New Jersey immediately ratified the proposed Constitution, but ratification by a total of nine states was required to enact the document. The process was hotly contested in many states and nowhere more so than in the key states of Virginia and New York. To persuade New Yorkers to ratify the proposed Constitution, Alexander Hamilton, James Madison, and John Jay collaborated on a series of essays collectively called *The Federalist Papers* and published during 1787–1788 in various New York newspapers under the joint pseudonym "Publius."

One of history's great political treatises, *The Federalist* argued that people were chiefly motivated by self-interest and, therefore, the establishment of a representative government, while valuable, was dangerous. Inherently selfish representatives might betray their trust, one faction might oppose and oppress another, and passions might well overcome rational decision. Investing certain central authority in the government was presented as a means of defending against these dangers. Of particular significance was the tenth *Federalist* essay, written by James Madison. Rejecting the common belief that republican government was possible only for small states, Madison argued that liberty, justice, and stability were actually more likely to be attained in a large area with a numerous and varied population.

The Federalist presented a strong enough case in favor of the new Constitution to tip the balance in New York, thirty delegates voting for ratification, twenty-seven against. The vote in Virginia was also close—eighty-nine to seventy-nine—and that came about when the Anti-Federalist protest that the Constitution failed to address the rights of individuals was answered by a promise that a "Bill of Rights" would be added. When New Hampshire became the ninth state to ratify the Constitution on June 21, 1788, the document became law, and was put into effect officially on March 4, 1789.

1789

Election of George Washington

One of the many innovations the new Constitution introduced into the United States government was the office of president, and in April 1789, a month after the document had been put into effect on March 4, the new Senate convened to count ballots cast by members of the electoral college for the first president of the United States. The result surprised no one and pleased just about everyone. George Washington was elected unanimously, with John Adams as his vice president.

In effect, that first election was rigged. For it was with the implicit understanding that Washington would be elected that the framers of the Constitution created a strong executive branch. The thought of having fought a long and painful revolution to get free of King George III only to embrace some new tyrant was a chilling one. Washington, however, had not only demonstrated a genius for leadership in commanding the Continental Army, he had also exhibited great skill as a statesman in presiding so productively over the contentious Constitutional Convention. Perhaps most important of all, he possessed the character of a true republican. Such was his popularity after the Revolution that, had he so chosen, Washington could have become absolute dictator of the United States or even the new nation's new king. Instead, he eagerly withdrew to his beloved Virginia plantation, Mount Vernon, and only with considerable reluctance did he answer his country's call to office.

Washington was inaugurated in New York City on April 30, 1789. Although the Constitution was in place, Washington's immediate task was to create much of the American government and, most important of all, to give shape to the office of president. He rapidly created key executive departments, naming Thomas Jefferson as secretary of state, Henry Knox as secretary of war, Alexander Hamilton as secretary of the treasury, Samuel Osgood as head of the post office, and Edmund Randolph as attorney general. Certain of these departments Washington organized into a close body of presidential advisors, the Cabinet.

Washington understood that his administration would set the pattern for future presidents. The chief quality he introduced was restraint. He studiously avoided conflict with Congress, believing it was not the chief executive's duty to propose legislation. He also opposed the formation of political parties—although, by the time of his second term, two competing parties had, indeed, been formed: the conservative Federalists, headed by John Adams and Alexander Hamilton, and the liberal Democratic-Republicans, headed by Thomas Jefferson.

Washington could have been president for life, but it is powerful evidence of his unwillingness to become a tyrant that he declined to stand for a third term, and the two-term presidency thereafter became a

> FDR was a beloved president, to whom the nation was intensely grateful, but Congress and the people were fearful of allowing any other man or woman in the future to become president for life. On February 26, 1951, Congress approved the Twenty-second Amendment to the Constitution, restricting future presidents to no more than two terms.

hallowed tradition until the twin crises of the Depression and World War II prompted the nation to elect Franklin Delano Roosevelt to a third and a fourth term.

In classical times, Romans set one honor above all others, reserving it for their greatest leaders: the title of "*Pater Patriae*," Father of His Country. Almost immediately, the free citizens of a new nation bestowed this epithet on George Washington.

1791

The Bill of Rights

The framers of the Constitution aimed to create as concise and elegant a document as the needs of government would permit. They believed it unnecessary to provide an explicit guarantee of individual rights because the Constitution clearly stated that the government is one of "enumerated powers" exclusively. That is, the government can take no action and can assume no authority except those actions and that authority explicitly provided for in the Constitution. Anti-Federalists and many others regarded this as an insufficient safeguard against tyranny and clamored for a "bill of rights."

At the behest of Congress in 1789, James Madison painstakingly examined, weighed, and synthesized the rights already included in several state constitutions, especially the Virginia Bill of Rights, which had been adopted in 1776. He then produced a set of twelve amendments to the Constitution. The first two—which had to do with an adjustment to the proportion of congressional representatives to population and the regulation of compensation for legislators—were rejected, but the other ten, enumerating and guaranteeing individual rights, were ratified on December 15, 1791, as the Bill of Rights.

The First Amendment protects freedom of religion, freedom of speech, freedom of the press, and the right of popular assembly for the purpose of petition for redress of grievances. The Second Amendment guarantees the right to bear arms, and the Third Amendment strictly limits the quartering of soldiers in private homes. The Fourth Amendment forbids unreasonable searches and seizures and requires search-and-seizure warrants to be specific—not blanket documents—and to be issued only upon probable cause. The Fifth Amendment mandates grand jury indictments in major criminal prosecutions, prohibits "double jeopardy" (being tried more than once for the same crime), and guarantees that no one need testify against himself or herself. This amendment also forbids taking private property for public use without just compensation and prohibits deprivation of life, liberty, or property without due process of law. The Sixth Amendment guarantees a speedy public trial by jury. It further specifies that the accused must be fully informed of the charges, must be confronted with the witnesses against him or her, must have the power to subpoena witnesses for his or her defense, and must have access to legal counsel. The Seventh Amendment guarantees jury trials in civil cases, and the Eighth prohibits excessive bail, unreasonable fines, and "cruel and unusual punishments."

The Ninth and Tenth amendments are special. The Ninth explicitly provides that the enumeration of rights in the Constitution does not nullify or deny other rights, which are retained by the people. The Tenth Amendment expresses the "doctrine of reserved powers": All powers not explicitly delegated to the United States are reserved to the states or the people.

1798

Trouble with Citizen Genêt

The Treaty of Paris, which ended the American Revolution in 1783, stipulated (among many other things) that all British interests were to evacuate the frontier forts of the "Old Northwest" (roughly the region encompassing the present states of Ohio, Indiana, Illinois, Michigan, and Wisconsin). Despite the treaty, many British traders remained in the region and, in some cases, incited the local Indians against American settlers. Simultaneously, on the high seas, Royal Navy ships periodically stopped and boarded American merchant vessels and abducted sailors who were—often arbitrarily—deemed British subjects; these individuals were then "impressed" into service on British men-o'-war. For their part, the British also had grievances, complaining that the United States breached the terms of the Treaty of Paris by failing to pay prerevolutionary debts owed to British creditors and by refusing to compensate Loyalists for property seized during the Revolution.

President George Washington did not want a new war with Britain, and so commissioned Chief Justice John Jay to negotiate a new treaty to secure evacuation of the frontier forts and to see to the settlement of debt and boundary disputes. The so-called Jay Treaty, concluded on November 19, 1794, mollified the British, but greatly alarmed the French, who feared that their erstwhile ally, the United States, was about to join forces with their greatest rival.

These fears were not entirely unjustified. Most Americans recoiled from the bloody excesses of the ongoing French Revolution (1789–1799), and, just a year before the Jay Treaty was concluded, Washington had coolly rebuffed the overtures of Edmond Charles Edouard Genêt, a French diplomat sent to the United States to secure U.S. aid for France in its war with England. Although Washington gave him the cold shoulder, "Citizen Genêt" (as French revolutionary etiquette styled him) was warmly greeted by some of the American public, and Genêt chose to interpret this reception as a show of universal popular support. In defiance of the president, he hired American sea captains to raid British vessels in U.S. coastal waters. To Washington's stern warning that he was violating U.S. sovereignty, Citizen Genêt replied with a threat to make a direct appeal to the American people. At this, Washington asked the French government to recall him.

In France, by this time, a new revolutionary party, the Jacobins, had replaced the Girondists, the party to which Genêt belonged. The Jacobin government sent a new foreign minister to the United States and asked Washington to send Genêt back—under arrest. Observing strict neutrality, Washington refused to compel Genêt to return to a Jacobin guillotine. Grateful, Genêt chose to become a U.S. citizen and settled into quiet respectability as the husband of New York governor George Clinton's daughter. It was a happy ending for Genêt and for the sovereignty of the fledgling American republic, but this episode, in combination with the Jay Treaty, brought France and the United States to the brink of war.

1797

The XYZ Affair

I n an effort to heal the growing breach between the United States and France, President Washington sent a new foreign minister, Charles Cotesworth Pinckney, to France, but the French legislative body known as the Directory refused to receive him. Washington's successor, John Adams, dispatched to Paris a commission, consisting of Pinckney, John Marshall, and Elbridge Gerry, in the hope of averting outright war by concluding a new Franco–American treaty of commerce. This time, in October 1797, French prime minister Charles Maurice de Talleyrand-Perigord sent three agents to greet the American commissioners in Paris. The agents told them that before a treaty could even be discussed, the United States would have to loan France $12 million *and* pay Talleyrand a personal bribe of $250,000. Indignant, on April 3, 1798, Adams submitted to Congress the correspondence from Pinckney, Marshall, and Gerry, which designated the French agents as "X," "Y," and "Z." Congress, in turn, published the entire portfolio, and in this way the public learned of the "XYZ Affair."

The XYZ Affair ignited a small-scale, undeclared, but perilous naval war between the United States and France, and, even more dangerous, created a counterrevolutionary, antidemocratic backlash in American government, which threatened some of the liberties so recently won in the War of Independence.

1798

The Alien and Sedition Acts

Passed during the staunchly Federalist administration of President John Adams in an atmosphere of deteriorating relations with radically revolutionary France, the Alien and Sedition Acts consisted of the Naturalization Act (June 18, 1798), which required immigrants seeking U.S. citizenship to have been resident in the country for fourteen years instead of the originally mandated five; the Alien Act (June 25), which authorized the president to deport any alien he deemed dangerous; the Alien Enemies Act (July 6), which authorized the president, in time of war, to arrest, imprison, or deport nationals of any enemy power; and, most infamous of all, the Sedition Act (July 14), which banned any assembly convened "with intent to oppose any measure . . . of the government." The act also outlawed printing, uttering, or publishing anything "false, scandalous, and malicious" concerning the government.

The Sedition Act alone was an outrageous infringement of the Constitutional rights to peaceable assembly and to free speech. But even the legislation relating to naturalization and the status of aliens was a bold affront to democracy. The fact was that a great many of the leading Democratic-Republicans—the liberal party opposed to the conservative Federalists—were relatively recent refugees from turbulent Europe. They had not been resident in the United States for anything approaching fourteen years, and to postpone citizenship for them would greatly erode the power base of the fledgling opposition party. Thus, Adams and his party mounted a blatant assault on their Democratic-Republican opposition, with the tyrannical object of legislating it out of existence.

The Virginia and Kentucky Resolutions

When John Adams was elected president in 1796, the election law at the time provided that the runner-up would become vice president. This meant that Adams, a Federalist, had his Democratic-Republican arch rival, Thomas Jefferson, as his vice president. Jefferson declared that if the Alien and Sedition Acts were permitted to stand, "we shall immediately see attempted another act of Congress, declaring the President shall continue in office during life, reserving to another occasion the transfer of the succession to his heirs, and the establishment of the Senate for life." Fearing the transformation of a revolutionary democracy into a pseudo-monarchy, Jefferson drew up a set of resolutions attacking centralized governmental authority and promoting the sovereignty of the states. As vice president, however, he thought it inappropriate and disloyal for him personally to make the resolutions public, so he persuaded the legislature of Kentucky (which had become a state in 1792) to publish them on November 22, 1799. Jefferson's friend and political protégé James Madison had drafted a similar set of resolutions, which were published by Virginia on December 24, 1798.

The Virginia and Kentucky Resolutions argued that the Alien and Sedition Acts were unconstitutional and, therefore, not binding on the states. Jefferson's original draft maintained that a state not only had the right to judge the constitutionality of acts of Congress, but also to "nullify"—declare invalid—any acts it determined to be unconstitutional. The outright statement of nullification authority was too radical for the Kentucky legislature to accept, and so the passage was suppressed in the final draft of the resolutions.

Nevertheless, nullification was unmistakably implied in both the Kentucky and Virginia documents. Seeking to restore democracy to American government, Jefferson had articulated the position that the United States was a compact among the states, not among the people. While Jefferson did not contest with the federal government the powers specifically given it by the Constitution, he did hold that federal acts outside of the federal government's constitutionally enumerated powers were inherently unconstitutional and, therefore, had no binding force on the states.

The Virginia and Kentucky Resolutions galvanized opposition to repressive Federalism in the United States, and while they did not secure the immediate repeal of the Alien and Sedition Acts, they ensured that, for the most part, the laws would be short-lived. Moreover, the electorate repudiated Federalism and endorsed Jefferson's Democratic-Republican position by electing Jefferson over Adams in 1800.

The Louisiana Purchase

In his first inaugural address, Thomas Jefferson, third president of the United States, remarked the nation's great good fortune in possessing "room enough for our descendants to the thousandth and thousandth generation."

But did it really *possess* such room?

As much territory as the new nation had, it was also hemmed in. There was British Canada to the north and the vast Louisiana Territory of France to the west. Or did that land belong to Spain? Following the French and Indian War, France had ceded the territory to Spain, but in 1800, Napoleon secretly reacquired Louisiana in exchange for parts of Tuscany, which he pledged to conquer on behalf of Spain. No sooner was the Secret Treaty of San Ildefonso concluded, however, than Napoleon abandoned his plan to conquer Tuscany, and Spain reneged on the treaty. While France asserted possession of Louisiana, *Spanish* officials closed the Mississippi River to American trade in 1802. President Jefferson could not tolerate the disruption of western trade, but he was reluctant to support France's claims on the territory against those of Spain. The thought of aiding a rapacious conqueror like Napoleon to establish himself in America was appalling—and even if Napoleon did not choose to menace the United States, the ongoing warfare between France and England would, sooner or later, motivate Britain to seize Louisiana for itself.

Searching for a solution to the Louisiana crisis, Jefferson sent James Monroe to France and Spain to make an offer for the purchase of the port city of New Orleans and Spanish Florida. This would secure the Mississippi River for trade and would neutralize the Spanish along the East Coast. However, even as Monroe sailed to Europe, Napoleon pondered the fate of one of his large armies, which was bogged down in the disease-infested West Indies, fruitlessly tangling with rebels led by Haitian freedom fighter Toussaint Louverture. With little to be gained and much to be lost, Napoleon decided to withdraw from the Americas altogether and to focus exclusively on his European campaigns. In light of this decision, Louisiana became more of a French military liability than an asset, and Napoleon's minister, Talleyrand, asked the resident U.S. foreign minister, Robert R. Livingston, what Jefferson might be willing to pay, not for New Orleans alone, but for the entire Louisiana Territory. In the days before instantaneous communication, Livingston had to stall until Monroe arrived. When he did arrive, he made the greatest real estate deal the world has ever seen. For 60 million francs—about $15 million—he purchased 90,000 square miles of trans-Mississippi territory for the United States. The "Treaty for the Cession of Louisiana" was formally concluded on May 2, 1803, and antedated to April 30.

One of the conditions of the purchase was that the United States assume all financial claims of American citizens in Louisiana against France. If we discount from the purchase price the amount of this assumption, $3,750,000, then the territory was purchased at three cents an acre!

The Louisiana Purchase instantly expanded the territory of the United States by 140 percent. Eventually, the region of the purchase would contain Missouri, Nebraska, Iowa, Arkansas, North and South Dakota, Kansas, Minnesota, Montana, Wyoming, most of Louisiana, and portions of Colorado and Wyoming.

1803

The Expedition of Lewis and Clark

Thomas Jefferson's most immediate reason for making the Louisiana Purchase was to put vast distances between the United States and its European colonial neighbors. His next thought was that a great western territory could serve for the eventual peaceful—but mandatory—relocation of Indians currently living east of the Mississippi. But, deeper in his imagination, the American West meant much more to Jefferson than a solution to certain domestic and international problems. As early as 1792, Jefferson had written about the desirability of mounting a scientific expedition to explore the wonders of the West. Early in 1803, when he contemplated nothing more than the purchase of New Orleans, Jefferson twisted congressional arms to obtain $2,500 to finance such an expedition. He sold the project to Congress as a search for the fabled Northwest Passage, a water route connecting the Atlantic and the Pacific. Whether or not the president actually expected the expedition to find such a passage remains an open question, but what he had no doubt about was the scientific importance of the trek.

When he took office, Jefferson had hired his cousin, army captain Meriwether Lewis, as his private secretary. He became virtually a surrogate father to the twenty-seven-year-old Lewis, whose own father had died when he was eighteen. Seeing in the young man intelligence, courage, and resourcefulness, Jefferson appointed him to lead the "Corps of Discovery" through the vast West. As cocaptain of the expedition, Lewis chose his close friend William Clark, another very able army officer.

The Lewis and Clark expedition left St. Louis on May 14,

1804, and reached central North Dakota in November. The Corps wintered among the friendly Mandan Indians, from whom they gathered information on what lay ahead. Accompanied by a remarkable young Shoshoni woman, Sacagawea, who served as translator and guide, the Corps explored the Rockies and reached the Continental Divide on August 12, 1805. The expedition reached the Columbia River and the Pacific Ocean in November 1805. The second winter of the Corps of Discovery was spent exploring the Northwest coast, and the return trip east began in March 1806 and ended at St. Louis on September 23.

True, Lewis and Clark did not bring home news of a Northwest Passage, but their twenty-seven-month, 8,000-mile odyssey yielded a trove of geographical, biological, geological, and anthropological observations all meticulously and eloquently recorded in Lewis's journals. The explorers had discovered 122 animal species and subspecies, as well as 178 previously unknown plants. They made valuable and peaceful contact with great Indian tribes, thereby establishing the basis for profitable trade. They raised the curtain on the momentous drama of western settlement, a drama that would prove, at times, a tragedy, but also a great American epic that profoundly shaped the nation's subsequent history.

1803

Marbury v. *Madison*
Empowers the Supreme Court

The philosophical and political paths of John Adams and Thomas Jefferson, boon collaborators on the American Revolution, diverged sharply during the early days of the republic. Adams was a conservative Federalist, who believed in building a powerful central government, whereas Jefferson was a liberal who created the Democratic-Republican Party to promote a government in which most of the power rested with the states and the people. In the election of 1800, Jefferson defeated Adams in Adams's bid for a second term. Just two days before Jefferson was inaugurated, Adams, acting under the Judiciary Act of 1801, which he had championed, sought to ensure a Federalist judiciary by appointing a slate of conservative judges, marshals, and other judiciary officials. Moreover, although the Judiciary Act increased the number of federal circuit courts, thereby enabling Adams to appoint more judges, it limited the Supreme Court to five members, blocking Jefferson from appointing a Democratic-Republican to the high court.

President Jefferson lobbied for the repeal of the Judiciary Act, which was finally repealed on March 8, 1802, and replaced by a new Judiciary Act restoring the sixth Supreme Court seat and slashing the number of federal circuit courts. Prevented by the 1801 act from dismissing Federalist judges, Jefferson, acting on the new law, simply pulled the offices out from under many of Adams's "midnight appointees." But he was not completely successful in removing Federalists from government. Just two days before Jefferson's inauguration, Adams appointed William Marbury justice of the peace for Washington, D.C. Rushing headlong to complete his last-minute appointments, Adams failed to distribute—that is, actually issue—Marbury's and other appointments. Thus, when Jefferson entered office, Marbury, although *appointed* justice of the peace, had yet to *receive* his appointment. After spending months deftly dodging Marbury's attempts to secure his appointment, in February 1803, Jefferson formally directed his secretary of state, James Madison, to withhold the appointment, which, he claimed, was invalid because it had not been distributed before the repeal of the 1801 Judiciary Act.

An outraged Marbury petitioned the United States Supreme Court for a writ of mandamus, a court order to the secretary of state demanding that he distribute the commission. As a staunch Federalist, Chief Justice John Marshall might have been expected to sympathize with Marbury's plight. But Marshall was also a statesman determined to be a good steward of what was, after all, a branch of a government still evolving. He understood that if he simply issued the writ, he would put the court in direct opposition to the president, a situation he believed harmful to the fledgling government. Yet, if he denied the writ, he would forever diminish the authority of the Supreme Court by appearing to defer to the will of the chief executive.

Marshall plotted a third course. Ruling that Marbury had been wrongfully deprived of his commission, Marshall also declared that Section 13 of the Judiciary Act of 1789, the act that empowered the Supreme Court to issue writs of mandamus and under which Marbury had filed suit, was unconstitutional. The reason was this: Section 13 added to the Supreme Court's "original jurisdiction" by improperly giving the high court jurisdiction in a case that should be heard by a lower court. Thus, Marbury's suit was thrown out. However, the victory was not for Jefferson and his party, but for the Supreme Court. Marshall's ruling in the case of *Marbury* v. *Madison* forever established the momentous authority of the Supreme Court to perform "judicial review"—

that is, to review particular cases from lower courts and, if necessary, make decisions regarding them on the basis of a judgment on the constitutionality of the laws that apply in the case. This gave the Supreme Court the awesome power to set aside any statutes of Congress the court judged unconstitutional.

1807

Jefferson's Embargo

The end of the eighteenth century and the early years of the
nineteenth saw the wars of the French Revolution followed
by the Napoleonic Wars. The United States struggled to remain neutral in these great conflicts, but when neither the French
nor the English could score a decisive victory, they began to prey
on the commerce of neutral nations, including the United States.
The British even resumed the practice of "impressment," boarding
American commercial vessels, examining their crews, and pressing
into Royal Navy service any men judged on the spot to be British
subjects. British warships also seized U.S. vessels attempting to enter French ports.

Jefferson did not want to go to war with Britain over these violations of sovereignty. Instead, he pushed through Congress the
Non-Importation Act, which barred the importation of many English goods. But, on June 22, 1807, the ongoing crisis exploded
when a British warship, the *Leopard,* fired on the U.S. Navy
frigate *Chesapeake* off Norfolk Roads, Virginia. British officers
boarded the *Chesapeake* and seized four men they claimed to be
deserters from the Royal Navy. Amid national outrage and a
clamor for war, Jefferson instead championed passage of the Embargo Act of December 22, 1807. This legislation sought to punish
Britain and other European powers economically by prohibiting
all exports to Europe and severely restricting imports from Britain.

The search for an alternative to war was admirable, but the
embargo proved to be a self-inflicted economic wound. It severely

crippled the American economy and created, in effect, a nation of smugglers and lawbreakers. In the meantime, relations between the United States and Britain continued to deteriorate, and calls for war grew louder.

1812

Rise of the War Hawks

From the perspective of today, the War of 1812 seems a particularly obscure conflict. Many assume that it was fought primarily over the issue of "impressment," the British practice of abducting sailors from U.S. merchant ships and, if they were unilaterally deemed British subjects, pressing them into service aboard Royal Navy warships. In fact, shortly before the United States declared war on June 18, 1812, Britain agreed to end its impressment policy.

The real cause of the War of 1812 was land hunger. Western congressional representatives—dubbed War Hawks—pushed for war with Britain because doing so would provide two important opportunities to acquire new territory. Spanish Florida, which encompassed modern Florida, but which extended as far west as the Mississippi, was a possession of Britain's ally Spain. War with Britain would mean war with Spain, and American victory in that war would mean the acquisition of Spanish Florida. War with Britain would also give the United States another opportunity to invade Canada and, perhaps, add that vast territory to the nation's continental empire. Finally, in the "Northwest" (that is, the upper Midwest), British interests, some Canadian-based, were arming Indians against American settlers. Westerners wanted to put a stop to that.

And so war was declared—with precious little thought given to just how unprepared the United States was for it. The nation's regular army consisted of about 12,000 men in widely scattered outposts, led mainly by inexperienced officers who were, in effect, political patronage appointees. Its navy included no more than a handful of ships. The British, in contrast, had the greatest army and navy in the world.

1812

American Defeats

American military planners drew up a grandiose strategy to invade Canada in three places: from Lake Champlain to Montreal, from New York across the Niagara frontier, and from Detroit into so-called Upper Canada.

On July 12, 1812, sixty-year-old William Hull, governor of Michigan territory, led a militia force across the Detroit River into Canada, his objective to capture Fort Malden, which defended the entrance to Lake Erie. Believing himself outnumbered, Hull delayed his assault on the fort, which gave the British commander, Isaac Brock, ample time to get his regulars into position. In the meantime, the great Indian warrior Tecumseh, allied with the British, led an attack that chased Hull out of Canada and back to Fort Detroit. There Hull and his 1,500 men hunkered down until Brock's and Tecumseh's troops showed themselves. Hull surrendered Fort Detroit without firing a shot.

On the Niagara frontier, New York militia general Stephen Van Rensselaer led 2,270 militiamen and 900 regulars in an assault against Queenston Heights, Canada. On October 13, Brock, newly arrived from victory in Detroit, pinned down the portion of Van Rensselaer's force that had crossed into Canada. The rest just looked on, refusing to cross the international boundary. American defeat here was total.

This left the principal U.S. force, 5,000 men under General Henry Dearborn, waiting to invade Canada via Lake Champlain. On November 19, however, just as the invasion was about to step off, the militia contingent of Dearborn's force declared fighting across international boundaries a violation of the Constitution.

The men refused to fight, and Dearborn had no choice but to withdraw.

The collapse of these early offensives laid the West open to British invasion and to devastating raids by British-allied Indians. Fortunately, they did not take full advantage of their own early victories, but the war that the War Hawks had begun to gain new territory for the United States now greatly imperiled the continued existence of America's western frontier.

1813

Battles of Lake Erie and the Thames

During the summer of 1813, William Henry Harrison, territorial governor of Indiana, assembled an army of some 8,000 men while a bold young naval officer, Oliver Hazard Perry, built, from scratch, an armed flotilla on Lake Erie. On September 10, Perry engaged the British fleet in a fierce battle that resulted in nothing less than the destruction of the British naval presence on Lake Erie. He conveyed to Harrison one of the most famous military messages in American history: "We have met the enemy, and they are ours."

Perry's victory at the Battle of Lake Erie cut off supplies to British land forces and sent them in a general retreat from Detroit. Harrison overtook the retreating army on October 5, 1813, and fought the British and their Indian allies at the Battle of the Thames. Not only did this result in a decisive British defeat in the West, but it also brought the defeat and death of Tecumseh, in whose leadership was the last real hope of halting the American invasion of Indian lands in the West.

1814

Burning of Washington, D.C.

The American victories of 1813 brought relief to the West, but, on the East Coast, British forces continued to prosecute the war vigorously. By 1814, the British plan was to campaign in New York, along Lake Champlain and the Hudson River, with the object of severing New England from the rest of the country; simultaneously, the British planned on taking New Orleans, thereby blocking the vital Mississippi artery. Finally, while these operations were being executed, an army would attack along the Chesapeake Bay, keeping U.S. military forces occupied and preventing them from interfering at New York and New Orleans.

Late in the summer of 1814, U.S. resistance to the Chesapeake Bay attack collapsed as Major General Robert Ross led British forces to victory in the Battle of Bladensburg, Maryland, on August 24. Sweeping aside the feeble remnants of American resistance, Ross invaded Washington, D.C., and set fire to most of the public buildings, including the Capitol and White House. President James Madison and most of the government fled into the countryside.

1814

"The Star-Spangled Banner"

With Washington in flames, Robert Ross marched against Baltimore. During this, the low point of American fortunes in the War of 1812, a young Baltimore attorney, Francis Scott Key, was detained in Baltimore Harbor aboard a British warship. He watched anxiously through the night of September 13–14, 1814, as Ross bombarded Fort McHenry, the principal defense of the city. To Key's great astonishment and relief, he saw, "by dawn's early light," that the American flag, the "star-spangled banner," yet waved. Fort McHenry had held out against the British onslaught, Baltimore remained in American hands, and Ross soon withdrew. On September 14, Key penned the words to what would become the United States national anthem.

The words of "The Star-Spangled Banner" were original, but the tune they were later set to had been written in 1777 by the Englishman John Stafford Smith. Composed as a setting of a tavern verse, "To Anacreon in Heaven," the tune was applied to Key's verse by about 1820. It did not become the official national anthem until President Herbert Hoover proclaimed it so on March 3, 1931.

Battle of Lake Champlain

While Washington burned and Baltimore resisted attack, a large force of 10,000 British soldiers, all veterans of the just-concluded Napoleonic Wars, marched south from Montreal. Their objective, ultimately, was New York City, and they intended, en route, to cut off New England from the rest of the country. The United States had no land forces sufficient to resist such an invasion, but, on September 11, 1814, American naval captain Thomas MacDonough engaged, defeated, and destroyed the British fleet on Lake Champlain. This spectacular victory was sufficient to send into retreat the 10,000-man land force, which rightly feared being entirely cut off from any source of supply.

The victory on Lake Champlain gave the American negotiators considerable strength as they hammered out a treaty with their British counterparts in the Flemish city of Ghent. That treaty, which ended the War of 1812, was signed on December 24, 1814. It restored the "status quo ante bellum"—the situation as it had been before the war. The War of 1812 had been dangerous and very costly for the United States, which gained no territory or other consideration as a result of it. Yet many judged it nothing less than a "a second war of independence." For better or worse, the United States had stood up to the greatest military power in the world—and had not lost.

1814

Battle of Horseshoe Bend

L ike the American Revolution before it, the War of 1812 was not just a conflict between Americans and British, but also involved the Indian allies of these powers. Most Indian tribes that did not remain neutral sided with the British during the War of 1812 in the belief that a British victory would curb American incursions into Indian lands.

On March 27, 1814, Andrew Jackson, at the time a minor frontier political figure, led a successful campaign against the hostile "Red Stick" Creek Indians and defeated them at the Battle of Horseshoe Bend, in present-day Alabama. This brought an end to a phase of the War of 1812 sometimes referred to as the Creek War. The treaty that resulted forced the Creeks to yield to the United States about two-thirds of their tribal lands, a massive cession that instantly pushed American settlement from the Tennessee River out to the Gulf of Mexico. The victory also thrust Jackson into national prominence. A second victory would prime him, ultimately, for the White House.

1815

Battle of New Orleans

n 1814, even the most momentous news traveled at the stately pace of wood and sail, and so neither Andrew Jackson nor British major general Edward Pakenham received word of the Treaty of Ghent before they met in battle at New Orleans.

Pakenham led 7,500 British veterans from Jamaica to attack New Orleans, which was defended by 3,100 Tennessee and Kentucky volunteers, in addition to local militiamen and hangers-on, all under the command of Jackson, fresh from his triumph at Horseshoe Bend.

Jackson's outnumbered forces repulsed two British attacks. Then, on January 8, 1815, having suffered severe losses—including the fatal wounding of Pakenham—the British withdrew. Although the battle came after the war had ended, it gave Americans the sweet taste of victory, and it let them feel that the War of 1812, for the most part a costly mistake, had been an American triumph. As for Jackson, his fortune was made. Catapulted to national prominence, he was destined to become a two-term president who brought to the federal government the common touch and was the first representative of the American frontier to hold the reins of national power.

1817

The Rush–Bagot Agreement

I n 1817, President James Monroe's acting secretary of state, Richard Rush, and British minister to the United States, Charles Bagot, negotiated the Rush–Bagot Agreement, definitively establishing the U.S. border with Quebec, which had been a sore spot in relations with British Canada. Even more important, the agreement established a precedent of a nonfortified, open border between the United States and Canada.

These days we take our cordial relations with our northerly neighbor for granted, but things didn't start out that way: Americans had invaded Canada during the Revolution and, again, during the War of 1812. Ever since Rush–Bagot, however, we've been on the most cordial of terms, with border relations the friendliest in the world. The relationship is certainly rare in history, perhaps even unique.

The Erie Canal Is Built

During the administration of James Monroe (1817–1825), westerners pushed for federal assistance in building the roads the West urgently needed in order to foster its commerce and economy. The president consistently vetoed such projects, however, for he did not believe in showing federal favor to any particular region. His attitude did not kill the projects, but, on the contrary, spurred development of an alternative link between the East Coast and the nation's vast inland realm.

As early as 1699 a French engineer named Vauban advocated building a canal between Lake Erie and Lake Ontario. By the beginning of the nineteenth century, when the Allegheny Mountains were effectively the western frontier, many Americans were coming to realize that the so-called Northwest Territories—the region that would later become Illinois, Indiana, Michigan, Wisconsin, and Ohio—were extremely rich in timber, minerals, and fertile farmland. The problem was transporting the produce and resources of this region back to markets in the East. In 1800, Gouverneur Morris, U.S. senator from New York, proposed building a great canal from the Hudson River to Buffalo, a growing commercial center on Lake Erie. As usual, the federal government would have none of it, but Governor De Witt Clinton of New York was excited by the prospect of a water link from Buffalo to Albany, on the upper Hudson River, which would thereby connect New York City, principal metropolis of the Northeast coast, with the great West.

Such a canal would be no small undertaking, since the distance between Buffalo and Albany was almost 400 miles. Yet, as

Clinton wrote in 1816, "As an organ of communication between the Hudson, the Mississippi, the St. Lawrence, the Great Lakes of the north and west and their tributary rivers, the canal will create the greatest inland trade ever witnessed," transforming New York City into "the granary of the world, the emporium of commerce, the seat of manufactures, the focus of great moneyed operations. . . . And before the revolution of a century, the whole island of Manhattan, covered with inhabitants and replenished with a dense population, will constitute one vast city." The following year, Clinton persuaded the state legislature to authorize $7 million for construction of a canal 363 miles long, 40 feet wide, and 4 feet deep.

After eight years of intensive labor, the canal was completed and, on October 26, 1825, Governor Clinton set out from Buffalo in the canal boat *Seneca Chief* along with two other boats to formally open the Erie Canal. The journey into New York Harbor took nine days—much faster than freight could be carted overland. Some 150 vessels and thousands of New Yorkers greeted the arrival, and Clinton emptied two barrels of Lake Erie water into the ocean at New York City in a ceremony contemporary publicists grandiosely dubbed the "Marriage of the Waters" between the Great Lakes and the Atlantic.

Before the canal, overland freight rates from Buffalo to New York City were $100 per ton. After the canal, rates dropped to $10 per ton. In 1829, 3,640 bushels of wheat traveled down the canal from Buffalo. By 1837, the figure was 500,000 bushels, and in 1841 the number of bushels topped one million. The success of the Erie Canal ignited a spectacular canal-building boom. By 1840, the United States was veined by 3,326 miles of canals.

Boundaries Settled, Territories Acquired

The Convention of 1818, hammered out by President Monroe's secretary of state John Quincy Adams and the British government, tackled the thorny issue of the Oregon Territory—the land west of the Rocky Mountains, extending from the forty-second parallel north to 54 degrees 42 minutes. The War of 1812 had failed to settle the boundary between the United States and British Canada here, and the 1818 convention called for joint U.S. and British occupation. True, this was nothing more than a temporary solution to ultimate possession of a very hotly contested region, and it by no means put the boundary dispute to bed, but it *was* a solution—a peaceful solution—and it showed that England was now quite willing to take American sovereignty seriously.

On February 12, 1819, Secretary Adams concluded another treaty, this one with Luis de Oñis, Spain's minister to the United States. It secured possession of both western and eastern Florida for the United States. With the acquisition of this territory, a principal objective of the War of 1812 was belatedly realized.

More difficult, however, was figuring out the precise border between the United States and Mexico, which was, until the Mexican Revolution of 1822, a colonial possession of Spain. Adams wanted a border that would pull Texas into American territory, but Spain was unwilling to relinquish both Texas and Florida to the United States, so the secretary of state finally agreed on a boundary at the Sabine River—the western boundary of the present-day state of Louisiana—and renounced any claim to Texas. This renunciation survived into the era of Mexican independence; however, after Texas won its independence from Mexico in 1836, the border issue would flare up again and, ultimately, become a cause for war between Mexico and the United States.

The busy Department of State concluded yet one more key treaty, this one with the czar of Russia, who had laid claim to the California coast as far south as San Francisco Bay. Adams managed to persuade his ministers to settle for a position north of the 54-degree-42-minute line, so that Russia would no longer be a third contender for the Oregon Territory. The czar retained his claim to Alaska—but, at the time, no one in the United States could imagine a use for that frozen wasteland.

1820

The Missouri Compromise

Since the ratification of the Constitution in 1787, the people of the United States had lived a lie, namely that a democratic nation could exist half free and half slave. That lie raised its ugly head whenever the balance between slave and free states was threatened. In 1818, the United States Senate consisted of twenty-two senators from free states and twenty-two from slave-holding states. Ever since independence, the balance between the non-slaveholding North and the slaveholding South had been precariously preserved with the addition of each state. But now the territory of Missouri petitioned Congress for admission to the Union—as a slaveholding state. The balance was in jeopardy, and Congress scrambled to find a new way to perpetuate the same old lie.

New York representative James Tallmadge introduced an amendment to the Missouri statehood bill allowing persons who were slaves in the present Missouri Territory to remain slaves after statehood, but banning the introduction of new slaves into the state. Furthermore, all slaves born in the state would continue as slaves until they reached twenty-five years of age, whereupon they would be automatically emancipated. In this way, slavery would be gradually eliminated from Missouri. The House of Representatives, which contained a free-state majority, passed the Tallmadge amendment, but the Senate, evenly divided between slave states and free, rejected it—and then promptly adjourned without reaching a decision on Missouri statehood. Only after the Senate reconvened did a long and agonizing debate begin.

The northern senators held that Congress possessed the authority to ban slavery in new states. The southerners countered that new states had the same right as the original thirteen: to determine for themselves whether they would allow slavery or not. After much wrangling, a compromise was reached in March 1820. It was grudgingly agreed that Missouri would be admitted to the Union as a slave state, but, simultaneously, that Maine (which had been a part of Massachusetts and was now seeking statehood in its own right) would be admitted as a free state.

Thus, the balance was preserved—for the present. But the Missouri Compromise also looked toward the future, stipulating that a line be drawn across the Louisiana Territory at a latitude of 36 degrees 30 minutes, north of which slavery would be forever banned—except in the case of Missouri. No one was truly pleased with the Missouri Compromise, but it did hold together the increasingly fragile Union for three more decades.

Texas Colonized

The Louisiana Purchase of 1803 added a large amount of territory to the United States, and many poured in to settle it. Yet, vast as the Louisiana Territory was, it seemed only to whet the appetite for more land. In the 1810s, Augustus Magee, a U.S. army officer stationed in the Louisiana Territory, befriended one Bernardo Gutierrez, who had been fighting for Mexican independence from Spain. Together, Magee and Gutierrez led an expedition into Texas, where they captured the lightly held villages of Nacogdoches, Goliad, and San Antonio. But then Magee died—no one knows why—and the expedition abruptly ended. Shortly after this, in 1819, Dr. James Long of Natchez, Mississippi, led another expedition to Texas, hoping to carve out of the region an independent state; he was soon defeated by Spanish colonial forces.

In 1820, Moses Austin, a Missouri lead miner, took a different tack. He traveled to San Antonio—in peace—and sought government permission to establish an American colony in the area. The Spanish government responded with a modest grant, but Moses Austin fell ill and died in 1821 before he could actually begin the project of settlement. On his deathbed, he asked his son, Stephen F. Austin, to carry out his plans. The young man was bookish and introverted—hardly a born leader—but he promised his dying father that he would do his best.

In the meantime, Mexico had won independence from Spain and made to Stephen Austin an even more generous grant than the Spanish government had offered his father. Soon, Austin led more than 1,200 American families to Texas, and by 1836 the American population of Mexican Texas had exploded to 50,000.

The Monroe Doctrine

The Napoleonic Wars, which spanned 1803 to 1815, were, in significant measure, *world* wars. Combat reached the American hemisphere, particularly South America, where, by overthrowing old regimes in Europe, the Napoleonic Wars sparked widespread revolution in the colonies. After Napoleon's final defeat in 1815, Spain started making noises about reclaiming the South American colonies it had lost. Britain, which now enjoyed highly profitable trade relationships with the new South American republics, asked the United States to join it in a stand against Spanish interference in South America. But instead of joining hands with the British in protesting any Spanish incursion into South America, President James Monroe included in his 1823 state of the union message to Congress the four principles we now call the Monroe Doctrine. He declared, in the first place, that the Americas were no longer available for colonization by any power. Second, he pointed out that the political system of the Americas was basically and essentially different from that of Europe. Third, he warned that the United States would consider any interference by European powers in the affairs of any of the Americas a direct threat to United States security. Finally, he pledged that the United States would not interfere with existing colonies, nor with the internal affairs of European nations, nor would it participate in any European wars.

It was a bold doctrine for a nation that, in 1823, possessed no standing army and a navy of minuscule proportions. But the Monroe Doctrine has endured into the present, exerting a powerful influence on our nation's foreign policy as the United States fashioned itself the guardian of the hemisphere. A stance of great strategic importance, it has also served, at times, to justify imposing the American will on smaller republics, especially in Central America and the Caribbean.

Congress "Removes" the Indians

"An Act to Provide for an Exchange of Lands with the Indians Residing in Any of the States or Territories, and for Their Removal West of the River Mississippi"—known more simply as the Indian Removal Act—was signed into law on May 28, 1830 by President Andrew Jackson, and, for that reason, the policy of "Indian removal" has always been associated with him. However, the idea of relocating Indians living east of the Mississippi River to specially reserved Indian Territory in the West did not originate with Jackson. The very first president of the United States, George Washington, talked of finding some equivalent of a "Chinese Wall" to separate Indians and whites, and Presidents Jefferson, Madison, and Monroe all contemplated the issue. It was President John Quincy Adams who laid the administrative groundwork for the legislation that was finally enacted during the Jackson administration.

The Indian Removal Act was not a government-decreed land grab, nor did the law itself mandate the *forcible* eviction of the Indians. Rather, it provided for land exchanges supplemented by re-settlement funds, subsidies, and annuities. Nor was the law overtly motivated by government-sanctioned racism—although racism certainly played a part in Indian removal. As John Quincy Adams saw it, the legislation was key to averting a constitutional crisis. On December 20, 1828, the legislature of Georgia enacted a law to bring all Indian residents of the state under state jurisdiction within six months. Like Georgia, other southern states, desirous of appropriating Indian lands, contemplated similar legislation aimed at circumventing federal laws protecting Indian lands and

Indian rights. The state legislation came after President Adams repeatedly denied southern requests for the federal removal of the Indians. The president was even prepared to send federal troops into Georgia and other southern states in which Indian rights were being violated and lands confiscated. A showdown between federal authority and states' rights was brewing, and civil war loomed. Adams decided to defuse the issue by resettling the Indians of the Southeast in the West.

While the 1830 law outlined a fundamentally voluntary exchange of eastern lands for western lands, in practice Indian removal was tragically very different. Most often, Indians were coerced or duped into making land exchanges. Typically, government officials would secure an agreement from compliant individual Indians, then would hold the agreement as binding, regardless of whether or not a majority of the tribe concurred. Once even a dubious agreement was concluded, the government believed itself entitled to remove *all* Indians of the tribe, by force, if necessary.

1831

Rebellion of Nat Turner

Throughout history, wherever slavery was practiced, fears of slave rebellion loomed, and, in the American South, such anxieties were occasionally justified. Nat Turner was a slave and charismatic lay preacher. He assembled a band of fellow slaves on the Southampton County, Virginia, plantation of Joseph Travis and, just before dawn on August 22, 1831, led them in killing every white member of the Travis household. After this, they raked the countryside, killing every white they encountered during the next twenty-four hours—fifty-five in all. The white response was equally swift and terrible. Not only were Turner and fifty of his followers captured and tried, twenty were summarily hanged, and white avengers then launched out on a rampage of indiscriminate killing and torture of whatever blacks were unfortunate enough to cross paths with them.

Horrific as the Turner rebellion and its aftermath were, equally destructive was the widespread panic created throughout the South, which hardened southern antagonism to growing antislavery efforts in the North. The lines of coming battle were being drawn.

1831

Abolitionists Lose Patience

The very year that saw Nat Turner's Rebellion also witnessed the emergence of a new newspaper in the North. William Lloyd Garrison was a liberal New Englander from Newburyport, Massachusetts, who became coeditor of a moderate abolitionist newspaper called the *Genius of Universal Emancipation.* But Garrison soon abandoned moderation and, on January 1, 1831, published the first issue of the *Liberator,* a radical abolitionist periodical that demanded nothing less than the immediate emancipation of all slaves.

The eloquent and impassioned *Liberator* electrified the abolitionist movement. Garrison became the most powerful white voice in support of abolition, and he was among those who pushed the slavery issue beyond compromise.

Nullification Crisis

By the early nineteenth century, cotton, in the American South, was king, and the biggest customer for southern cotton was England, which spun the crop into cloth, then exported the finished cloth to the United States. Because of its higher quality, British fabric was more eagerly sought after in the United States than domestic-milled cloth. The result was that northern textile industries increasingly suffered. Through the first twenty-five years of the nineteenth century, the South enjoyed almost completely free trade with England and its other European customers. U.S.-imposed tariffs and duties were all but nonexistent. This was a great boon to the agricultural economy of the South, but it was a drag on the fledgling industrial economy of the North. To prod Americans into buying American-made goods, such as domestic cotton cloth, Congress passed a strongly protective tariff law in 1828, levying a heavy duty on all imported manufactured goods. Northerners welcomed the tariff, while southerners took to cursing it as the "Tariff of Abominations."

In response to the 1828 tariff, John C. Calhoun, from South Carolina and, at the time, vice president under John Quincy Adams, became the architect of a profound crisis. He composed an anonymous pamphlet entitled *South Carolina Exposition and Protest,* which argued that any state could pronounce the federal tariff "null and void" if that state deemed it unconstitutional.

Now, the notion of nullification was not original with Calhoun. No less than two founding fathers, James Madison and Thomas Jefferson, had introduced the nullification concept in their Virginia and Kentucky resolutions of 1798 and 1799 opposing the

Alien and Sedition Acts. Despite this precedent, Calhoun had a hard time recruiting support for nullification; most of the southern states repudiated the doctrine. In any case, the timely election of Andrew Jackson, who had campaigned, in part, on a platform of tariff reform, stole Calhoun's thunder. But the promised reform was slow in coming and, when it came, it proved deeply disappointing to the South. The Tariff Act of 1832, passed during the Jackson administration, so offended Calhoun that he promptly resigned as Jackson's vice president and stood for election to the Senate. He won, and, at his instigation, the state of South Carolina called a convention that, on November 24, 1832, enacted an Ordinance of Nullification forbidding collection of tariff duties in the state. Another South Carolina senator, Robert Y. Hayne, upped the ante to an even more dangerous level when he embellished Calhoun's nullification theory with the additional argument that not only could a state nullify an unconstitutional law, it could also, as a last resort, withdraw from the Union itself. In response, Massachusetts senator and legendary orator Daniel Webster delivered his most famous speech, defending the powers of the federal government versus the alleged rights of the states: "Liberty and Union, now and forever, one and inseparable!"

Nullification brought the nation to a crisis, a stark showdown between the will of a single state and the law of the land. The scope of the crisis reached far beyond the Tariff of 1832. Underneath it all, Calhoun and his cohorts were fighting for the perpetuation of an economy based on slavery. They clearly saw that slavery would, someday, be abolished by a northern majority in Congress. Calhoun was quite capable of doing the math, and he understood that such a majority, someday, was inevitable. The nullification doctrine seemed the only means of circumventing the democratic principle of majority rule, especially if the doctrine was linked to the threat of secession.

Calhoun took heart in the belief that Andrew Jackson, a southerner after all, would now certainly back down on the tariff. Instead, Jackson responded to nullification on December 10, 1833, with a declaration that not only asserted the constitutionality of the tariff, but denied the power of any state to prevent enforcement of a federal law. The president vowed to use federal troops to enforce the collection of duties, and he secured from Congress passage of a Force Act, which empowered him to do so.

The Force Act might well have brought on civil war, not in 1861 but in 1833. However, having made his point, Jackson then supported a compromise tariff, which mollified the South. War had been averted—for the present—but nullification and the concepts of states' rights and secession would not go away. Even after the South had fought and lost the Civil War, the doctrine of states' rights would resurface in the twentieth century as an excuse for dodging the force of federal civil rights legislation.

1836

Fall of the Alamo

By 1836, the Texas colony Stephen Austin had founded in 1821 had grown to 50,000 Americans. The local Mexican population was only 3,500. During the 1830s, the burgeoning American majority chafed under Mexican rule. Many objected in particular to Mexican laws forbidding slavery. Many were disturbed by cultural and religious differences with the Mexicans: The colonists were predominantly Protestant while the Mexicans were overwhelming Catholic. Austin, believing his colony was hardly prepared to fight a war of independence, repeatedly negotiated terms of peaceful coexistence with the ever-tumultuous Mexican government. He drafted a proposed constitution to make Texas a full-fledged Mexican state, and in 1833 traveled to Mexico City to seek an audience with Antonio López de Santa Anna, the country's new president. Austin waited five months before he was granted an audience; then Santa Anna rejected the plea for statehood. As Austin rode back to Texas, he was arrested, returned to Mexico City, and imprisoned there for the next two years. At last released in 1835, Austin was broken in health and returned to Texas sufficiently embittered to urge Texans to support an internal Mexican revolt against Santa Anna. It was this that triggered the Texas Revolution.

Against the advice of Sam Houston, who became the de facto leader of the Texas revolution, a small force of Texans under militia colonel William B. Travis took a defensive stand behind the walls of the decayed Spanish mission called San Antonio de Valero, but nicknamed the Alamo because it was close to a grove of cottonwoods (*alamos* in Spanish). Santa Anna entered San Antonio on February 25, 1836. A number of noncombatants, mostly women and children, now took refuge with the Alamo garrison, and, at the last minute, reinforcements arrived, bringing the number of the Alamo defenders to 189 (some recent scholars believe the number was over 250).

Santa Anna unleashed a weeklong artillery bombardment, which—quite incredibly—failed to kill a single Texan, even as the defenders' grapeshot and rifle fire took a heavy toll among the attackers. However, the artillery did batter down the Alamo walls faster than the defenders could repair them, and, on March 6, Santa Anna deployed 1,800 men to storm the fortress. It was a clumsy attack that cost the Mexicans about 600 killed, but sheer numbers prevailed. After an hour and a half of fighting, almost all of the Alamo's defenders had fallen, and the old mission was in Santa Anna's hands. Davy Crockett—the legendary Tennessee frontiersman who had volunteered to defend the Alamo—and the few other prisoners Santa Anna took were summarily executed. The women and children who had sought refuge in the Alamo were released, however, and Santa Anna charged one of their number, Susannah Dickerson, to tell all of Texas what had happened at the Alamo. He was confident that her tale of horror would extinguish any further rebellion. He was, of course, mistaken.

1836

Independence for Texas

L ed by Sam Houston, a small army of Texans rallied to the battle cry of "Remember the Alamo!" Houston mustered only about 800 Texans against 1,250 Mexicans under Santa Anna at the Battle of San Jacinto, west of the San Jacinto River, just off Galveston Bay, on April 21, 1836. But he led them brilliantly, advancing on Santa Anna's forces as they were settling in for their afternoon siesta. He ordered his men to hold their fire until his main column was just sixty yards from the Mexicans. Then, with a shout of "Remember the Alamo!" Houston ordered the attack.

The battle, which gained Texas its independence, was over in fifteen minutes. Six hundred thirty Mexican troops were killed— many frankly slaughtered in revenge for the Alamo and for the earlier execution of prisoners at Goliad, Texas. Texan forces lost nine killed and thirty-four wounded, including Houston, who had taken a musket ball in the right leg. Santa Anna temporarily escaped, but was soon captured. Houston spared his life in exchange for his signature on the Treaty of Velasco on May 14, 1836, whereby Mexico granted the full and complete independence of Texas.

1837

"The American Scholar": Milestone in American Culture

In an age before movies, radio, and television, the public lecture was a popular form of entertainment, and even speeches delivered before special audiences—such as the Harvard chapter of the Phi Beta Kappa Society—sometimes received wide attention. In 1837, Ralph Waldo Emerson, who would soon gain a reputation as the dean of American men of letters, was just getting his literary start. When he spoke before the Phi Beta Kappa audience on August 31 of that year, he made an impact that is difficult to appreciate or even understand today. People listened—and they were changed by what they heard. The author and physician Dr. Oliver Wendell Holmes, Sr. (father of the famed Supreme Court justice), called the speech "our intellectual Declaration of Independence."

The title of the speech, "The American Scholar," was hardly one to set the world on fire, but the message electrified and inspired not only American intellectuals, but Americans in general. By the late 1830s, Americans were justly proud of their international and historical standing as political pioneers, but in matters cultural, intellectual, and aesthetic, they remained the vassals of old Europe, slavishly adhering to European standards of art, of literature, of philosophy, and thereby stunting the development of American creativity. In his speech, Emerson called on the rising generation of the nation's cultural creators to strike out on bold new intellectual and artistic paths, just as the founding fathers had dared to blaze new political and moral trails. Democracy demanded a democratic art and science and philosophy. And just as a government dedicated to liberty was a vast improvement on ancient governments shackled by kings and queens and deference to them, so an art, literature, science, and philosophy produced with true independence by a democratic people was bound to be an improvement on the cultural pursuits of the outmoded continent across the sea. If American writers and artists complained that, in contrast to Europeans, they had no rich native history to draw on—no great myths and legends—Emerson countered that Americans did not *suffer* from the absence of such a history, but were blessed by *freedom* from it. Nothing of an outworn past need retard intellectual and aesthetic progress in America. Instead, Americans were in an enviable and unique position to be pioneers not just of human settlement, but also of the human spirit and the human mind. Soon, Emerson argued, it would be Europe that followed the American lead.

Between Emerson's 1837 speech and the Civil War in 1861, American arts and letters enjoyed a sudden and spectacular renaissance that stunned and continues to stun the world. The naturalist philosopher-poet Henry David Thoreau began writing, the poet Walt Whitman published his *Leaves of Grass,* Edgar Allan Poe raised the horror tale to a height of uncanny psychological penetration, Nathaniel Hawthorne created profound allegories of the soul tormented by personal history, and Herman Melville expanded the novel into a book about the universe within each of us and beyond each of us. The literary and philosophical works of this "American Renaissance" (as later literary historians called it)—triggered, it seems, by Emerson's message—transported America from the backwaters of world culture to a leading position in the thought and art of the nineteenth and twentieth centuries and of our present day.

The Trail of Tears

Pursuant to the Indian Removal Act of 1830, some northeastern tribes were peacefully resettled in Indian Territory. However, many of the Indians of the Southeast, members of the so-called Five Civilized Tribes—Chickasaw, Choctaw, Seminole, Cherokee, and Creek—militantly resisted removal. The army was called out and, under extreme coercion, about 100,000 of these people were marched off to Indian Territory (the present state of Oklahoma and some surrounding territory) during the 1830s. About one-quarter of this number died en route.

Most infamous among the removals was the Cherokee trek of 1838–1839 along what generations of Cherokees have called the "Trail of Tears." Concentrated in Georgia, the Cherokee tribe was politically sophisticated. The tribe's majority, organized into the Nationalist Party, appealed to the U.S. Supreme Court in 1832 to protest abuse and land swindles suffered at the hands of Georgia. In *Worcester* v. *Georgia* (1832), Chief Justice John Marshall declared the state's actions unconstitutional, but President Jackson refused to use federal power to enforce the high court's decision. Instead, he advised the Indians to resolve their difficulties by accepting removal. At Jackson's direction, a removal treaty, the Treaty of New Echota (December 29, 1835), was negotiated with a minority Cherokee party, called the Treaty Party, which represented perhaps 1,000 out of 17,000 Cherokees. Although, then, the treaty was rejected seventeen to one, the government held it as binding on all of the Cherokees, and, during the summer of 1838, Major General Winfield Scott began a mass roundup of Cherokees and confined them for the rest of the summer in what were, in fact, concentration camps. During the fall and winter of 1838–1839, Scott marched them under armed escort 1,200 miles to Indian Territory. They were cold, short of food, and often abused by their military guards, who raped women, robbed everyone, and killed anyone who made trouble. Four thousand of the 15,000 who started on the journey perished.

A Georgia soldier recalled years after the Trail of Tears trek: "I fought through the Civil War and have seen men shot to pieces and slaughtered by thousands, but the Cherokee removal was the cruelest work I ever saw."

Invention of the Telegraph

In the nineteenth century, space, vast space, was the great American blessing—and curse. There was plenty of land to accommodate a burgeoning population, and yet how could a nation—one nation—be held together over such a vast territory? How could Americans communicate with one another?

The answer, it turned out, was technological rather than political, but the person who supplied the solution was no technologist. He was a painter. Born in Charlestown, Massachusetts, in 1791, Samuel F. B. Morse earned a solid reputation as an artist. He twice studied abroad, and, on the return voyage from his second trip, he struck up a conversation with another passenger, a British scientist named Thomas Jackson. These chats literally sparked an idea in Morse's imagination: Why not use electrical current as a medium through which communication might be transmitted?

Once home, Morse laid aside his brushes and set about inventing what he called the telegraph. That word was not his invention. It had been used to describe any number of signaling systems, typically employing semaphore flags or lanterns displayed on hilltop towers, at least as early as the beginning of the nineteenth century, and the word itself was compounded of two Greek roots—the "tele" portion meaning distant, and the "graph" part signifying writing: distant writing. But the idea of harnessing the still highly novel (and, thus far, pretty useless) phenomenon of electricity to transmit intelligible speech was groundbreaking.

Morse read the scientific journals of his day and learned that, in 1819, the Danish scientist Hans C. Oersted (1777–1851) had discovered the principle of "induction" when he noticed that a wire carrying an electric current deflected a magnetic needle. Several scientists had followed up on this discovery by experimenting with deflecting-needle telegraphs. Two men, William F. Cooke and Charles Wheatstone, actually installed a working deflecting-needle telegraph along a railway line in England in 1837—but the technology was too fragile and unreliable to be developed much further. Morse read that, in 1825, William Sturgeon had invented the electromagnet—a coil of wire wrapped around an iron core, which magnetized the core only as long as current flowed through the coil. Building on this, and further inspired by the electromagnetic experiments of Michael Faraday and Joseph Henry, Morse began working on a telegraph receiver based on the electromagnet. When energized by a current from the line—that is, when the remote operator pressed a switch ("telegraph key")—Morse's electromagnet attracted a soft iron armature, which was designed to make marks on a moving piece of paper. Depending on the duration of the electrical impulse received, the armature would inscribe a dot (if the remote telegraph key had been depressed for a fraction of a second) or a dash (if it had been held down a bit longer). Not only did Morse invent a robust electromagnetic telegraphic transmitter and receiver, he also created a logically coded system of short *dots* and longer *dashes* for transmitting the alphabet with the device.

Once Morse was confident that he had perfected a practical device, he persuaded Congress to finance the world's first long-distance telegraph line, between Washington, D.C., and Baltimore, a distance of about forty miles. On May 24, 1844, he transmitted the first telegraphic message over that wire: "What hath God wrought?"

Within a decade of Morse's first message, the nation's original forty miles of wire stretched to 23,000, and the telegraph was well on its way to annihilating distance itself.

Black America Gains a Voice

Frederick Douglass was born into slavery in 1817 on a Maryland plantation. His master sent him to Baltimore to learn the skill of ship caulking. The young man had already been taught the alphabet by his master's wife, and, while apprenticing in Baltimore, he taught himself how to write by tracing the letters of the names of ships painted on their prows. In 1838, Douglass obtained seaman's papers from a free black. Using these, he made his escape to New Bedford, Massachusetts, and freedom. Ever since he had learned to read and write, Douglass was a voracious reader and soon discovered William Lloyd Garrison's *Liberator*. By 1841, he had added eloquence to literacy, and he found himself in great demand as a lecturer under the auspices of the Massachusetts Anti-Slavery Society. Douglass was so impressive an orator that many whites, even those who meant well, simply refused to believe that he had ever actually been a slave. As this skepticism became increasingly persistent, Douglass was moved to write, in 1845, his autobiography, the *Narrative of the Life of Frederick Douglass*, an unflinching account of slavery and liberation, which not only portrayed the inhumanity of slavery, but, even more important, exhibited to the world the intense humanity of the slaves.

Five thousand copies of *Narrative* were sold within four months of its first printing, and six new editions were published between 1845 and 1849. Douglass published two later versions, *My Bondage and My Freedom* (1855) and *The Life and Times of Frederick Douglass* (1881).

1845

The "Great American Pastime"

Games resembling baseball had been played in England and America for years. They were called "one o'cat," "rounders," "base," and even "baseball." By the mid-nineteenth century, social-athletic clubs were formed in American cities to play these games. One such club, a Manhattan group calling itself the Knickerbocker Base Ball Club, wrote down the rules of their game in 1845—and to this event may be assigned the birth of "professional" baseball in the United States.

Within twenty years of the Knickerbockers' codification of the rules, baseball became the most popular game in America, and before the end of the nineteenth century, it was being called the "great American pastime."

Texas Statehood and a California Revolution

Having won its independence from Mexico in 1836, Texas existed as a republic while United States legislators argued over admitting it to the Union as a new state. There was the usual problem over upsetting the legislative balance between slave and free states by admitting a slave state, and there was also the near certainty that taking on Texas would mean war between the United States and Mexico. For expansionists, who saw such a war as a means of acquiring much southwest territory, the prospect of the conflict was both necessary and inviting. For others, especially those in the Northeast, picking a fight with Mexico seemed both unwise and immoral.

As both England and France made overtures of alliance to the Republic of Texas, the president and Congress at last acted, and Texas was admitted to statehood on December 29, 1845. As predicted, this brought the United States and Mexico to the verge of war. Then, when President James K. Polk saw that England and France were now hungrily eyeing California—which was held so feebly by Mexico that it looked ready to drop into the hands of whoever was there to catch it—he offered Mexico $40 million for the territory. Not only did the Mexican president turn down the offer, he also rebuffed President Polk's emissary, refusing even to see him. This provoked Polk to authorize the U.S. consul at Monterey (California), Thomas O. Larkin, to organize California's small but powerful American community into a movement for U.S. annexation. At the same time, John Charles Frémont—a daring and headstrong western explorer surveying prospective transcontinental railroad routes for the U.S. Bureau of Topographical Engineers—marched into California and took over the incipient independence movement, the so-called Bear Flag Rebellion, proclaiming the Bear Flag Republic on June 14, 1846. After a skirmish or two, California independence was secured. By this time, however, the short-lived Bear Flag Rebellion had dissolved into the events of the U.S.–Mexican War. For, as Mexico saw it, the rebellion in California only added insult to the injury inflicted by the annexation of Texas, whose border with Mexico the Mexican government disputed.

1846

The U.S.–Mexican War Begins

After the United States admitted Texas to the Union and precipitated a rebellion in California, Mexican troops laid siege to Fort Texas—present-day Brownsville—on May 1. President Polk dispatched troops to the new state and, on May 13, 1846, declared war on Mexico. General Zachary Taylor, marching to the relief of the fort, faced 6,000 Mexican troops with a mere 2,000 Americans, but nevertheless defeated the enemy in the May 8 Battle of Palo Alto.

That contest established the pattern for the rest of the war. Typically, American forces were significantly outnumbered by the Mexican troops, which, however, were so poorly led and indifferently equipped (chronically supplied with faulty gunpowder and ammunition) that the Americans, enthusiastic and commanded by highly competent officers, almost always prevailed. On May 9, Taylor was victorious at Resaca de la Palma, a dry riverbed just north of the Rio Grande, and he advanced onto Mexican soil.

In the meantime, early in June, *official* U.S. action got underway against the Mexicans in California as Stephen Watts Kearny led the "Army of the West" from Fort Leavenworth, Kansas, to California via New Mexico. Along the way, Kearny captured Santa Fe on August 15 without firing a shot. Before Kearny even reached California, he was intercepted by the legendary Indian fighter Kit Carson, who told him that, on August 17, Commodore Robert F. Stockton had announced the annexation of California. A brief spasm of resistance was put down in December and January, and California was secure.

In New Mexico, during the winter of 1846–1847, resistance

was more violent. On January 19, 1847, the citizens of Taos killed the local sheriff and a deputy, then murdered Governor Charles Bent as well as any other Americans they could find. Colonel Sterling Price—who would later serve the Confederacy as a general—made short work of the so-called Taos Rebellion.

"Civil Disobedience"

In the American West and South, the war with Mexico was so popular that recruiting offices had to turn applicants away. In the Northeast, however, especially in New England, many saw the war as an unjust display of naked aggression, and they protested it.

Henry David Thoreau, the American naturalist, philosopher, and essayist, protested the U.S.–Mexican War by refusing to pay a poll tax used, he claimed, to help finance the conflict. In July 1846, Sam Staples, the Concord, Massachusetts, constable and tax collector, personally demanded payment. Thoreau refused and was clapped into the local jail. The next morning a still-unidentified woman, probably Thoreau's aunt, paid the tax on his behalf (and without his permission), and Thoreau was released.

In 1849, Thoreau used this episode as the subject of an essay, "Civil Disobedience." He wrote: "Under a government which imprisons any unjustly, the true place for a just man is also a prison." There is, he declared, a higher law than the civil one, and only those who follow this higher law are truly free. When civil law and higher law conflict, the only appropriate choice is civil disobedience.

Although the essay was little read in the nineteenth century, it received widespread attention in the twentieth, and it inspired and instructed such leaders of nonviolent revolution as Mohandas Gandhi and Martin Luther King, Jr.

1846–1848

Victory Against Mexico

A s the U.S. "Army of the West" conquered California—what had been Mexico's northern provinces—and the "Army of the Center" secured the Texas–Mexico borderlands, the "Army of Occupation" marched deep into Mexico itself. Monterrey (Mexico) fell to General Zachary Taylor on September 24, 1846, but, in the meantime, the astoundingly resilient Antonio López de Santa Anna, who had been living in Cuban exile after a popular rebellion ended his dictatorship of Mexico, offered to help the United States rapidly win the war in return for $30 million and safe passage to Mexico. American officials declined to pay him, but he was allowed to return to his homeland, and, no sooner did he arrive than he mustered an army intended to defeat Zachary Taylor. By January 1847, Santa Anna had assembled 18,000 men, about 15,000 of whom he sent against Taylor's 4,800-man force at Buena Vista. After a two-day battle, Taylor defeated the far superior force on February 23.

At this point, however, President Polk, worried that Taylor would become a military hero and, therefore, a political rival, replaced him with General Winfield Scott, an apolitical veteran of the War of 1812. Scott launched an invasion of Vera Cruz on March 9, 1847, and fought a daring advance all the way to Mexico City. On September 13, Chapultepec Palace—the seemingly impregnable fortress guarding the capital—fell to Scott, and on September 17, 1847, Santa Anna surrendered.

Peace terms were hammered out in the Treaty of Guadalupe Hidalgo (ratified by the U.S. Senate on March 10, 1848). In exchange for a payment of $15 million and a U.S. pledge to assume various claims against Mexico, the Mexican government ceded to the United States New Mexico (which also included parts of the present states of Utah, Nevada, Arizona, and Colorado) and California and renounced claims to Texas above the Rio Grande. Five years later, with the $10-million Gadsden Purchase, the United States acquired more territory from Mexico, thereby completing the acquisition of the land that makes up the continental United States today.

The Mormon Trek

From the beginning, one of the cornerstones of American liberty has been freedom of religion, yet no religion in American history has been more persecuted than the Church of Jesus Christ of Latter-Day Saints, the Mormons. Founded as a result of a mystical visitation upon fifteen-year-old Joseph Smith, Jr., in 1820, the church grew rapidly, but Smith and his followers were hounded out of each place in which they attempted to settle—upstate New York, Ohio, and Missouri. The Mormon town finally founded as Nauvoo, Illinois, prospered, but after Smith and his brother were lynched in 1844, church leader Brigham Young made plans to resettle the Mormons in the Far West, in a place so remote that the people would finally be free of persecution.

During the winter of 1845–1846, all of Nauvoo built wagons and other necessities for the great trek. With the logistical brilliance of a great general, Young planned and executed a 1,400-mile overland migration of successive waves of several hundred Mormon "Saints" (as the people called themselves) at a time. They settled in the Salt Lake valley of present-day Utah, where Young laid out a utopian city, built around a central Temple Square.

The Mormon Trek was one of the first of the great mass migrations to the West, and it was unique in that it resulted in the establishment of a "theo-democracy," which, ultimately, was integrated into the United States and came to coexist with neighbors and government alike.

1848

Seneca Falls Convention
Addresses the Rights of Women

Well before the middle of the nineteenth century, thoughtful women—and plenty of men, too—awoke to the realization that the United States Constitution disenfranchised not only black slaves, but also women. Indeed, most of the early feminists in the United States were active on behalf of both women's rights and abolition; they saw both slavery and the oppression of women as essential issues of human rights that deserved to be linked. While attending the World Anti-Slavery Convention in London in 1840, Elizabeth Cady Stanton met Lucretia Mott, at the time the most outspoken and most visible American female abolitionist. In 1833, Mott had founded the Philadelphia Female Anti-Slavery Society, but, astoundingly, the organizers of the World Anti-Slavery Convention denied her a seat as an official delegate because she was a woman. This moved Mott to broaden her human rights focus to the cause of equality for women.

After returning to the United States from England, Stanton and Mott became energetic leaders of a women's suffrage movement, and organized a conference at Seneca Falls, New York, held during July 19–20, 1848. Attended by 240 women and men, it was the first public meeting in the United States devoted to women's rights. The Seneca Falls Conference produced the "Seneca Falls Declaration of Sentiments," which, modeled on the Declaration of Independence, catalogued the abuses women commonly suffered in a male-dominated society, government, and nation.

From the *"Seneca Falls Declaration of Sentiments,"* 1848:

We hold these truths to be self-evident: that all men and women are created equal. . . .

The history of mankind is a history of repeated injuries and usurpations on the part of man toward woman, having in direct object the establishment of an absolute tyranny over her. . . .

Now, in view of this entire disfranchisement of one-half the people of this country . . . we insist that they have immediate admission to all the rights and privileges which belong to them as citizens of the United States.

1849

The California Gold Rush

On January 24, 1848, James Wilson Marshall, a foreman on the northern California ranch of German immigrant Johann Augustus ("John") Sutter, rode out to inspect the race (a channel for waterflow) of a new mill that had been built on the property. He was suddenly attracted by something shiny in the sediment collected at the bottom of the race. He looked at it. He felt it. It was gold.

Surprisingly enough, Marshall's discovery did not immediately set the countryside on fire, but, after a matter of weeks, word spread, and Sutter found that his employees were deserting him to pan for gold. Ranch operations fell apart, and, even worse, Sutter had failed to purchase the property *before* he built the mill, so his land claims were invalidated. Around John Sutter, everyone (it seemed) was getting rich while he himself faced financial ruin.

While Marshall's discovery caused a big stir in California's central valley during 1848, it was neither Sutter nor Marshall who broadcast the discovery to the world. Sam Brannon, a renegade Mormon living near San Francisco (called at the time Yerba Buena), saw the discovery of gold as an opportunity to prosper—not from grubbing for the ore, but by supplying hordes of hopeful prospectors with pans, picks, shovels, tents, clothing, food—everything they needed, and at prices he could virtually dictate. Brannon used the local newspaper he owned to publicize the discovery of "Gold! Gold from the American River!" Within two weeks, Yerba Buena emptied out, plummeting from a population of a few thousand to a few dozen, as men dropped their tools and left their jobs to prospect on the south fork of the American River.

As word of gold spread east, similar scenes played out in city after city, town after town, farm after farm. Men dropped their tools where they worked, bid farewell to employers—and often to families as well—and set out on the long trek to California.

For some few of the hundreds of thousands who made the California trek over the next several years, the danger, the cost, and the effort were well worth it. But most prospectors found in California nothing more than hard lives, mean spirits, and perhaps just enough gold to pay for meals, shelter, and clothing, all at extravagantly inflated prices. Some found much less than even this, and died, like Sutter himself, ruined. Still others—most of those who came—soon gave up prospecting and took up farming or some other occupation. In this manner, the population of California and the Far West grew.

There were still others, men like Brannon, who decided that the real money in the Gold Rush was not on a riverbed or in the ground, but in the pockets of those who came in quest of ore. Collis Huntington and Mark Hopkins, for example, made a fortune selling miner's supplies. Charles Crocker grew so rich from his expanding dry goods mercantile operation that he started the bank that still bears his name. Leland Stanford parlayed his own mercantile pursuits into a political career that culminated in the California state house and in the founding of the great Palo Alto university named for him. And one Levi Strauss hit upon the idea of using denim reinforced with metal rivets to make pants even a prospector couldn't destroy. They were called blue jeans.

The Compromise of 1850

The territory of California had been officially transferred to the United States by the Treaty of Guadalupe Hidalgo, which ended the Mexican War on February 2, 1848. But on January 24, 1848, just a few days before the treaty was signed, gold was discovered in the territory, and by 1849, tens of thousands of prospectors were pouring into California. The explosion of population suddenly made statehood an urgent issue—and that, of course, raised a familiar question: Would the territory be admitted as a slave state or free?

Back in 1846, Congress, seeking a means of bringing the U.S.–Mexican War to a rapid conclusion, had debated a bill to appropriate $2 million to compensate Mexico for "territorial adjustments." To this bill, Pennsylvania congressman David Wilmot proposed an amendment, which became known as the Wilmot Proviso. It would have barred the introduction of slavery into any land acquired by the United States as a result of the U.S.–Mexican War. This provoked South Carolina's John C. Calhoun to formulate, once and for all, the South's opposition to federal intervention in the slavery issue. Calhoun proposed four resolutions:

> *First:* Territories, including those acquired as a result of the war, are to be deemed the common and joint property of the states.
>
> *Second:* With respect to the territories, Congress acts as agent for the states and, therefore, can make no law dis-

criminating among the states or depriving any state of its rights with regard to any territory.

Third: Any national law governing slavery violates the Constitution and the doctrine of states' rights.

Fourth: The people of a state have the right to form their state government as they wish, provided it is republican in form.

Having loudly and clearly laid down his resolutions on behalf of the South, Calhoun issued a stern warning: Fail to maintain a balance between the conflicting demands of the North and the South, and a "civil war" would surely ensue.

Partly in response to Calhoun's resolutions, the Wilmot Proviso was scrapped, and a new compromise was reached in 1850, which enunciated the principle of "popular sovereignty," an enactment of the fourth of Calhoun's resolutions, allowing the people of a territory to determine by popular vote whether they would seek admission to the Union as a free state or a slave state. In the immediate case, California was admitted as a free state, and the territories of Utah and New Mexico were created, each to be subject to popular sovereignty on the issue of slavery.

1854

The Kansas–Nebraska Act

n 1854, when the territories of Nebraska and Kansas applied for statehood, Congress looked at the Compromise of 1850 and decided to repeal and replace it. Whereas the 1850 compromise applied popular sovereignty (the right of citizens of a state to decide whether or not their state would be slave or free) to some of the territory acquired as a result of the U.S.–Mexican War, the 1854 legislation extended popular sovereignty beyond this territory and, in the process, rubbed out the geographical barrier to slavery created by the Missouri Compromise of 1820. The situation had been explosive in 1820 and was explosive again in 1850. Now, the Kansas–Nebraska Act was as a match applied to a fuse.

There was never any doubt that Nebraskans, who were free-soil northerners, would vote themselves a free state. But Kansas, south of Nebraska, was an entirely different matter. On the eve of statehood, pro-slavery Missourians and antislavery Iowans streamed into the territory, each side vying to create a majority for the popular sovereignty vote. The Missourians proved faster and more numerous than the Iowans and elected a pro-slavery territorial legislature to ensure that Kansas would enter the Union as a slave state. Once this was done, many returned to Missouri, whereas the Iowans remained. Thus, Kansas became a slave territory with an abolitionist majority, and the result was a chronic condition of bitter civil warfare between the slavery and free-soil factions: a prelude to civil war on a national scale.

Bleeding Kansas

In the wake of the Kansas–Nebraska Act of 1854, intimidation, ambush, arson, murder, and aggression followed by retribution and revenge—all over the issue of whether Kansas would be free-soil or slave—became so commonplace that the nation dubbed the emerging state "Bleeding Kansas."

This was typical: In 1856, pro-slavery "border ruffians" raided the abolitionist town of Lawrence, Kansas, setting fire to a hotel and several houses, destroying a printing press, and then killing a number of townspeople. By way of payback, one May night, John Brown, a radical abolitionist who had taken command of the Kansas Free Soil Militia, led four of his sons and two other followers in an attack on pro-slavery settlers along the Pottawatomie River. Brown and his men used sabers to kill five unarmed settlers.

In 1861, Kansas would be admitted to the Union, not as a slave state, but a free one. This hardly brought peace. As "Bleeding Kansas" was a prelude to the Civil War, the Civil War itself, once under way, brought to Kansas a particularly ugly brand of guerrilla violence. As for John Brown, he would go on, in 1859, to lead a raid on the federal arsenal at Harpers Ferry, Virginia, with the object of arming the slaves for a general revolt. He thus became a radical martyr to the cause of abolitionism and his action a curtain raiser on the drama that broke and then transformed the United States of America.

The Dred Scott Decision

Dred Scott was a Missouri slave who belonged to a U.S. Army surgeon, John Emerson, of St. Louis. As a military officer, Emerson served in several posts. Transferred first to Illinois and then to Wisconsin Territory, he took Scott with him to each new assignment. When Emerson died in 1846, Scott returned to St. Louis, where, at the urging of abolitionist lawyers who volunteered their services to him, he sued Emerson's widow for his freedom, arguing that he was now legally a citizen of Missouri, having been made free because of his long residence in Illinois, where slavery was banned by federal law (the Northwest Ordinance), and in the Wisconsin Territory, where the provisions of the 1820 Missouri Compromise made slavery illegal. When a Missouri court ruled against Scott, his lawyers appealed to the United States Supreme Court, which handed down its decision in 1857.

The Supreme Court's antislavery northern justices sided with Scott, while the pro-slavery southerners upheld the Missouri court's decision. Chief Justice Roger B. Taney, native of the slave-holding state of Maryland, wrote the majority opinion, which held that neither enslaved blacks nor, for that matter, free blacks were citizens of the United States; therefore, they had no right to sue in federal court. This point, outrageous though it was, would have been sufficient to settle the case, but Taney wanted the decision to go further, much further. He held that the Illinois law banning slavery had no force on Scott once he returned to Missouri, a slave state. Furthermore, he concluded that the law that applied in Wisconsin was also without force, because the Missouri Compromise was unconstitutional in that it violated the Fifth Amendment, which bars the government from depriving an individual of "life, liberty, or property" without due process of law—and slaves were manifestly property.

Anyone who abhorred slavery found the Dred Scott decision nothing less than obscene. Had the United States come to this? That the highest court in the land was emboldened to use the Bill of Rights to *deny* freedom to a human being? This outrage alone was sufficient to galvanize abolitionist sentiment throughout the nation. But the implication of the Dred Scott decision went beyond even moral outrage. Because Taney had defined slavery as nothing more or less than an issue of property, a Fifth Amendment issue, a constitutional issue, his decision made it incumbent on the federal government to protect slavery in every state, whether or not slavery was practiced in a particular state. That is, even in a free state, a slave remained the property of his or her owner, and, like any other item of property, could not be taken from the owner without due process of law. Thus, the decision put slavery beyond any further compromise. The constitutional rights of slaveholders had to be universally upheld. In this there was no choice—so long as slavery itself legally existed. To free even a single slave— legally—slavery itself had to be abolished, and not just in some states, but nationally. Without the possibility of a middle course, Taney's decision made civil war all but inevitable.

1859

Oil Boom

Before the middle of the nineteenth century, Americans used oil distilled from whale blubber to fill their oil lamps. Unlike so-called rock oil—a kerosene product distilled from surface shale rocks—whale oil burned clean and bright. The trouble was that the demand for whale oil had caused the mammal to be hunted to near extinction. Fortunately, a new type of Austrian lamp was just beginning to appear in the United States, which was designed to burn the shale oil—and burn it cleanly. Suddenly, there was a substantial market for petroleum from the ground.

By the late 1850s, a number of oil companies were formed, including the Rock Oil Company of Connecticut. The company's founders heard that oil was seen floating on water near Titusville, Pennsylvania. They purchased property there and hired Edwin Drake to find the underground source of the oil. Drake consulted a drilling expert, William Smith, and the two men sunk a well, which, on August 27, 1859, at a depth of sixty-nine feet, struck oil. The Titusville well was the first that tapped oil at its source, and it almost immediately launched a great industry. By the 1880s, drilling for oil became a nationwide enterprise.

John Brown's Raid on Harpers Ferry

I n 1857, John Brown moved to Boston from Kansas, where he had led militant—and extravagantly violent—antislavery forces. In Boston, capital of the northern abolition movement, Brown gained the financial backing of leading abolitionists. He laid plans to raid the federal arsenal at Harpers Ferry, Virginia (today West Virginia), with the intention of arming local slaves and fomenting a massive uprising.

Brown and his small band of raiders, which included four of his sons, invaded the town of Harpers Ferry, cut telegraph lines, and occupied the arsenal on October 16. Some of Brown's men rode through the countryside, menacing plantation owners and freeing slaves;

> "I, John Brown, am now quite *certain* that the crimes of this *guilty land* will never be purged *away* but with Blood." —John Brown, note intended to be read after his execution

however, the massive, spontaneous slave rebellion Brown had anticipated did not materialize, and, on October 17, U.S. Marines, under the operational command of U.S. Army colonel Robert E. Lee, marched into Harpers Ferry. When Brown refused to give up the arsenal, Lee's troops rushed the facility, killed ten of Brown's men, and took the rest, four men, including Brown, prisoner.

John Brown, tried for treason, conspiracy, and murder, was found guilty and hanged on December 2, 1859. Abolitionists were quick to paint him as a martyr to the cause of freedom, and certainly his violent example made any further talk of compromise on the issue of slavery seem pale, weak, and useless.

1860

Susan B. Anthony Wins Key Rights for Women

After the Seneca Falls Conference of 1848, some delegates continued to work toward the twin causes of abolition of slavery and women's suffrage. But another leading delegate, Susan B. Anthony, decided to focus exclusively on the cause of women's rights. Anthony organized grassroots female suffrage organizations throughout New York state, and she became the first-ever political lobbyist on behalf of a social cause, successfully persuading New York state legislators to pass the Married Women's Property Act of 1860. This landmark law secured for women the basic rights of holding property, of earning wages and retaining the wages they earned, and of petition for custody of children in cases of divorce. In no other state at the time did women have these rights.

Anthony succeeded in transferring the topic of women's rights from the arena of moral theory directly into law, politics, and the economy. The New York legislation became a model for the other states.

1861

The Fall of Fort Sumter

South Carolina became the first state to secede from the Union on October 20, 1860. Six more quickly followed; then, shortly afterward, another four. War did not begin, however, until the following year. Discounting a signal gun fired a few moments earlier, the first shot of the Civil War came at 4:30 A.M. on the morning of April 12, 1861, when Edmund Ruffin, a choleric South Carolina pro-slavery newspaper editor, pulled the lanyard on one of the many cannon trained on Fort Sumter. Major Robert Anderson, commandant of the fort located in Charleston Harbor, held out for two days of continuous bombardment, during which some 4,000 rounds fell on the fort, before he finally surrendered on April 14. Miraculously, no one, in all that fire, had been hurt. As for Anderson and his command, the chivalrous Louisiana general P.G.T. Beauregard allowed him and his command to withdraw with full military honors. At West Point, years earlier, Anderson had been Beauregard's artillery instructor.

From the moment the war began, similar ironies were seen. Brother officers, comrades at arms, now found themselves on opposite sides of a geographically defined conflict. Sometimes, members of the same family suddenly became enemies. People understood this right away. What almost no one saw, however, was that Fort Sumter would be the only battle without casualties. Before it was over, four long years in the future, at least 618,000 Americans, most of them very young, would be dead.

The Civil War Goes Badly for the North

At the outset of the Civil War, the South didn't seem to have a chance of winning independence. Its population, economy, and industrial base were dwarfed by those of the North. Yet the South did have a leg up in military leadership. The cream of the U.S. Army officer corps was predominantly southern and felt allegiance to their home states. Thus, the Confederate forces were better led than those of the North, especially early in the war. The southern war strategy was, for the most part, defensive, which meant that troops would be defending their homeland against the equivalent of foreign invaders. That conferred a great advantage of morale. And the North? What was the North fighting for? As some saw it, it was to free the slaves—and relatively few white northerners were willing to lay down their lives for that. As President Abraham Lincoln saw it, the fight was not to free the slaves, but to save the Union. But there were many northerners who didn't even believe this was worthwhile. As General Winfield Scott said of the states that had left the Union, why not simply "let the wayward sisters depart in peace"?

Perhaps, then, northerners shouldn't have been stunned (as they were) when the Confederates won victories at Bull Run (July 21, 1861), the battles of the Seven Days (during the Peninsula Campaign of Union commander George B. McClellan), the Second Battle of Bull Run (August 29–30, 1862), Fredericksburg (December 13, 1862), and Chancellorsville (May 2–4, 1863). Despite its superiority of resources, the North had all it could do just to stay in the fight through the early summer of 1863.

1862

The Homestead Act

With the nation torn North from South, President Lincoln was eager to bind East and West closer together. He signed into law, on May 20, 1862, the Homestead Act, a piece of legislation that immediately began to shape the American destiny. The act gave 160 acres of public land in the West as a homestead to "any person who is the head of a family, or who has arrived at the age of twenty-one years, and is a citizen of the United States, or who shall have filed his declaration of intention to become such." This wasn't a free gift, but it required very little cash—something westerners and would-be westerners were always short of. For a modest filing fee, the homesteader obtained his 160 acres, and then, to "perfect" his claim (establish permanent ownership), he had to live on the land for five years and make certain improvements, the most important of which was the construction of a dwelling. After these requirements were met, the homesteader was granted clear title to the land. There were also alternatives to this process. A homesteader could "preempt" the land after a mere six months' residence by purchasing it at the bargain rate of $1.25 per acre, and if the settler could scrape together $50—no mean sum in the 1860s—he could add an additional 40 acres to his original 160 and even purchase additional lots of 40 acres each, at $50, up to a maximum of 160 added to his original grant.

As public policy, the Homestead Act was unprecedented in nothing less than the history of the world. To begin with, few of the world's "civilized" nations had any free land to distribute, but those that did typically distributed territory at the whim and prejudice of some ruler. By the close of the nineteenth century, under the Homestead Act, about 600,000 farmers had received clear title to some 80 million acres of formerly public land. It opened the West to tens and then hundreds of thousands.

1862

The Emancipation Proclamation

On a personal level, it is clear that Lincoln abhorred slavery. "As I would not be a slave, so I would not be a master," he once wrote. But, as president, he believed himself bound by his oath of office to uphold the Constitution, which clearly protected slavery in the slave states. Of more immediate concern was Lincoln's fear, in the midst of civil war, that any attempt simply to declare the slaves free would drive the four slaveholding border states—Maryland, Delaware, Kentucky, and Missouri—still nominally loyal to the Union, into the Confederate fold, while in those portions of the Confederacy currently under Union military occupation, such a declaration might well incite renewed rebellion. So Lincoln moved slowly, so slowly that, on August 19, 1862, Horace Greeley, the highly influential editor of the *New York Tribune,* published an open letter to the president on behalf (he said) of the 20 million citizens of the loyal states. He called for immediate emancipation. Lincoln replied:

> My paramount object in this struggle *is* to save the Union, and is *not* either to save or destroy Slavery. If I could save the Union without freeing *any* slave, I would do it; and if I could save it by freeing *all* the slaves, I would do it; and if I could do it by freeing some and leaving others alone, I would also do that. What I do about Slavery and the colored race, I do because I believe it helps to save this Union; and what I forbear, I forbear because I do *not* believe it would help to save the Union.

Nevertheless, Lincoln did edge closer to an emancipation proclamation, but he decided to issue it only on the heels of some Union army victory. Coming after a string of Union defeats, it would only ring hollow and desperate. While the Battle of Antietam on September 17, 1862, resulted in something of a bloody draw, it could at least be *construed* as a Union victory. So Lincoln chose the moment to issue, on September 23, 1862, the Preliminary Emancipation Proclamation.

The document freed no slaves; instead, it merely served warning on slaveowners living in states "still in rebellion on January 1, 1863," that their property would be declared, after that date, "forever free." Only after the January 1 deadline had passed—and the Civil War continued—did Lincoln issue the "final" Emancipation Proclamation. Even that document gave freedom only to those slaves living in areas of the Confederacy that were not under the control of the Union army. In the Union-occupied South, owners still held their slaves, as did owners in the border states.

Timid as the Emancipation Proclamation may strike us from a twenty-first-century perspective, the document did much to galvanize the North's resolve to see the war through to total victory. It elevated the struggle to the highest possible moral plane, and it made the abolition of slavery the single most visible issue of the war. It also laid the legal foundation for subsequent constitutional amendments that abolished slavery, that ensured full citizenship for freedmen, and that enfranchised all persons "regardless of previous condition of servitude."

The Emergence of General Grant

The principal focus of the Civil War was on its eastern theater. Here, until Gettysburg, the Union's performance was a heartbreaking disappointment. In the meantime, in the war's western theater, an obscure Union general named Ulysses S. Grant was scoring the kind of major triumphs sorely missed in the battles of the East. Shiloh (April 6–7, 1862) was the usual bloody struggle, but Vicksburg, which yielded to Grant's long siege on the day after Meade's victory at Gettysburg, July 4, 1863, and Chattanooga, which fell to the North on November 25, 1863, were signal victories that gave the Union control of large territories. Coupled with U.S. Navy flag officer David Farragut's capture of New Orleans in April 1862, Grant's victory at Vicksburg gave the Union control of the Mississippi River, thereby cutting the Confederacy in two and denying it a major source of transport and supply.

In 1864, after having appointed and fired a series of mediocre (or worse) commanding generals, Lincoln recognized Grant as the dogged, relentlessly aggressive commander the Union Army so badly needed. Appointed general in chief, Grant set about inexorably forcing Lee's army back toward the Confederate capital of Richmond, Virginia. Grant's secret? He was a superb tactician, but, most of all, he understood the grim equation of this war: The North had more men than the South, more money than the South, more railroads than the South, and more industry than the South. The North could afford to "spend" more of all these resources—paramountly, the men—than the South. If the North stayed in the fight, Grant understood, the Confederacy would inevitably exhaust itself.

Gettysburg

During the early summer of 1863, the South's principal commander, Robert E. Lee, boldly abandoned the defensive strategy that had served the Confederate forces so well and took the offensive by invading Pennsylvania. During July 1–3, 1863, at a Pennsylvania crossroads town called Gettysburg, Confederate and Union forces clashed. The first day went badly for the North, but General George G. Meade's field subordinates managed to hold their positions and prevent a rout. On the second day, the tide turned, and on the third day, following a massed charge by the Confederates—so-called Pickett's Charge—which was as dashing as it was desperate, Lee's army was defeated.

Had the Union lost the engagement, it is quite possible that the northern will to continue the fight would have been broken, leading to some negotiated, compromise settlement with the secessionist states. But Meade not only turned back the Confederate army at Gettysburg, his forces also dealt the South a defeat that discouraged both England and France, which had been courting the Confederacy at least to some degree, from supporting the rebel cause. Undeniably, Gettysburg marked the turning point of the war. At the same time, that war was hardly over. While the Union army had achieved much, Meade failed to pursue the defeated Lee, whose army was allowed to escape, beaten but intact, back to the South.

The Fall of Atlanta and the March to the Sea

Grant bore down steadily on Lee's Army of Northern Virginia. Lee sometimes out-generaled him, but even when he was defeated, Grant continued to advance, always forcing Lee to spend precious blood against him. While Grant fought the bitter Wilderness Campaign in Virginia through May and June of 1864, his chief lieutenant, William Tecumseh Sherman, advanced through Tennessee and Georgia to Atlanta, a key rail hub, which he captured, occupied, and finally burned (September–November 1864) before continuing on his infamously destructive "march to the sea."

Grant concentrated on destroying Lee's Army of Northern Virginia while Sherman made real the most terrifying kind of modern combat—"total war," war waged not just against an opposing army but against the entire "enemy" population. It was war intended to kill the people's will to fight by attacking their means of sustenance and survival. Sherman cut a swath of destruction from Atlanta to Savannah, then worked his way north, aiming to catch Lee in a great pincers between his forces and those of Grant.

1864

The Thirteenth Amendment

Congress did not wait until the war was won to formalize and extend the provisions of the Emancipation Proclamation with the Thirteenth Amendment to the Constitution. As with most amendments, its language was simple:

> *Section 1.* Neither slavery nor involuntary servitude, except as a punishment for crime whereof the party shall have been duly convicted, shall exist within the United States, or any place subject to their jurisdiction.

> *Section 2.* Congress shall have power to enforce this article by appropriate legislation.

But its implications were profound. The Senate passed the amendment on April 8, 1864. Representatives argued in the House but they, too, passed it, on January 31, 1865. The measure was ratified on December 18, 1865.

1865

The War Ends

Under the grinding pressure of "total war," the South fought on, hoping to salvage some possibility of a negotiated peace in preference to abject surrender.

Union general Philip Sheridan defeated Confederate general George E. Pickett at Five Forks (April 1, 1865), and, after an almost yearlong siege, Grant took heavily fortified Petersburg, Virginia, key to the Confederate capital city of Richmond. On April 2, 1865, Richmond—from which the Confederate government had fled—fell to him. Then, one week later, at Appomattox Court House, General Robert E. Lee surrendered his Army of Northern Virginia to General Grant, effectively, if not officially, ending the Civil War.

The great and daunting task that remained was, in the words of President Lincoln's Second Inaugural Address, to "bind up the nation's wounds" and restore the Union. Lincoln, who proposed a policy of "malice toward none and charity for all," was perhaps the only national leader capable of successfully guiding such a task.

1865

Assassination of Abraham Lincoln

On the evening of April 14, 1865, with the Civil War all but over, an unimaginably careworn Abraham Lincoln sought a few hours' diversion at a Ford's Theater performance of a popular comedy, *Our American Cousin*. At about 10 P.M., John Wilkes Booth, a popular matinee idol and well-known southern sympathizer, entered the theater, approached the door of the president's private box, found that the lock was broken (he may well have known that it would be), opened the door, and calmly leveled his derringer between Lincoln's left ear and spine. He squeezed the trigger.

Among the 1,675 members of the audience, few heard the report of the tiny weapon. The dull pop made little impression on Mrs. Lincoln, seated next to her husband, nor on Major Henry Rathbone, seated in the presidential box with his fiancée, Clara Harris. Booth was familiar with the script of *Our American Cousin*, and he had timed his shot to coincide with the play's biggest laugh—just after Harry Hawk, playing Mr. Trenchard, says, "Wal, I guess I know enough to turn you inside out, you sockdologizing old mantrap."

When Rathbone realized an intruder was present, he tangled with Booth, who stabbed him in the shoulder, then leaped down from the box to the stage. He caught his right spur in the Treasury Regiment flag that festooned the box. As a result, his left leg took the full impact of his fall, and a bone snapped just above his instep. Turning to the audience, the actor shouted the state motto of Virginia: "Sic semper tyrannis!"—Thus ever to tyrants!—then limped into the wings, fell, recovered, and ran, lopingly, out of the theater. No one in the bewildered audience thought to give chase.

Booth was on the loose twelve days before he was run to ground, about midnight on April 26, at a tobacco farm near Port Royal, Virginia. Shot and fatally wounded, he was never brought to trial. On the very day of Booth's death, General Kirby Smith surrendered the last Confederate military unit to General E.R.S. Canby. It was, officially, the final day of the Civil War.

1866

The First Cattle Drive

In large numbers, Texans went off to fight in the Civil War, leaving behind their homes—and their cattle. By the end of the war, millions of head of Texas cattle ranged freely across the state. With the Texas economy in ruins, the cattle offered wealth on the hoof. Strays abounded, and if a man could round up a stray and brand him, that animal was his. In this way, large herds were accumulated after the war, and the profession of cowboy came into its own.

Charlie Goodnight had been mustered out of the Texas Rangers after the war and, with old-time cattleman Oliver Loving, he put together a postwar herd of some 5,000 head and decided to make a fortune by driving 2,000 of them from Texas to the new Indian-fighting army outposts in Colorado. Soldiers demanded beef, and government provisioning contracts were highly lucrative. Together, Goodnight and Loving pioneered the Goodnight–Loving Trail, which became one of four principal cattle trails and marked the beginning of the trail-drive industry. That business produced more than beef, of course. It gave rise to the cowboy, certainly the most celebrated and beloved worker in American history; the subject of legend, of dime novels, and of film—a national icon.

Reconstruction Begins

The tragedy of Abraham Lincoln's violent death was even worse than probably anyone at the time could have imagined. John Wilkes Booth had killed perhaps the only man capable of beginning and fostering the healing of the nation. Lincoln had been determined to fight the war to absolute victory, but, once the war had been won, he did not want the South punished. He favored amnesty and other steps to heal the nation. As a healing gesture, in 1864, he had chosen a Democrat, a Tennessean, as a running mate. Now, thanks to Booth, that man, Andrew Johnson, was president. Loud, boorish, abrasive, and given to drink, Johnson was universally unloved. Like Lincoln, he favored amnesty and healing, but he lacked Lincoln's charisma, eloquence, intelligence, and moral force. His clumsy efforts to jam down congressional throats generous treatment for the former Confederacy resulted in a legislative rebellion. Congress both feared and resented an amnesty that restored power to the very individuals who had brought about the rebellion. Moreover, while the Republican Party was the majority party of the North, the Democratic Party was the majority party of the South, and the Republican Congress had no desire to allow the Democratic Party to revive. Finally, there was genuine moral outrage over the manner in which the former Confederate states, while ostensibly freeing the slaves in compliance with the Thirteenth Amendment, actually kept them in bondage, denying them the vote and their other rights.

So Congress and President Johnson always found themselves on opposite sides concerning "Reconstruction," the process of reincorporating the former Confederate states into the Union. In

1866, over Johnson's veto, Congress passed the Freedman's Bureau Act and the Civil Rights Act to assist blacks in their transition from slave life to freedom and to assure that African Americans would be deemed full citizens of the United States. Congress pushed through the Fourteenth Amendment, which explicitly extended citizenship to everyone "born or naturalized in the United States," forbidding states to enact laws "which shall abridge the privileges or immunities of citizens of the United States," and guaranteeing the voting rights of all citizens. All of this was noble and just, but, typical of Reconstruction in the absence of Lincoln, the Fourteenth Amendment also included measures of naked vengeance: Section 3 barred former Confederates from holding federal—*or state*—offices unless individually pardoned by a two-thirds vote of Congress, and Section 4 repudiated debts incurred by the former Confederate government and also repudiated compensation for "the loss of emancipation of any slave."

The only former Confederate state to ratify the Fourteenth Amendment was Tennessee, and when the others refused, Congress passed a series of harsh Reconstruction Acts, which put all of the former Confederacy, save Tennessee, under military government. Only after the states drafted and approved acceptable state constitutions, fully enfranchising blacks, were the military governments removed. But, even then, Reconstruction was not finished. More federal laws were passed, intended, on the one hand, to assure equal rights for African-American citizens, to establish state-supported free public schools, to provide more equitable conditions for labor, and to apportion taxes more equitably, but also clearly intended to punish and keep punishing the South. Burdensome taxes were levied. Corruption became universal and crippling. In a vengeful frenzy, those who administered Reconstruction thrust illiterate former slaves into high-level positions in state and local governments. The result, of course, was only to increase chaos and corruption, and to trigger self-righteous bitterness, acts of defiance against the federal government, and, worst of all, brutal acts of terror against blacks.

In the absence of Lincoln, Reconstruction created a climate of sectional division and resentment that endured well into the twentieth century and, by casting southern blacks into the unwilling role of scapegoat, fostered in the South a new kind of racism, founded not, as slavery had been, on mindless assumptions of black racial inferiority but on naked racial hatred.

Impeachment of Andrew Johnson

No one thinks Andrew Johnson was an effective president. His efforts to prevent Congress from punishing the South with harsh Reconstruction measures were well intended, but clumsy, inept, ineffectual, and alienating. As the Civil War had challenged the basic democratic concept of national union, the rapidly escalating war between Johnson and Congress challenged the equally basic democratic concept of separation of powers and the system of checks and balances. Congress sought to seize executive powers, even as President Johnson tried to thwart Congress by interfering in the execution of the Reconstruction laws it had passed.

The struggle between the two branches of government reached its point of greatest crisis on March 2, 1867, when, over Johnson's veto, Congress passed the Tenure of Office Act. This law barred the president from dismissing, without senatorial approval, any civil officeholder who had been appointed with senatorial consent. Part of the general effort to usurp as many executive prerogatives as possible, the act was immediately and specifically aimed at preventing Johnson from removing a member of his own cabinet, Secretary of War Edwin Stanton, who was strongly allied to the cause of the Radical Republicans. With typical absence of understanding or finesse, Johnson defied the law by dismissing Stanton in 1868. This moved the House of Representatives to vote the impeachment of Andrew Johnson.

Under the Constitution, only the House of Representatives may bring impeachment charges against the president, who is then tried before the Senate. The charges brought against Johnson were weak and transparently motivated by partisan politics. The Tenure of Office Act was dubious at best, and Johnson's defiance of it, though heavy-handed, was intended to bring the law to a constitutional challenge before the Supreme Court. Congress prevented this by voting articles of impeachment, and, from March through May 1868, the Senate held a trial. The key votes, on May 16 and 26, 1868, fell only one short of the two-thirds majority required for conviction and removal from office. Seven Republicans, all men of conscience, voted with Johnson's supporters. What would have been, in effect, a coup d'etat was averted, but the gulf between Andrew Johnson and Congress was so deep and wide that the president, though he continued to hold office, was effectively neutralized as a political leader at a time when the wounded nation required leadership above all else.

1869

A Golden Spike Defeats Distance

The idea of building a transcontinental railroad was discussed seriously just two years after the very first American railroad, the Baltimore and Ohio, began operation in 1830. In 1832, Hartwell Carver, a physician from Rochester, New York, published some articles in the *New York Courier and Enquirer* proposing the construction of a railroad on 8 million acres of government land from Lake Michigan to Oregon Territory. Over the years, many more schemes were proposed, even the most feasible of which became political footballs and resulted in nothing but talk.

As often happened with great American enterprises, it took the exertions of a single inspired individual to transform visions into reality. Theodore Dehone Judah, the son of a Bridgeport, Connecticut, Episcopal priest, turned to engineering instead of the Good Book, and became a builder of railroads. He tirelessly publicized, raised money, and lobbied Congress. Then, in 1860, he discovered a relatively easy pass through the formidable California Sierra. With a partner, a mining town druggist named "Doc" Strong, he recruited seven backers, including four whose names and fortunes would be forever linked with the transcontinental railroad: Collis P. Huntington and Mark Hopkins, partners in a hardware store; Leland Stanford, a wholesale grocer; and Charles Crocker, a dry goods merchant. Now backed by real money, Judah secured passage of the Pacific Railway Act of 1862, authorizing two companies—the Union Pacific, starting from the east (Omaha, Nebraska) and building west, and the Central Pacific, moving eastward from Sacramento, California—to begin construction. Judah then traveled back to California to light a fire under his backers. When they balked over laying track farther east than the California–Nevada state line, he set off back to Washington in search of new backers. He took the quickest route available at the time: a ship to Panama, a difficult overland trek through the isthmus jungle, and another ship up the east coast of Central and North America. In Panama, however, he contracted typhoid fever and, weeks later, died.

But by this time, the Civil War had made construction of the railroad a top priority for the Lincoln administration. The Pacific Railway Act was only the first of several pieces of legislation that granted huge tracts of land to the railroads, not only for laying track but as parcels that could be sold to finance construction. This scheme was given momentum with liberal government loan packages, and yet, even with finance and authorization in place, the project stalled. Finally, in 1865, President Lincoln called on Oakes Ames, a prominent industrialist who made his first fortune manufacturing shovels (he was therefore nicknamed the "ace of spades"), and asked him to "take hold" of the project.

Ames instantly recruited investors in a corporation created by Union Pacific vice president Thomas Durant and named after the company that had financed the French railway system a decade earlier, Crédit Mobilier. For major investors, it was the mother of all sweetheart deals. Run by the directors *of* the Union Pacific, Crédit Mobilier was paid *by* the Union Pacific to *build* the Union Pacific. The scheme culminated in a spectacular scandal—yet it did get the transcontinental railroad moving.

Led by a U.S. Army engineer, Grenville Mellon Dodge, the Union Pacific began laying prodigious lengths of track—266 miles in 1866 alone. The Central Pacific, which had to lay track in the mountains, carving paths out of slopes and bridging vast chasms, advanced more slowly. The bulk of work on both railroads fell to immigrant laborers. Irish hands built most of the Union Pacific, while Chinese "coolies" endured racial slurs and even racial violence to build the Central Pacific.

The cost of the railroad was in the millions, of course, but the amount of graft paid out by the tycoons to government officials and others is incalculable. And local governments themselves were liberal with bribes of their own. A town could be made or ruined, depending on whether or not the railroad passed through it. Western municipalities ponied up huge sums to bend the advancing line this way or that. As for the workers—the Irish, the Chinese, and the others—they were regarded as little more than expendable commodities. The politics, the graft, the exploitation, the racism, the waste, all were part of the transcontinental railroad—and yet, so were the dreams, the will, the muscle, the vision, and the courage of many men.

On May 10, 1869, at Promontory Summit (often mistakenly identified as Promontory Point), Utah, railroad tycoon Leland Stanford—aided by workers—wielded a sledgehammer to drive home a ceremonial "golden spike" to join the rails of the eastbound Central Pacific with the westbound rails of the Union Pacific. From sea to shining sea, the nation was now bound by bands of iron.

1876

The Telephone

Born in Scotland, Alexander Graham Bell became a distinguished teacher of the deaf, first in England and then in the United States, where, in Boston, he opened a school for the deaf in 1872. His interest in sound and speech led to experiments with two devices: a harmonic telegraph (an instrument to transmit multiple telegraph messages simultaneously over a single line) and a device to record sound waves graphically (so that the deaf might *see* sound). In 1874, the two ideas suddenly merged in Bell's imagination, and he began to think that if he could "make a current of electricity vary in intensity precisely as the air varies in density during the production of sound," then he could "transmit speech telegraphically."

It was a brilliant insight into converting one form of energy, sound, into another, electricity, and Bell spent the next two years intensively working on it. He was tinkering with a version of the device when he accidentally spilled battery acid in his lap. In pain, he called to his assistant, Thomas Watson, who was in the next room, stationed at the receiver. Watson heard Bell's call—"Mr. Watson, come here; I want you"—not through the door, but through the receiver. The telephone had been born, and within a very few years, it became a ubiquitous and indispensable feature of modern civilization.

1876

Yellow Hair Falls at the Little Bighorn

Late in the spring of 1876, Philip Sheridan, in overall command of army operations against the Indians, laid out the latest of many campaigns to force the Sioux onto reservations. He ordered General Alfred Terry, leading a force from the east, Colonel John Gibbon from the west, and General George Crook from nearby Fort Fetterman to converge on the Yellowstone River, where major Sioux camps were believed to be. Among Terry's command was the Seventh Cavalry, led by George Armstrong Custer.

Custer had graduated from West Point in 1861 at the very bottom of his class, but in the Civil War he had commanded troops with a combination of heroism and utter disregard for their lives and his. This catapulted him to promotion as brigadier general of volunteers at age twenty-three, then, two years later, to the same rank in the regular service—at twenty-five, the youngest general in the history of the U.S. Army. Like many other officers, Custer reverted to lower rank after the Civil War, but he soon climbed back to colonel, was given the Seventh Cavalry, and sent to fight Indians—who, in reference to his flamboyantly long blond locks, dubbed him "Yellow Hair." Courageous, to be sure, Custer was also hungry for glory—at the expense of the Indians as well as the men of his command.

On the morning of June 17, 1876, Crook, with more than 1,000 men, halted for a rest at the head of the Rosebud Creek in Montana. Sitting Bull led Sioux and Cheyenne against Crook's position, and the cavalry was forced into retreat after a fierce six-hour fight. After the Battle of the Rosebud, the Sioux established a camp. In the meantime, Terry's column linked up with Gibbon's at the mouth of the Rosebud, both commanders unaware of Crook's retreat. Gibbon's and Terry's officers, including Custer, convened in the cabin of the Yellowstone River steamer *Far West* to lay out a campaign strategy. They believed they would find a Sioux encampment on the stream the Indians called the Greasy Grass and the whites called the Little Bighorn. Their plan was to attack. Custer was to lead his Seventh Cavalry up the Rosebud, cross to the Little Bighorn, then advance down the Bighorn valley from the south as Terry and Gibbon marched up the Yellowstone and the Bighorn to block the Indians from the north. Thus, Sitting Bull would be caught in the jaws of a pincer.

What none of the officers knew was that the "camp" was really a large village, populated by perhaps as many as 7,000 Sioux, including many warriors.

On June 25, when his scouts sighted a Sioux camp and warriors, Custer resolved to attack immediately, before the always-elusive enemy could flee. He did not pause to determine just how many Sioux were present. Instead, he led his men across the divide between the Rosebud and the Little Bighorn, dispatching Captain Frederick W. Benteen with 125 men to the south to make sure the Sioux had not moved into the upper valley of the Little Bighorn. As Custer drew nearer to the Little Bighorn, he spotted about 40 warriors and sent Major Marcus A. Reno, with 112 men, after them. Reno was to pursue the warriors back to their village, while Custer, with his remaining men, more than 200, charged the village from the north.

Reno's 112 men, in pursuit of the 40 warriors seen earlier, were soon engulfed by masses of Sioux. In the meantime, Custer had ascended a bluff, saw now that the Sioux encampment was vast—later estimates vary wildly, from 1,500 to 7,000, but certainly far in excess of the Seventh Cavalry's 600 men—and he saw that Reno had advanced right into it. Custer summoned his bugler, Giovanni Martini, and handed him a note to deliver to Benteen, ordering him to bring the ammunition packs and join the fight. The errand would save Martini's life. He was the last surviving cavalryman to see Custer alive.

Warriors led by Gall, a Hunkpapa Sioux chief, charged across the Little Bighorn and waded into the knot of cavalry troopers. While Gall pressed in from the south, Crazy Horse pushed in from the north. For Custer and his command, it was over in less than an hour. They died, all of them.

More than 200 men, including Custer, were killed on the Little Bighorn battlefield. Congress authorized an increase in the army's strength, but the defeat so demoralized the army that no attempt at reprisal was made until November. Nevertheless, the defeat of George Armstrong Custer, a brilliant tactical victory for the Sioux warriors, was, ultimately, a strategic disaster for the Native Americans. Before the Little Bighorn, white public opinion wavered between hatred of and sympathy for the Indians. Afterward, most American citizens were prepared to let the army do whatever it deemed necessary to confine the Indians to their reservations.

1876

The Disputed Hayes–Tilden Election

On election night, 1876, Republican presidential candidate Rutherford B. Hayes, governor of Ohio, went to bed believing he had lost to the Democratic governor of New York, Samuel J. Tilden. But dawn brought a different story—and an election dispute that would go on for four months amid charges of voter fraud, intimidation and even murder of black voters in the South, manipulation of ballots by partisan election judges, the threat of lawsuits, and a recount of votes in contested states.

The popular vote gave Tilden a 250,000-ballot lead over Hayes. This fact did not discourage Hayes supporter Daniel Edgar Sickles from pointing out that the fate of Hayes could yet be determined by contesting electoral votes in Oregon, Louisiana, South Carolina, and Florida. If at least some of these disputed electoral votes could be delivered to Hayes, he would win.

The resulting electoral battle raged wildly and with no end in sight before the March 4, 1877, inauguration date. There was talk of authorizing the current secretary of state to serve as interim chief executive. Many in the South were actually discussing secession, and some were already setting up rival governments. Just two days before the inauguration deadline, Congress authorized a bipartisan Electoral Commission even as legislators negotiated a behind-the-scenes deal to decide the issue. In essence, the deal was this: The South would give the election to Hayes in return for his pledge to bring full home rule to the southern states and an immediate end to the military-enforced Reconstruction governments that had been established in the wake of the Civil War. If this meant that the rights of African-American citizens were to be sacrificed, well—so be it.

The southern legislators agreed to a commission composed of eight Republicans and seven Democrats, who voted straight down party lines to rule in favor of Hayes. As for the country, it held together—after a fashion; for the rift between North and South was wide, and the gulf between white and black Americans deepened. As for Hayes, he bore throughout his single presidential term the mocking title of "His Fraudulency."

1879

Edison's Incandescent Electric Lamp

orn in Milan, Ohio, in 1847 to a family of modest means, Thomas Edison was an intensely curious and always restless boy, who so exasperated his teachers that he soon left school, although he continued to read voraciously. His maverick ways and his continual questioning, tinkering, and experimentation vexed his conventional father, who worried that his son was "addlepated," but his mother, always supportive, encouraged Edison and did the best she could to further his education by tutoring him at home. In his teens, Edison secured a job as an itinerant railway telegrapher and, in his twenties, embarked on a career as an inventor, beginning with devices that built on, improved, and extended the telegraph in various ways. By the time of his death, in 1931, he held 1,093 patents, a still-unbroken record for any individual.

The most famous of his inventions was, of course, the incandescent electric light. Edison spent many months of exhausting experimentation and failure. Electric arc lighting already existed, but it was intensely brilliant and impractical for widespread domestic and industrial use. Edison saw that the task before him was (as he put it) to "subdivide the light," and he further saw that finding just the right material to use as a filament was the key to solving this problem of subdivision. As he worked on this, he also envisioned a whole new industry—an industry devoted to generating electrical power for the masses, for the world.

But finding the filament, this little bit of material, proved to be a daunting task. Edison set about collecting thousands of candidate items, from exotic metal wires to a hair plucked from the beard of one of his assistants, and he tediously tried each, observing and evaluating how each worked—and failed to work. At long last, he discovered the virtues of carbonized cotton, which glowed brightly in a vacuum and had a reasonably long life—forty hours, at first. He told a reporter that he had tried some ten thousand materials before he hit upon carbonized cotton. When the reporter marveled that he had never become sufficiently discouraged to quit, Edison replied in a manner that revealed his brute-force approach to technology: "I didn't fail ten thousand times. I successfully eliminated, ten thousand times, materials and combinations which wouldn't work."

On December 31, 1879, he offered a public demonstration of the lamp and was awarded a patent the next month. Shortly after this, Edison oversaw the first commercial installation of electric lights, on the steamship *Columbia,* belonging to the Oregon Railroad and Navigation Company. By 1881, he had built the world's first central electric power plant, the Pearl Street Station in lower Manhattan.

Very soon, all of urban America—and much of the urban world—was being electrified. Rural areas followed more slowly, but follow they did, and by the end of Edison's life electric lighting and electric appliances were part of the very tissue of modern civilization. This American inventor had transformed life itself.

1881

Tuskegee Institute Founded

Like many African Americans of the nineteenth century, Booker T. Washington, born in 1856 at Rocky Mount, Virginia, had a future with precious little to hope for. He was a slave, and the emancipation that came after the Civil War brought scarcely brighter prospects. At the age of nine, Washington moved with his family to Malden, West Virginia, where he worked at a salt furnace and, later, in a coal mine. His primary education was virtually nonexistent, but he prepared himself sufficiently to enroll in the Hampton Normal and Agricultural Institute at the age of sixteen while working as a janitor to support himself. Washington graduated three years later, taught for two years, studied theology for another year, then decided on a full-time career as a teacher. He joined the staff of Hampton Institute, where he created a program for educating American Indians.

In 1881, Washington answered the call to head a new school for blacks in remote Tuskegee, Alabama. As with his own early life, there was little promising about the place, which consisted of two run-down buildings and very little else. Washington christened the place Tuskegee Normal and Industrial Institute, and decided that he would of-

> **During a speech** given at the Atlanta Cotton States and International Exposition on September 18, 1895, Booker T. Washington spread out the fingers of his hand and raised it in front of his face: "In all things that are purely social, we can be as separate as the fingers, yet one as the hand in all things essential to mutual progress."

fer young black Americans a broad but vocationally practical education. For what he believed in was not theoretical equality for African Americans, but hard-nosed, practical economic self-determination. Achieve that, he declared, and political and civil rights would—in the fullness of time—come.

Many whites, even southerners, were willing to work with Washington, who politely assured would-be donors, southern white employers, and southern governors that young black men would get from Tuskegee an education that would keep them down on the farm and in the basic trades. But as the civil rights movement began to grow and develop, and especially with the founding of the National Association for the Advancement of Colored People (NAACP) in 1909, the "accommodationist" and "compromise" view of Booker T. Washington came under increasing attack by progressive African Americans. Still, for blacks whose early twentieth-century horizons rarely extended further than the poverty of a sharecropper's field, Tuskegee offered hope—real hope that could be counted in the dollars of a decent wage. For better or worse, Booker T. Washington became the leading spokesman for African-American "social progress" at the turn of the century. He offered a hard compromise: black acceptance of disfranchisement and segregation in exchange for white encouragement of black progress in economic and educational opportunity.

How the Other Half Lives

Like many other New Yorkers of the late nineteenth century, Jacob August Riis was an immigrant. He had come from Denmark in 1870 and had spent his first seven years in the city struggling with poverty until, at last, he found his calling as a newspaper reporter. Riis worked in lower Manhattan, in offices adjacent to some of the most notorious slums in the city. Where others were repulsed by these neighborhoods, Riis was fascinated, and he appointed himself the chronicler—with pen and camera—of the slums.

He observed and wrote for two decades, finally producing in 1890 a masterpiece of sociology and journalism, *How the Other Half Lives*. As political reformer Theodore Roosevelt put it, the book was "an enlightenment and an inspiration," revealing to more fortunate Americans a world they had chosen to ignore and allowing them to ignore it no more. How effective was Riis's book? The evidence is clear. Prior to its publication in 1890, there were no serious efforts to rebuild the slums. After 1890, such efforts swept the nation.

The Death of Sitting Bull

During the 1880s, a Native American religious movement the whites called the Ghost Dance began spreading through many of the western Indian reservations. It was essentially a peaceful movement, the Indians' stoic and highly spiritual acceptance of defeat in this world and a hope for victory in the next. Yet, among the Teton Sioux, the Ghost Dance took on militant overtones that white authorities found ominous and menacing. So, on November 20, 1890, cavalry and infantry reinforcements were sent to the Pine Ridge reservation in Dakota Territory. Their arrival only fanned the flames of rebellious discontent, and some 3,000 Indians defiantly gathered on a plateau at the northwest corner of Pine Ridge dubbed the Stronghold.

Brigadier General John R. Brooke, commander of the Pine Ridge area, held talks with the militants, but the anger continued to simmer, and Brooke's commanding officer, Major General Nelson A. Miles, transferred his headquarters to Rapid City, Dakota Territory. In the meantime, the most revered and influential of Sioux leaders, Sitting Bull, a figure who combined military skill with profound moral and religious force, began actively espousing the Ghost Dance at Standing Rock Reservation, also in Dakota Territory.

The government agent in charge of Standing Rock, James McLaughlin, understood that, for many Indians, Sitting Bull was the very embodiment of their cultural and spiritual identity. A major uprising could easily form around such a man. McLaughlin decided to neutralize Sitting Bull by arresting him—as quietly and as quickly as possible. Instead of calling in troops to do the job, he deployed Native American reservation policemen. But on December 15, 1890, the arrest went terribly wrong, a riot broke out, and, in the melee, the legendary Sitting Bull was shot dead. The death of Sitting Bull symbolized the eclipse of Native American culture by the forces of Euro-American culture.

1890

Massacre at Wounded Knee
Ends the Indian Wars

The killing of Sitting Bull during a botched arrest attempt on December 15, 1890 created an explosive situation on the Sioux reservations. Fearing an uprising, army commander Nelson A. Miles decided to arrest Chief Big Foot of the Miniconjou Sioux, a well-known leader of the Native American Ghost Dance movement, which whites believed was at the heart of the incipient rebellion. What Miles did not know was that Big Foot, having decided that the Ghost Dance offered nothing but desperation and futility, had abandoned the faith. Miles was also unaware that Chief Red Cloud, a Pine Ridge reservation leader friendly to the whites, had invited Big Foot to travel from his home on the Cheyenne River to Pine Ridge to exercise his considerable influence in persuading the would-be leaders of uprising to surrender.

Miles deployed troops in a dragnet across the prairies and badlands to intercept all Miniconjous and, in particular, Big Foot. On December 28, 1890, a squadron of the Seventh Cavalry, the outfit of the slain George Custer, tracked down Big Foot—who was seriously ill with pneumonia—and about 350 Miniconjous camped near a Dakota stream called Wounded Knee Creek.

The troops waited and watched. That evening, reinforcements arrived, and, by morning, 500 cavalrymen, under Colonel James W. Forsyth, surrounded Big Foot's camp. Determined to take no chances, Forsyth positioned on the surrounding hills four Hotchkiss guns, rapid-firing Howitzer-like artillery pieces. With these in place, he ordered his men to disarm the Indians in an orderly fashion and take them to the rail line, where a train would "remove them from the zone of military operations." The procedure was routine; the soldiers quietly entered the Indian camp and began their search for guns.

During the search, a medicine man named Yellow Bird, outraged by the presence of the troops, began dancing wildly and urging the others to resist. He reminded them all that they wore sacred "ghost shirts," which would protect them against the white men's bullets. Next, Black Coyote, described by another Indian as "a crazy man, a young man of very bad influence and in fact a nobody," menacingly lofted his Winchester above his head as the cavalrymen moved about the throng, collecting weapons. Black Coyote loudly protested that the rifle had cost him dearly and that nobody was going to take it from him. The soldiers responded provocatively, crowding around him, shoving him, taking him by the shoulders and spinning him around.

While attention was focused on Black Coyote, a rifle was fired. Was it Black Coyote's? Was it another Indian's? Was it the carbine of a trooper? Was it fired on purpose? Was it fired by accident? Whoever fired and for whatever reason, it was enough to unleash rifle fire on both sides. However, at this point, few of the Indians were still armed, and hand-to-hand combat broke out. Almost as soon as the fighting began, it ended, with the Indians making a break.

To prevent the escape of the Miniconjous, Forsyth ordered the Hotchkiss guns to open up. They fired at a rate of almost a round a second, targeting men, old men, women, and children. In less than an hour, Big Foot and 153 other Miniconjous were dead. So many others staggered, limped, or crawled away that no one knew or knows just how many died at Wounded Knee. Probably, some 300 of the 350 who had been camped at the creek finally perished. Casualties among the Seventh Cavalry were twenty-five killed and thirty-nine wounded, most of them victims of Hotchkiss rounds.

The U.S. Army called the event the "Battle of Wounded Knee," but the public, even those hardened against the Indians, called it a massacre. On December 30, a combination of hostile and hitherto friendly Sioux factions ambushed the Seventh Cavalry near the Pine Ridge Agency. Elements of the Ninth Cavalry came to the rescue, and General Miles marshaled 3,500 troops around the Sioux who had assembled along White Clay Creek, fifteen miles north of the Pine Ridge Agency. Chastened by Wounded Knee, Miles moved with patient restraint, gradually contracting the ring of troops around the Indians, all the while asking for their surrender and pledging good treatment in return.

Even the most determined among the Sioux leaders were persuaded now that their cause was lost, and, on January 15, 1891, the Sioux formally surrendered to the army.

1892

Opening of Ellis Island

In his message to Congress on December 1, 1862, Abraham Lincoln called the United States the "last, best hope of earth." Before and after that day, millions proved him right. From all over the Earth, from places that failed humanity politically, economically, or spiritually, people have poured into America, a nation of immigrants.

The greatest waves of immigration came in the late nineteenth and early twentieth centuries, when the demands of burgeoning American industry began to outweigh the concerns of those who wanted to bar entry to "foreigners." The labor of the immigrant was cheap, and employers looking for unskilled and semiskilled workers to feed newly emerging assembly lines and do the heavy lifting required to build bridges and to raise the nation's first skyscrapers welcomed, first and foremost, the Irish, then people from southern and eastern Europe as well. The end of that century saw the coming of Italians, Greeks, Turks, Russians, and Slavs. With these came, for the first time, large numbers of Jews, who added a distinctive new element to the nation's blend of ethnic identities and religious faiths.

The urban centers of the East Coast and the Midwest had little trouble assimilating the new immigrants, although their lives in these cities were by no means easy. Many immigrants had been promised a land whose streets were paved with gold. More often, the reality was a dark and crowded slum. Yet no slum could screen the world of promise and opportunity that did, indeed, lay beyond this street or that. If there were no golden nuggets to pick off the American pavement, there was plenty of hope. But if the cities of the East and Midwest accepted immigrants, the West and South-west resisted. Employers in these regions had no scruples against hiring "foreigners," but they didn't want them to enjoy the bene-fits of citizenship. In the Southwest, migrant labor from Mexico provided a cheap source of temporary farm workers, and, far-ther north, Asians—especially Chinese—were prized for their efficiency, determination, and endurance. Yet naturalization laws barred them from attaining U.S. citizenship, and, by 1882, anti-Asian prejudice resulted in passage of the first of a series of Chinese Exclusion Acts, which blocked even the temporary immigration of Chinese laborers. As for the Mexican migrants, au-thorities winked. Big farmers—agribusiness—wanted cheap labor, and federal legislators as well as local authorities were willing to oblige.

As the nineteenth century drew to a close, American authori-ties recognized the need for a centralized immigration processing facility—a doorway, as it were, to America. Chinese exclusion meant that this portal would not be built on the Pacific coast, but on the Atlantic. In 1890, the United States Bureau of Immigration was created. In New York City, the chief point of immigrant entry was Castle Garden, a disused military fortress at Battery Park, on the southern tip of Manhattan. It was woefully inadequate to han-dle the immigrant flood, and the new immigration bureau decided to move operations to Ellis Island in upper New York Bay. Named for Samuel Ellis, who owned the island in the 1770s, it had been purchased by the federal government from the state of New York in 1808 for use as an arsenal and fort. The Bureau of Immigration saw it as an ideal immigration facility, a *cordon sanitaire,* sepa-rated from the mainland by water, so that immigrants could be received, examined for disease, quarantined if need be, then ad-mitted to the mainland—or deported.

The first of the Ellis Island immigration station buildings was opened on January 1, 1892. During the fifty-two years of its oper-ation, from 1892 to 1943, Ellis Island processed more than 12 mil-lion immigrants; during the height of its operation, it sometimes did so at rates of a million people a year.

1898

Explosion of the *Maine* Provokes the Spanish–American War

By the close of the nineteenth century, the people of the Spanish colony of Cuba, just ninety miles off the coast of Florida, hungered for independence from Spain. Sentiment in the United States was mostly friendly to the independence movement. After all, since 1823, with proclamation of the Monroe Doctrine, the United States had regarded itself as the chief steward of the Americas and didn't like the imperial presence of European powers in its hemisphere. Despite popular sentiment, which was whipped up and shaped by leading "yellow journalists," paramountly Joseph Pulitzer and William Randolph Hearst, President Grover Cleveland and his successor, William McKinley, resisted intervening in Cuban affairs. But in February 1896, Spanish general Valeriano Weyler began to take particularly brutal steps to "restore order" in Cuba. He set up "reconcentration camps" for the incarceration of known rebels as well as other citizens accused of supporting or sympathizing with the rebels. Hearst's papers branded the Spanish general "Butcher Weyler," and correspondents reported in graphic detail a host of acts of violent repression.

In the heat of growing war fever, President McKinley ordered the battleship *Maine* into Havana Harbor for the purpose of protecting American citizens and interests there. Those "interests" were not exclusively ideological, but also financial. By the late nineteenth century, great American business concerns had invested heavily in Cuba, especially its highly productive sugar plantations. While revolutionary unrest posed a threat to those investments, the prospect of a *successful* revolution, bringing independence from Spain, was most promising to business. If the United States could ensure the establishment of an independent Cuban government that was nevertheless beholden to the United States and that was inclined to make provisions favorable to business, U.S. investors stood to profit handsomely. To some, even more inviting was the prospect not of an independent Cuba, but of a Cuba formally annexed to the United States.

On February 15, 1898, with war fever running high in the United States, the battleship *Maine* suddenly blew up, with the loss of 266 crewmen.

A naval court of inquiry hurriedly concluded that the ship had struck a Spanish mine. (Modern analysts agree that no such thing happened; the ship's powder magazine spontaneously exploded,

Telegram from Charles Dwight Sigsbee, captain of the U.S.S. *Maine:*

HAVANA, February 15, 1898.

SECRETARY OF THE NAVY,
Washington, D.C.:

Maine blown up in Havana Harbor at 9.40 tonight, and destroyed. Many wounded and doubtless more killed or drowned. Wounded and others on board Spanish man-of-war and Ward Line steamer. Send light-house tenders from Key West for crew and the few pieces of equipment above. No one has clothing other than that upon him. Public opinion should be suspended until further report. All officials believed to be saved. Jenkins and Merritt not yet accounted for. Many Spanish officers, including representatives of General Blanco, now with me to express sympathy.

Sigsbee.

and no hostile action had been involved.) The American people raised the cry of "Remember the *Maine* . . . to hell with Spain!"— a deliberate echo of the battle cry of Texas independence three-quarters of a century earlier: "Remember the Alamo!"

Spain did its best to avert war by accelerating the withdrawal of its troops from Cuba, but the U.S. Congress voted a resolution to recognize, immediately, Cuba's independence. This left Spain no choice. It declared war on the United States on April 24, 1898.

A "Splendid Little War"

The first American military action of the Spanish–American War took place not in Cuba, but in the Spanish-occupied Philippine Islands. At the outbreak of war, Commodore George Dewey sailed the U.S. Asiatic Squadron from Hong Kong to Manila Bay, where, on May 1, he attacked the Spanish fleet and, in a spectacular battle, sank all ten warships in the bay. Following this, 11,000 U.S. troops landed at Manila and, coordinating their operations with the guerrilla forces of Filipino rebel leader Emilio Aguinaldo, rapidly defeated the Spanish army in the islands. In July, Spanish Guam also fell to the United States, which picked up Wake Island as well, at the time claimed by no one—other than the people living there. Congress quickly passed a resolution annexing to the United States the commercially important Hawaiian Islands.

In the meantime, action got under way on Cuba. On May 29, an American naval fleet blockaded and bottled up the Spanish fleet at Santiago Harbor while, in June, 17,000 American soldiers landed at Daiquiri and assaulted Santiago. The war's great make-or-break land battle, at San Juan Hill on July 1, included a magnificent charge up adjacent Kettle Hill by the all-volunteer Rough Riders, led by Theodore Roosevelt, who had resigned as assistant secretary of the navy to accept a colonelcy of the volunteers.

On July 3, after the American victory at San Juan Hill, Spanish admiral Pasqual Cervera decided to run the U.S. naval blockade of Santiago Harbor. After four hours of battle, almost all of Cervera's fleet was at the bottom of the harbor. On July 17, 24,000 Spanish troops surrendered, and Madrid sued for peace nine days later. John Hay, McKinley's secretary of state, summed up the ten-week conflict by calling it a "splendid little war."

The Course of American Imperialism

By the terms of the peace settlement that ended the Spanish–American War in 1898, Spain withdrew from Cuba and ceded to the United States Puerto Rico and Guam. It also sold the Philippines to the United States for $20 million. Immediately, America established a territorial government in Puerto Rico, but it was less sure about what to do with Cuba. In April 1898, Senator Henry M. Teller of Colorado, like many others alarmed by the prospect of unbridled United States imperialism, proposed an amendment to the U.S. declaration of war against Spain. It stipulated that the United States "hereby disclaims any disposition or intention to exercise sovereignty, jurisdiction, or control over said island except for pacification thereof, and asserts its determination, when that is accomplished, to leave the government and control of the island to its people." The United States established a military government on the island "to restore order" while Cubans drafted their own constitution. In the meantime, however, the Teller Amendment was succeeded by the Platt Amendment, introduced by Senator Orville Platt of Connecticut in February 1901. This gave the United States "the right to intervene for the preservation of Cuban independence, the maintenance of a government adequate for the protection of life, property, and individual liberty. . . ." The Platt Amendment was used as the basis by which an "independent" Cuba became a virtual puppet of U.S. interests. This relationship persisted even after the Platt Amendment was abrogated on May 29, 1934, and continued until the 1959 revolution led by Fidel Castro.

As for the Philippines, Aguinaldo proclaimed Filipino independence in defiance of the Treaty of Paris, by which Spain sold the islands to the United States, and a guerrilla war broke out between Filipino freedom fighters and the U.S. army of occupation. Only after World War II would the United States grant the Philippine Islands full and complete independence.

Despite the moral and political conflicts associated with the Spanish–American War and its outcome, the episode established the United States as an emerging world power, a status that U.S. participation in World War I and then World War II would confirm and enlarge in the twentieth century.

Birth of the Movie Industry

Cinema is one of those complex inventions that never really was "invented," at least not at any single moment and by any one person. What was the first movie? We could go back to the shadow plays of fifteenth-century Europe, which used a lantern to project the shadows of puppets and was a technique borrowed from Java via the Middle East. We could go back to various experiments exploiting the persistence of vision phenomenon, most famously the zoetrope, patented almost simultaneously in 1867 in England and the United States, a device that used thirteen slots and thirteen pictures spinning around in a metal cylinder. By varying the number of pictures, figure movement was simulated. Then there was the work of British photographer Eadweard Muybridge, who developed the zoopraxiscope, which combined sequenced still photographs to create a "moving picture" representing the events of specific periods of time. In 1889, using a film base devised by American photography pioneer George Eastman, Thomas A. Edison invented the first movie film. It was not until 1891 that he patented a movie camera to expose the film and 1894 that he came up with the kinetoscope, a means of viewing the developed motion picture.

Edison's kinetoscope was not a projector, but a single-viewer "peep" device. The Lumiere brothers, Auguste and Louis, produced what most film historians consider the first real movie show with the presentation of their Lumiere Cinematographe to a paying audience at the Grand Café in Paris on December 28, 1895. After seeing the Lumiere Cinematographe, another Frenchman, Georges Méliès, magician-owner of the Theatre Robert-Houdin in

Paris, decided to purchase filmmaking equipment and turned out a series of extraordinary short films, including early experiments with color, and at least one film incorporating "special effects," the 1902 *A Trip to the Moon,* which was also the world's first science fiction movie.

Despite the great success of *A Trip to the Moon* and other films, Méliès was soon driven out of business by pirates and swindlers. Thomas Edison did not intend to suffer a similar fate. In 1893, he built the world's first movie studio. Christened the "Black Maria" because it looked like a police paddy wagon, it was an ungainly building on the grounds of his Menlo Park, New Jersey, workshop and could be rotated 360 degrees to take advantage of available sunlight. Here was produced the earliest surviving copyrighted film, *Fred Ott's Sneeze, January 7, 1894,* which was nothing more or less than a portrayal of an Edison employee sneezing. In 1896, the Edison Company began turning out minute-long "shorts" and ten-minute "one-reelers" on a regular basis.

In 1903, Edwin S. Porter, a former Edison Company cameraman, directed for the Edison Company *The Great Train Robbery,* a ten-minute, fourteen-scene "epic" that was advertised as "a faithful duplication of the genuine 'Hold Ups' made famous by various outlaw bands in the far West." In fact, the plot was inspired by a real event, which occurred on August 29, 1900, when four members of Butch Cassidy's famed Hole-in-the-Wall gang stopped the Union Pacific's No. 3 on its way to Table Rock, Wyoming. The robbers forced the conductor to uncouple the passenger cars from the rest of the train and then blew up the safe in the mail car. They made off with some $5,000 in cash.

To tell the story, Porter introduced innovative techniques that would become cornerstones of filmmaking, including parallel editing—cuts that show chronologically parallel as well as overlapping action, minor camera movement for added realism, and shooting on loca-

The Great Train Robbery can be viewed online, for free, at memory.loc.gov/ammem/edhtml/gtr.html.

tion (parts of New Jersey made to look like the Wild West). Editing was complex and exciting, and, for the first time in movie history, the camera was allowed to pan.

The Great Train Robbery was tremendously successful. Movies became the poor man's theater, then quickly evolved into the first truly mass medium, not only entertaining America, but helping the nation, as the preeminent exporter of movies, to become an international cultural capital.

Invention of the Airplane

Before the end of the eighteenth century, people were flying in hot-air balloons, but the true dream of flight had always been to emulate the birds—not just to float in air, but to soar, at will, swiftly, and in whatever direction one chose. Gliding dates back to at least the year 1000, when a Benedictine monk named Elmer of Malmesbury launched himself from the tower of Malmesbury Abbey, England, and soared for some 600 feet before crashing to Earth and breaking both legs. Some 900 years later, in 1892, the two sons of a bishop—this one of the Church of the United Brethren of Christ—started making and selling bicycles in Dayton, Ohio. The "Bishop's boys," as townspeople called them, made a fine living from their shop, with plenty of money left over to finance what soon became their real passion: aeronautics. In 1896, the Bishop's boys—Wilbur and Orville Wright—avidly read an account of the death of Otto Lilienthal, a German builder of gliders, who had been killed in the crash of one of his own machines. From this point on, they bought every aeronautical book and magazine they could find. By 1899, when they had completed their first man-carrying biplane kite, they had already methodically consulted the Weather Bureau—precursor of today's National Weather Service—to determine the best location for testing flying machines. Following the bureau's advice, the Wrights took their aircraft to the beach at Kitty Hawk, North Carolina. Here they perfected the most efficient manned gliders ever produced to that time. Then, in December 1903, they fitted a 170-pound, twelve-horsepower gasoline-fueled motor to a 750-pound gossamer craft fashioned of fabric and wood. On the morning of December 17, the boys flipped a coin. When it came up heads, Orville, without further discussion, assumed his position at the controls. It was not a seat in a cockpit, for there was no seat and there was no cockpit. Orville Wright lay on his belly across the bottom wing, the engine coughed into life, and the aircraft rolled down a rail track the Wrights and a handful of assistants had laid on the sand. It took off and flew for twelve seconds, over a distance of about 120 feet.

That first day, the Wrights made three more flights, Wilbur managing to keep the aircraft aloft for almost a minute and over a distance of 852 feet. Then they returned quietly to

"Success. Four flights Thursday morning. . . . Inform press. Home Christmas." —Orville and Wilbur Wright, telegram to their father

Dayton, where they continued their experiments at Huffman Prairie, a local cow pasture, until, by 1905, they had achieved a flight of thirty-eight minutes' duration over a distance of twenty-four miles. Securing necessary patents in 1906, they toured a flabbergasted world during 1908–1909, the year in which they began manufacturing aircraft commercially. Just more than 900 years had passed since the flight and crash landing of Elmer of Malmesbury. Sixty-six years after Kitty Hawk, three Americans would fly to the moon, and two would walk on it.

1908

The Model T

Henry Ford was born on a Dearborn, Michigan, farm, but it was machines, not crops, that interested the boy, who soon apprenticed himself to the owner of a machine shop. After working as an itinerant farm-machinery repairman and a sawmill operator, Ford became chief engineer for the brand-new Edison Illuminating Company generating station in Detroit.

Electricity wasn't the only cutting-edge technology that intrigued Ford. "Horseless carriages" had started to appear on the streets of a few cities, and Ford tinkered together his first automobile in 1896. He went to work for a builder of custom-made cars, then designed and built a racer—the 999, capable of an astounding sixty miles per hour—and, at last, organized the Ford Motor Company in 1903.

By the beginning of the twentieth century, there were hundreds of small automobile manufacturers in the United States. At first, Ford's company was no different from these. But, in 1908, he hit on something to set his operation apart. Cars were expensive, hand built for the wealthy. Ford saw that the materials were not costly, but the skilled labor to fashion them into an automobile was. He set about designing a car that could be mass produced, and he created the assembly line to mass produce it.

The car was the Model T, which, in 1908, sold for $850, cheaper than any custom-built car, but still more expensive than most people could afford. Between 1908 and 1913, Ford perfected his assembly line, thoroughly breaking down, streamlining, and standardizing the production process. In 1908, he manufactured 10,607 cars. By 1916, when the assembly line was in full swing, he turned out 730,041, not priced at $850, but at $360—within the reach of the average American.

The Model T gave its owner unprecedented freedom and mobility. It triggered a demand for roads, which, in a remarkably short time, stitched the nation together as never before. It promoted as well the suburbanization of America, for the most part greatly improving the quality of life available to the average man and woman. Equally profound was the effect of the assembly line, which, for better or worse, forever changed the relationship between labor and management and, indeed, changed the nature of labor itself.

The NAACP Is Founded

Booker T. Washington, founder of the Tuskegee Institute in Alabama, and, at the end of the nineteenth century, America's most famous African-American leader, was not a fighter for civil rights or social equality. He advocated setting such issues aside and instead focusing black energy on achieving economic self-determination in the belief that, as this was achieved, social equality would follow. Washington's "gradualism" appalled many more progressive African Americans, and to hasten the process of racial equality, in 1909, a group of New York–based intellectuals and social activists—black as well as white—decided to create an organization to counter gradualism. They called it the National Association for the Advancement of Colored People (NAACP) and used it as a platform for public lectures, political lobbying, and popular social publishing. Its most effective organ, a magazine called *The Crisis,* was edited for many years by the distinguished writer, sociologist, and historian W.E.B. DuBois, the nation's first African-American Ph.D., with degrees from Fisk University, Harvard, and the University of Berlin.

The NAACP used its public programs and publications to raise the social consciousness of blacks as well as whites, to make them aware that there were alternatives to passive patience and gradual change. Added to its outreach and educational programs were well-financed and carefully planned legal efforts aimed at testing and ultimately overturning in the nation's courts discriminatory state and local legislation. By 1920 the NAACP claimed 90,000 members, nearly half of whom were southerners, and it was clear that this organization was the leading voice of African-American social progressivism.

1913

Income Tax Enacted

In February 1913, after ratification by the states, the Sixteenth Amendment gave the federal government the authority to levy taxes on personal income. In principle, there was nothing new about an income tax. The Old Testament speaks of tithing, the payment to the state of the tenth part of what one earns, and the U.S. government enacted a temporary income tax—from 3 to 5 percent—during the Civil War, beginning in 1862. Even earlier, back in 1812, when the government needed cash to finance the War of 1812, the Treasury Department thought seriously of adopting what was then the new British practice of taxing income, a tax Parliament used to finance the seemingly ceaseless Napoleonic Wars.

The first U.S. income tax was repealed after the Civil War, but the agency that had administered it, the Internal Revenue Service, remained in existence, and in 1894 Congress enacted the tax again. It was a popular measure, urged by the nation's farmers and urban laborers, who believed that the wealthy should pay more in taxes than the ordinary working man. Tested in the Supreme Court the following year in *Pollock* v. *Farmer's Loan & Trust Co.*, however, the 1894 income tax was ruled unconstitutional.

It was now clear to progressive reformers that public sentiment was high for the income tax and that the only way around the constitutional roadblock was to amend the Constitution. Progressive political thinkers were sufficiently alarmed by the concentration of wealth among a coterie of industrialists to prompt them to form an unlikely alliance with arch conservatives, who were always looking for a dependable way to raise money for national emergencies. This unique progressive–conservative coalition pushed the legislation through Congress and into the hands of the states for ratification.

The demands of the federal income tax began modestly enough. The law laid claim to 1 percent of taxable income above $3,000 for individuals or $4,000 for married couples. The rate was *graduated and progressive,* rising with income level. It hit its maximum—7 percent—for those with annual incomes in excess of $500,000. War brought a dramatic increase in the income tax. At the height of United States involvement in World War I, rates on the top income bracket temporarily shot up to 77 percent. With the Great Depression, the high-end rates increased sharply again, and when World War II bound federal revenue to national survival, the top rate reached a stratospheric 91 percent. Over the years, the tax code has been patched, shored, plugged, and punched through with a stupefying array of deductions, credits, subsidies, and exemptions. It is now the most complex body of public law ever enacted, and while most people agree (however reluctantly) that the income tax has become essential to financing the nation, there is absolutely no doubt about its effectiveness in having financed a multibillion-dollar tax-accounting industry.

1917

The Zimmermann Telegram

Woodrow Wilson was elected president of the United States in 1912 on a promise to improve government and to lead Americans to better lives. His many progressive reforms came swiftly and proved remarkably successful. Less than two years into his first term, on June 28, 1914, the assassination of the Austro-Hungarian Archduke Franz Ferdinand and his wife, the Grand Duchess Sophie, in Sarajevo, propelled Europe and the colonial empires associated with it into the bloodiest war fought on Earth up to that time. Initially, the German armies made a spectacular drive through France, sweeping all resistance before them. On the Eastern Front, the Germans and Austro-Hungarians held off, then repeatedly defeated the armies of mighty Russia. But after a month of ceaseless advance in the west, the German commander in chief was seized by a spasm of strategic uncertainty. He turned his southern forces, then dug in less than thirty miles outside of Paris. France was saved—or, at least, reprieved—and for the next four years, the flower of Europe's young manhood slaughtered each other along opposing lines of static trench works extending from the English Channel coast in the north to the Swiss border in the south.

Early in the war, most Americans were thankful that President Wilson managed to keep the United States neutral. In February 1915, he did warn Germany—whose U-boats glided under the Atlantic, targeting mostly British merchant and passenger vessels—that the United States would hold it strictly accountable for the loss of American lives in the sinking of neutral or passenger ships. Just four months later, on May 7, 1915, a U-boat torpedoed the

British passenger liner *Lusitania,* killing 1,200 people, including 128 Americans. This outrage elicited from many in America a clamor for war, but Wilson stayed the neutral course, and, in 1916, was reelected in large part on the strength of the campaign slogan, "He Kept Us Out of War!"

The *Lusitania* sinking brought United States diplomatic pressure on Germany to end unrestricted submarine warfare. The German kaiser yielded and ordered all U-boats to surface and warn passenger liners before attacking them, so that passengers and crew might abandon ship. Nevertheless, relations between the United States and Germany continued to deteriorate until, in February 1917, with the situation increasingly desperate on the Western Front, Germany announced the resumption of unrestricted submarine warfare—attack by submerged U-boats and without warning. Almost immediately, on February 3, the U.S.S. *Housatonic* was torpedoed and sunk. President Wilson responded by severing diplomatic relations with Germany. The next month, on March 1, the American public learned of the "Zimmermann Telegram," a coded message sent on January 19, 1917, from German foreign secretary Arthur Zimmermann to his nation's ambassador to Mexico outlining the terms of a proposed German–Mexican alliance against the United States. Publication of the telegram left little public sentiment for continued neutrality, and, on April 2, 1917, Woodrow Wilson asked Congress for a declaration of war. It was voted up on April 6.

The United States Mobilizes for War

President Wilson made it clear that America's entry into the "Great War" was not merely in retaliation for violations of U.S. neutrality, but "to make the world safe for democracy." With this statement, the president elevated the United States to the status of a world power. The U.S. Navy was already a reasonably formidable force, but the U.S. Army was downright puny. It numbered only about 200,000 men in 1917. Wilson led a spectacular mobilization that, by the end of the war in November 1918, would swell the army to four million men. The president directed the creation of a welter of war agencies, which essentially put private industry entirely under government control. He pushed through Congress, in May 1917, a Selective Service bill, by which 2.8 million men were drafted. In command of the AEF (Allied Expeditionary Force) was the highly capable General John J. Pershing. The navy sailed under the command of Admiral William S. Sims.

Pershing's arrival in Paris on June 14, 1917, with nothing more than a small staff, came at the nadir of Allied fortunes. One after the other, each major Anglo–French offensive had failed. Thoroughly demoralized, much of the French army mutinied. On the Eastern Front, the giant Russian army had folded, and the broken nation was tumbling headlong into a revolution that would end centuries of czarist rule, introduce communism into the world, and take Russia out of the war, instantly freeing up masses of German troops for service on the Western Front.

Despite the rapid pace of American mobilization, it would be October 21, 1917, before U.S. strength in Europe was sufficient to commit even a few units to battle. Not until the spring of 1918 did large masses of Americans make a significant impact on the fighting. But before he could even begin to command his forces against the Germans, Pershing found himself at war with his French and British allies, who demanded that U.S. troops be placed under their control. Wilson backed Pershing's resistance to this, and the American general retained full authority over U.S. troops. At home, Wilson conducted a campaign of his own, creating a powerful propaganda machine to generate tremendous support for what was, after all, a "foreign war." In instances where propaganda failed, the Wilson government used emergency war powers to censor the press and to silence critics. All of this contributed to the patriotic pressure put on America's young men, who enlisted in great numbers. Those who failed to enlist or, even worse, sought to avoid the draft, were branded as "slackers" and subjected to public humiliation. American idealism and democratic ideals were bolstered by commercially slick propaganda and repressive laws.

World War I: The American Battle Record

The American Expeditionary Force was not committed to battle in truly large numbers until June 1918, but once it was in the war, it fought exceedingly well, with great gallantry, and at a terrible cost in life. Between June 6 and July 1, 1918, the "Yanks" recaptured for the allies Vaux, Bouresches, and, after a hellish struggle, Belleau Wood, while also managing to hold the key Allied position at Cantigny against a crushing German offensive launched between June 9 and June 15.

As the spring of 1918 became summer, during July 18–August 6, 85,000 Americans ended the endless Western Front stalemate by defeating the Germans' last major offensive at the Second Battle of the Marne. This was followed throughout August by a series of Allied offensives—at the Somme, Oise-Aisne, and Ypres-Lys—in which U.S. troops played important roles.

In one great offensive, against the St. Mihiel salient during September 12–16, the Americans acted independently in a deployment of some 1.2 million men against the German supply lines between the

It was called the "Great War," and it was bigger and more terrible than any war that had come before it. A total of 65 million men and women served in the armies and navies of combatant nations during World War I. Of this number, at least 10 million were killed and 20 million wounded. Of the 2 million U.S. troops actually committed to combat, 112,432 died, and 230,074 were wounded. In monetary terms, the war cost the United States the equivalent of $32,700,000,000 in current dollars.

Meuse River and the Argonne Forest. The campaign, which continued until the very day of armistice, November 11, 1918, was both highly successful and terribly costly.

As it became apparent to Germany that American troops not only fought fiercely and well, but were available in seemingly inexhaustible numbers, pouring out of a nation that also ground out the weapons and matériel of war, the German government agreed to an armistice, which was set for the eleventh hour of the eleventh day of the eleventh month of 1918.

1919

The Treaty of Versailles and the League of Nations

World War I had cost America dearly, but it also gave the nation new prestige as a great world power. This was enhanced by the leadership role President Woodrow Wilson took in hammering out the peace in what he hoped would be a "war to end all wars." Tragically, the other three of the "Big Four"—as the heads of state of Great Britain, France, Italy, and the United States were called—were less interested in creating a new world of universal peace than in claiming immediate vengeance on Germany and disabling it from ever threatening the West again. Despite Wilson's valiant efforts, the Treaty of Versailles emerged as a relentlessly punitive document that, far from bringing world peace, created in Germany the desperate climate that, within a few years, produced Hitler and Nazi militarism.

As disappointed as Wilson was with most of the Treaty of Versailles, he believed he had triumphed in integrating into it the League of Nations, which he had reason to believe would become a credible force for preventing war. But Wilson, negotiating in Europe, was out of touch with the postwar temper of his own nation. The last thing most Americans wanted was further involvement with Europe and its destructive problems. When isolationist Republicans, led by Senator Henry Cabot Lodge, chairman of the Foreign Relations Committee, blocked United States participation in the League of Nations, Wilson, home again, decided to take his appeal directly to the American people. Despite his profound exhaustion, he embarked on a speaking tour of the West, only to collapse after a speech at Pueblo, Colorado, on September 25, 1919.

This was followed by a debilitating stroke after he returned to Washington, and, while he was incapacitated, chances for Senate approval of the League of Nations died. Confirming the nation's new mood of isolationism, the bland Warren G. Harding was elected to the presidency in 1920 and promised Americans nothing more or less than a "return to normalcy." The League, he announced, was "not for us." With that, the nation turned its back on developments in Europe, blithely ignoring the conditions and acts that, within two decades of the "war to end all wars," would produce a second world war.

1919

Prohibition Enacted

When the Eighteenth Amendment was passed by Congress on December 18, 1917 and ratified by two-thirds of the states on January 29, 1919, America was more than ripe for Prohibition. Typical of constitutional amendments, the language was brief and straightforward, its principal article stating, "After one year from the ratification of this article the manufacture, sale, or transportation of intoxicating liquors within, the importation thereof into, or the exportation thereof from the United States and all territory subject to the jurisdiction thereof for beverage purposes is hereby prohibited." The background history of Prohibition was, however, long, and its implications profound.

In the years leading up to the Civil War, the rural United States was swept by fundamentalist Christian religion that spawned a "Temperance Movement," which campaigned so successfully against the manufacture and sale of liquor that, by 1855, thirteen of thirty-three states had voted themselves dry. After the Civil War, the Woman's Christian Temperance Union and, in 1895, the Anti-Saloon League became increasingly powerful lobby organizations on local, state, and federal levels. Candidates for virtually every office were obliged to declare themselves "wet" or "dry" and, often, voters made their choices solely on this distinction. By 1916, twenty-one states outlawed saloons, and voters across the country, but principally in rural states, sent a dry majority to Congress. It was this majority that enacted the Eighteenth Amendment, passing it over the veto of Woodrow Wilson, who feared that Prohibition could never be enforced and would, in his words, create "a nation of lawbreakers."

And so it did.

At first, there was a kind of innocence about it all. Urban folk never wanted Prohibition, and now that they had it, they brewed up moonshine, bathtub gin, wine, and beer at home, often in the seclusion of their cellars. It was also not a very difficult matter to smuggle liquor across the borders with Canada or Mexico. Soon, neighborhood people started making or importing—bootlegging, it was called—the stuff for friends and neighbors and, later, for distribution by neighborhood restaurants, drug stores, and former saloon keepers. As for the cop on the beat, alienating the neighborhood by making a raid or an arrest just wasn't worth the trouble. And if he *was* inclined to enforce the law, a few dollars—or bottles—were usually sufficient to generate benign neglect.

Increasingly, however, people turned to professional criminals to slake their thirst. The immigrant experience in the United States was typically a hard road, and streetwise second-generation immigrants were always on the lookout for a shortcut. Crime held allure as the shortest cut of all. Moreover, often excluded from mainstream American society, ethnic immigrants found the fellowship and society they needed in *organized* crime, including the Irish gangs that sprang up in New York and other cities and the Italian Mafia, which, transplanted from its Sicilian seedbed, took root on American shores late in the nineteenth century. Prohibition, an opportunity to turn crime into big business by controlling the supply and distribution of an illegal substance much in demand, brought the American Mafia into full bloom. Far from producing a nation of hardworking, sober, reverent citizens, Prohibition created organized crime, which, in many cities, came to figure as a shadow government and terrorized, drained, and plagued the nation for decades to come—long after Prohibition was repealed by the Twenty-First Amendment, passed on February 20, 1933, and ratified on December 5 of that year.

1920

Women Get the Vote

Back in 1777, New Jersey, embroiled in the American Revolution, made a mistake in drafting its voting law. The statute specified that all "individuals" worth fifty pounds or more could vote. So, New Jersey *women* who met the fifty-pound criteria voted in 1777, and they were the only women who voted in the United States of America. Assuming the matter of gender was self-evident, New Jersey lawmakers failed to specify the word *men* when they drew up the law. The embarrassing oversight was soon corrected, and the loophole plugged. It was not until 1848, with the Seneca Falls Conference, that the organized women's suffrage movement began.

Before the Civil War, the women's suffrage movement was closely tied to the abolition movement. But, after the war, women suffragists became divided over whether or not to bind the campaign for women's right to vote with the campaign to ensure the enfranchisement of former slaves. Elizabeth Cady Stanton and women's rights activist Susan B. Anthony fought hard for constitutional amendments that would enfranchise both blacks and women, and Lucretia Mott was elected chair of an Equal Rights Association. But when the Fourteenth and Fifteenth Amendments, extending the vote to black men, failed to address women's rights, Stanton and Anthony broke with Mott's group to form the National Woman Suffrage Association, which opposed the Fifteenth Amendment because it enfranchised slaves, but not women. Yet another splinter group, the American Woman Suffrage Association, supported the Fifteenth Amendment as a necessary first step in the broadening of voting rights.

The fragmentation of the women's suffrage movement slowed progress on the issue until, in 1890, the National Woman Suffrage Association and the American Woman Suffrage Association merged under the leadership of Anna Howard Shaw and Carrie Chapman Catt to become the National American Woman Suffrage Association. It was this group that made the final, long push toward getting the vote for women. Under unrelenting political pressure, individual states began to give women the vote—in nonfederal elections. Wyoming was the first, in 1890, and several other western states followed suit. Nationally, Theodore Roosevelt's Progressive ("Bull Moose") Party endorsed women's suffrage in 1912, and, during World War I, President Woodrow Wilson endorsed a constitutional amendment granting women the right to vote as what he called "a vitally necessary war measure," for so many adult males were away at war.

With such a broad base of support, the Nineteenth Amendment was passed by Congress on June 4, 1919, and ratified by the states on August 18, 1920. Its principal clause, so long and difficult in coming to birth, could not have been simpler: "The right of citizens of the United States to vote shall not be denied or abridged by the United States or any State on account of sex."

1920

Birth of Commercial Broadcast Radio

The basic radio had been developed at the end of the nineteenth century by the Irish-Italian Guglielmo Marconi, but it was an American, Reginald Fessenden, who invented the first practical radio voice transmitter in 1906 and another American, Lee De Forest, who developed the vacuum tube, the heart of pre-transistor electronics. De Forest made a few stabs at broadcasting musical programming between 1907 and 1909, but it wasn't until November 2, 1920, that Pittsburgh's KDKA broadcast returns from the presidential election, thereby inaugurating the first regular commercial broadcasting. Over the next three years, 556 commercial radio stations went into operation nationwide, and by the end of the decade, radio had become a genuine mass medium, a viable alternative to newspapers and magazines for the mass dissemination of entertainment and information.

1923–1982

The Equal Rights Amendment

For the most part, the campaign for women's suffrage worked within the system: by lobbying, by selectively supporting candidates for elective office, and by generally raising public consciousness. At the radical fringe, however, was the Congressional Union's National Woman's Party, organized by Alice Paul, a University of Pennsylvania Ph.D. and Quaker activist. Paul, a militant advocate of women's suffrage and women's rights, was jailed three times in England and three times in the United States. In prison, she waged a hunger strike, was pronounced insane, and force-fed. Her followers picketed, also staged hunger strikes, and engaged in other forms of civil disobedience to support passage of a constitutional amendment that would not only give women the right to vote, but would explicitly confer on them equal rights with men.

The Equal Rights Amendment

Section 1. Equality of rights under the law shall not be denied or abridged by the United States or by any State on account of sex.

Section 2. The Congress shall have the power to enforce, by appropriate legislation, the provisions of this article.

Section 3. This amendment shall take effect two years after the date of ratification.

Paul drew up what she called the Equal Rights Amendment, which, even after women were granted the right to vote by the Nineteenth Amendment, languished for decades in Congress. When finally passed in the 1970s, the amendment failed to achieve ratification by the requisite two-thirds majority of states. An extension of the ratification deadline was given, but "ERA" died in 1982. The amendment was reintroduced during the 107th Congress (2001–2002), but has yet to gain passage.

1927

Lindbergh Flies the Atlantic

By 1927, the airplane had come a long way since the Wright brothers' first flight at Kitty Hawk, North Carolina, in 1903. Nevertheless, through the early 1920s, most people still regarded flying as something for daredevils and certainly not as an alternative to the train or the ship. Charles Augustus Lindbergh—University of Minnesota dropout; son of a Minnesota congressman; one-time stunt flier; former second lieutenant in the 110th Observation Squadron, 35th Division, Missouri National Guard; and sometime airmail pilot—loved the thrill of flight, but, even more, was determined to bring flying into the mainstream. When hotel owner Raymond Orteig put up a $25,000 prize—to be awarded to the first person or persons who crossed the Atlantic by plane, nonstop, between New York and Paris—Lindbergh saw an opportunity to demonstrate the potential of transoceanic flight.

Armed with the prospect of the Orteig prize, Lindbergh persuaded a group of St. Louis businessmen to finance construction of a suitable aircraft. Lindbergh researched several models before he commissioned the Ryan Aeronautical Company of San Diego, California, to customize a single-engine airplane especially for the flight. More cautious aviators would have chosen a twin-engine plane for the hazardous crossing. In case one engine failed, the pilot could reach land and bring the plane down on the other. But a twin-engine plane burned more fuel than a single-engine craft, and it generally required a two-man crew. Lindbergh wanted to save fuel, and he wanted to fly with the only person whose aviation skills he thoroughly trusted: himself. So the Ryan aircraft, christened *The Spirit of St. Louis,* was designed as a kind of flying fuel tank, with a single, large engine. Lindbergh even put a fuel tank in front of the cockpit, where, ordinarily, the windshield would be. He reasoned that he would encounter no obstacles over the water, that fuel was more important than a continuous straight-ahead view, and if he needed to see what was in front of him, he could poke his head out the window or use a small built-in periscope. The plane cost $10,580.

The 1920s loved daring deeds, and all eyes were focused on the tall, unassuming, boyishly handsome Lindbergh, dubbed by all the papers "The Lone Eagle." There was a very good chance that he'd go the way of earlier competitors for the Orteig prize. They crashed and burned or simply disappeared.

The night before his takeoff, from Long Island's Roosevelt Field (today the site of a shopping mall), the incessant clatter of reporters' typewriters kept Lindbergh awake. He had had almost no sleep when, at 7:52 on the morning of May 20, 1927, he began to roll down an unpaved airstrip turned to mud by a night of heavy rain. Lindbergh had stripped the plane of all unnecessary weight. "Unnecessary," as he saw it, included a parachute. Lindbergh reasoned that one would do him little good over the icy Atlantic anyway. However, loaded with fuel and mired in the mud, the stripped-down *Spirit of St. Louis* barely cleared the treetops at the end of the field.

For the next thirty-three hours twenty-nine minutes, an already sleep-deprived Lone Eagle battled fatigue, the elements, and the vagaries of dead-reckoning navigation as he made his way, alone, across the ocean.

On May 21, when he touched down at Le Bourget Field outside of Paris at 10:22 P.M. (local time), a groggy but elated Lindbergh was overwhelmed by the reception he was accorded. Thousands thronged him in Paris, and later, back home as well, in all the major cities of the United States. He was elevated to a heroic status that recalled, if anything, the champions of ancient Greece. Lindbergh, it seemed, had not only defied death, but had annihilated time and nullified distance. If those who acclaimed young Lindbergh envied his eagle-like freedom, they also felt that his feat had won a part of that freedom for everyone. In economic terms, Lindbergh's transatlantic flight raised a groundswell of commercial interest in aviation. In less than a dozen years, airlines inaugurated regularly scheduled transatlantic service, and life itself was, quite simply, transformed.

1929

The Stock Market Crash

The roar of the "Roaring Twenties" was not fueled exclusively by bootleg liquor, but also by money or, more precisely, by spending. During the decade, many Americans had a go-for-broke attitude and speculated in stocks in unprecedented numbers, frequently overextending themselves by purchasing securities "on margin," putting down as little as ten cents on the dollar in the hope that the stock price would rise fast and far enough to cover loans few could truly afford. So much stock was bought on margin—backed by dimes, not dollars—that much of it amounted to little more than paper. Well-financed industries poured cash into production, machinery, and plants to turn out more and more products that, however, were priced beyond the means of most consumers. Goods piled up and the prices fell, and industry laid off workers. If people with average incomes couldn't afford many of the goods being produced in profusion, people without incomes could afford even less. The marketplace continued to shrink, and as that happened, companies found themselves unable to make new hires. And this represented just the industrial sector of the economy. Long before the vicious cycle of increased production and reduced demand began, farmers were suffering from chronically low farm prices and high transportation costs.

There were warning signs of instability during the autumn of 1929, one of the most obvious being wildly fluctuating stock prices. On October 24, the market was caught up in a selling spree, which culminated five days later, on October 29. It was called "Black Tuesday," the day the bottom fell out.

Prices disintegrated. Value evaporated. Brokers "called" their margin loans, demanding immediate payment in full on loans used to purchase stocks that were now worthless. The investors didn't have the money. Many were ruined. The brokers collected the stocks—collateral for the margin loans they had made—but who was there to buy them? So brokers and brokerages went belly up, too.

On Black Tuesday, stocks lost an average of 40 points. This was at a time when the Dow-Jones Industrial Average peaked at 380. By the close of business on October 29, 1929, the Dow was at 230. In 1930, 1,300 banks failed. By 1933, another 3,700 would fail, and one out of four workers was jobless.

The "Bonus Army" Marches on Washington

Herbert Hoover had been elected president in 1928, when most Americans felt good about the economy and were pleased with the hands-off-business approach taken by government under Hoover's predecessor Calvin Coolidge. Known as "Silent Cal," Coolidge was notoriously tight-lipped, but he is remembered for having declared, "The business of America is business." And now, as the nation descended into economic depression, his fellow Republican, Hoover, came across as stunned and as fearful as his fellow Americans, assuring them unconvincingly that "prosperity was just around the corner."

Hoover did propose a number of relief programs, but he steadfastly insisted that it was up to the states and local governments to finance and administer them. In principle, this was prudent, but Hoover's policy was doomed for the very simple reason that state and local governments had no money. Hoover, who had made his reputation as a great humanitarian, brilliantly administering international relief efforts following the devastation of Europe after World War I, also cleaved to the steadfast belief that federal aid must not be given directly to individuals. Big-government intervention in private lives, he feared, would compromise the liberty, integrity, and initiative of the individual citizen.

The policies of Herbert Hoover were not callous, but they were ineffectual. Shantytowns constructed of boxes and crates bloomed like evil flowers across the American landscape to house the jobless and homeless. They were called "Hoovervilles," and the desperation they housed bred something approaching revolution. Already, revolutionary unrest had swept much of the world (for this depression was worldwide), especially Germany, badly crippled by the punitive Treaty of Versailles. In Italy and Germany, totalitarian government—fascism in Italy, National Socialism, and Nazism in Germany—offered some hope for recovery. Most Americans clung to democracy, but democracy was not putting beans on the table, and among intellectuals and some radical working men and women, communism seemed to offer a viable alternative.

How close did the United States come to revolution? One indication was the fate of the "Bonus Army" in 1932. Veterans of World War I were entitled by law to a cash payment, a so-called "bonus," payable in 1945. With conditions desperate in 1932, however, a movement arose to secure immediate payment of the bonuses. In May 1932, some 15,000 to 20,000 unemployed veterans marched on Washington in an effort to compel Congress to release their bonuses. This "Bonus Army" camped in the city and just outside it, at Anacostia Flats, Maryland. The House of Representatives took notice and did pass a bonus bill on June 15, only to have it voted down by the more conservative Senate. By the time this happened, the marchers' makeshift camp had grown into a sprawling "Hooverville" of crates, shacks, and shanties. When rioting broke out on July 28, President Hoover ordered General Douglas MacArthur to clear Pennsylvania Avenue of demonstrators. Although he also ordered MacArthur *not* to cross into Anacostia Flats, the general did just that, advancing against the unarmed Bonus Army—which included women and children—with units of cavalry, infantry, and armor, and making liberal use of tear gas and the flat of cavalry officers' sabers.

The assault on the Bonus Army was a national disgrace, and President Hoover, whipped by a storm of protest, managed to make matters worse by calling the Bonus Army nothing more than a "pack of criminals." Of what, the nation asked in response, were they guilty? Poverty? Joblessness? Despair?

Fortunately for the American democracy, 1932 was an election year. The people had available to them the same opportunity for revolution that had been available every four years since the election of George Washington. They could vote in a whole new government. And that is what they did.

FDR Is Elected on the Promise of a "New Deal"

I n 1921, the career of a promising young New York politician, Franklin Delano Roosevelt, seemed to have been ended by a crippling attack of polio, but, with buoyant optimism and smiling determination, FDR refused to give up, became the dynamic governor of New York, and in 1932 was elected president of the United States, earning 22.8 million votes to Herbert Hoover's 15.8 million.

He had promised the Depression-burdened nation a "New Deal," and in the first "Hundred Days" of his administration ushered through Congress radical and sweeping legislation aimed at relieving suffering, and at transforming the economic policies of the United States. New Deal measures included a Federal Deposit Insurance Corporation and tight federal regulation to prevent the devastation of bank failures; a Home Owners' Loan Corporation to help Americans buy—and keep—their homes; a Federal Securities Act to curb the kinds of careless activities that had contributed to the stock market crash of 1929; and a host of federally subsidized employment programs to give Americans jobs.

The New Deal introduced unprecedented government regulation of private enterprise, including aid to industry and price controls on the products produced. The federal government forged a close alliance with business through the National Industrial Recovery Act, which also protected the rights of labor and guaranteed collective bargaining. Farmers were the particular focus of FDR's New Deal. Programs subsidized farm prices and helped farmers secure credit. Great public works—most notably Boulder (now Hoover) Dam—harnessed the forces of nature itself to irrigate arid lands and to furnish raw power in the form of electricity.

But, most of all, there was the presence of Roosevelt himself. His courage, his vision, and his ability to communicate confidence and hope worked political magic in sustaining the nation through the worst economic crisis in its history. "We have nothing to fear," he declared in his first inaugural address, "but fear itself." And most Americans proved willing to take him at his word.

World's First Television Broadcast

As with motion pictures, the technology of television is so complex that we can't point to any one person as the "inventor" of TV. But if any individual comes close, it's Vladimir Zworykin, a Russian immigrant who, while working as an electrical engineer for Westinghouse, invented the "iconoscope" in 1924. A specially treated vacuum tube, the iconoscope transformed light into electrical impulses and electrical impulses back into light—in the form of an image projected electronically onto a phosphor-coated screen. Because it was capable of a two-way transformation—light to electricity, electricity to light—the iconoscope became the basis for the television camera as well as the familiar TV "picture tube," the heart of the television set.

Although technicians and scientists were excited by the iconoscope, it found no immediate commercial application. While working at RCA Laboratories in the 1930s, Zworykin developed the iconoscope into a genuine television system and, in 1933, demonstrated his invention by transmitting a television picture from New York to Philadelphia—the world's first TV broadcast.

And yet Zworykin hardly became a household name. No one—none of the great radio networks and not even RCA—leaped at the revolutionary technology. Half a dozen years crawled by before the first *public* television broadcast was made: In 1939, NBC aired live video of President Franklin D. Roosevelt addressing the nation as he opened the New York World's Fair. The broadcast caused a stir, including predictions that a great new medium had been born, but the sudden onset of World War II diverted most of America's technological effort to the war. Television, destined to revolutionize civilized life, had to be put on hold.

1940

The Mark I Computer

BM, the International Business Machine corporation, a leading manufacturer of calculating machines since 1924, joined forces with a team from Harvard University to create the Mark I, an electro-mechanical device that is generally acknowledged as the world's first genuinely programmable computer. The Mark I saw service during World War II as a device capable of making intensely complex calculations of the speed and trajectory of artillery shells.

Mark I was a gargantuan machine, eight feet high and fifty feet long. It was rendered obsolete in 1946 by ENIAC, which replaced all mechanical parts with vacuum tubes and was therefore the first fully electronic computer. Like Mark I, however, it was enormous: 3,000 cubic feet in volume, thirty tons in weight, and equipped with 18,000 vacuum tubes, which had to be changed almost continually.

Together, Mark I and ENIAC ushered in the electronic age, in which computers would become increasingly powerful and would play an ever larger role in daily life. By the 1970s and 1980s, with the advent of integrated circuits, miniaturization reduced the enormous volume of these early machines to a size that could be set upon a desk. The "personal computer," especially linked to the Internet, redefined computing and extended its reach into virtually every American life.

1941

Attack on Pearl Harbor

The United States remained neutral as a volatile situation developed in Europe, with Nazi Germany and fascist Italy hammering out the Rome–Berlin Axis in 1936 and the Empire of Japan concluding an alliance with Germany the same year. In 1938, Adolf Hitler annexed Austria to his Third Reich and then carved the Sudetenland out of Czechoslovakia, followed by all of Czechoslovakia and a part of Lithuania. Germany's military actions went unopposed in Europe, until on September 1, 1939, it invaded Poland. England and France declared war and World War II had begun.

American attention was nervously focused on Europe while Japan, having violated a 1922 international agreement, established the puppet state of Manchuko in Manchuria in 1932 and, by 1937, was engaged in a full-scale war of aggression against China. On September 27, 1940, Japan signed the Tripartite Pact with Italy and Germany, thereby creating the Berlin–Rome–Tokyo Axis. Relations between the United States and Japan deteriorated when President Franklin Roosevelt embargoed the export of scrap metal, oil, and other commodities to that country. Instead of curbing Japanese aggression, as Roosevelt had hoped, the embargo pushed the empire to attack. On Sunday, December 7, 1941, at 7:50 in the morning, carrier-launched Japanese aircraft struck without warning at Pearl Harbor, Hawaii, where some seventy-five major U.S. Navy ships were moored. The attack was over by ten o'clock, leaving eighteen U.S. ships sunk or badly damaged and more than 200 aircraft destroyed on the ground. The battleships *Arizona, West Virginia, Oklahoma,* and *California* were among those sunk, and the *Nevada* was badly damaged. Some 2,400 U.S. servicemen were killed, 1,300 wounded, and 1,000 missing, while the Japanese suffered fewer than 100 casualties, losing only twenty-nine planes and five midget submarines. The only bright spot in this military disaster was that the U.S. aircraft carrier fleet was not in port. It would form the powerful nucleus of the American response to Japanese aggression in the Pacific.

On December 8, President Roosevelt asked a joint session of Congress for a declaration of war, calling December 7, 1941, a "day which will live in infamy." The attack on Pearl Harbor was a spectacular tactical victory for Japan, but, strategically, it was a military blunder. It brought an end to the Great Depression in the United States as well as instant unity of purpose. The nation was forged into a weapon the likes of which the world had never before seen.

The Fall of the Philippines

In the days and weeks following Pearl Harbor, Imperial Japanese forces attacked Wake Island and Guam (both U.S. possessions), British Malaya, Singapore, the Dutch East Indies, Burma, Thailand, and the Philippines (at the time a U.S. commonwealth territory). On Guam, the small U.S. garrison was quickly overwhelmed and surrendered. On Wake Island, grotesquely outnumbered marines repelled a first Japanese attack, but were forced to yield to a second. Britain's crown colony of Hong Kong folded, as did Singapore, and then the Dutch East Indies. Burma, lifeline to China, fell—although Claire L. Chennault, a former U.S. Army Air Service captain now working as air advisor to China's Generalissimo Chiang Kai-shek, led his American Volunteer Group, the famed Flying Tigers, and their outnumbered and outclassed Curtiss P-40s in crippling action against the Japanese.

The cruelest blow in the Pacific came in the Philippines, where, despite a gallant defense through May 6, 1942, U.S. and Filipino forces under Lieutenant General Jonathan M. Wainwright surrendered and were subject to unspeakable brutality at the hands of their Japanese captors. The infamous Bataan Death March, in which prisoners were forced on foot from Corregidor to POW camps in Bataan, caused the deaths of 10,000 prisoners from abuse and starvation. Fortunately, the senior American commander in the Pacific, General Douglas MacArthur, escaped to Australia, promising those left behind on the Philippines, "I shall return." His pledge would not be redeemed until 1944.

1942

Japanese-American Internment

At the time of the Japanese attack on Pearl Harbor, some 120,000 persons of direct Japanese descent were living in the United States. Of these, about 80,000 had been born in this country and were citizens. As early as December 11, 1941, just four days after Pearl Harbor, the FBI rounded up and detained 1,370 Japanese Americans as "dangerous enemy aliens"—although they were, in fact, Americans. The first public call for putting Japanese Americans "under federal control" came on December 22, 1941, from the Agriculture Committee of the Los Angeles Chamber of Commerce. The source was significant. For years, Japanese-American farmers had enjoyed great success in California, Oregon, and Washington, running their farms so efficiently that many Anglo farmers couldn't compete. Doubtless, many Americans were very fearful of Japanese Americans and the acts of sabotage they might commit, but it is also true that the war provided a convenient means for sweeping away years of agricultural competition.

On January 5, 1942, U.S. draft boards classified all Japanese-American selective service registrants as enemy aliens. On January 29, U.S. Attorney General Francis Biddle established "prohibited zones," forbidden to all enemy aliens. German and Italian as well as Japanese aliens were ordered to leave San Francisco waterfront areas immediately. The next day, Earl Warren, at the time California's attorney general, but destined to gain fame beginning in the 1950s as a liberal chief justice of the Supreme Court and eloquent voice of civil liberties, declared that, "unless something is done," the presence of Japanese Americans on the West Coast "may bring about a repetition of Pearl Harbor." Early in February, the entire West Coast congressional delegation appealed to President Franklin D. Roosevelt to order the removal of "all persons of Japanese lineage . . . aliens and citizens alike, from the strategic areas of California, Oregon and Washington." On February 19, President Roosevelt signed Executive Order 9066, authorizing the secretary of war to define military areas "from which any or all persons may be excluded as deemed necessary or desirable." As carried out by Secretary of War Henry Stimson and the man he put in charge of the operations, Lieutenant General John DeWitt, this meant that Japanese Americans, citizens and noncitizens alike, living within 200 miles of the Pacific Coast had to evacuate.

More than 100,000 persons were moved to internment camps in California, Idaho, Utah, Arizona, Wyoming, Colorado, and Arkansas. The camps were spartan, and many of the internees suffered great financial hardship and loss. Worst of all, the forced removal of Americans—the deprivation of liberty and property without due process of law—seemed flatly unconstitutional. Yet the only significant opposition to the removal came from Quaker activists and the American Civil Liberties Union. Suits brought before the Supreme Court, including *Hirabayashi* v. *United States* and *Korematsu* v. *United States,* failed. The high court upheld the constitutionality of the executive order.

Some young Japanese men—about 1,200—won release from the camps by enlisting in the United States Army. They were segregated in the 442nd Regimental Combat Team (which also consisted of some 10,000 Japanese Hawaiian volunteers—the Hawaiians had not been confined to camps), and they fought in Italy, France, and Germany. The 442nd amassed a remarkable record of heroism, becoming the

"You fought not only the enemy, but you fought prejudice—and you have won." —President Harry S Truman, addressing the 100th Battalion, 442nd Regimental Combat Team, on its return from Italy, July 1946

most decorated unit for its size and length of service in American military history.

On December 17, 1944, Major General Henry C. Pratt issued Public Proclamation No. 21, which, effective January 2, 1945, allowed the "evacuees" to return to their homes. Some were able to take up their lives where they had left them; others found themselves financially and emotionally devastated. All court cases seeking recompense from the government failed until 1968, when the United States reimbursed many who had lost property because of their relocation. In 1988, Congress appropriated funds to pay a lump sum of $20,000 to each of the 60,000 surviving Japanese-American internees.

1942

The Doolittle Raid on Tokyo

During the early months of World War II, the news from the Pacific was bleak. In a spectacular effort to raise American morale, Lieutenant Colonel James Doolittle of the U.S. Army Air Forces led an extraordinary surprise bombing raid against Tokyo on April 18, 1942, using sixteen twin-engine B-25 bombers launched from the aircraft carrier *Hornet*. The pilots were well aware that the bombers could not carry sufficient fuel to return to any American base, nor were they designed to land on an aircraft carrier. The plan was to bomb Tokyo, then find landing places in China and seek safe haven among Chinese resistance fighters. From here, it would be up to each crew somehow to find a way home.

The raid was launched, and although the damage inflicted on Tokyo was minor, the psychological effect was incalculable—both upon the shocked Japanese and upon the elated American public, signaling the intention of the U.S. military to take the offensive as soon as possible.

Battle of Midway

Early in May 1942, the U.S. Navy sank or disabled more than twenty-five Japanese ships in action that prevented Japan from extending its conquests deep into the south Pacific and, equally important, checked Japanese efforts to sever supply lines to Australia. Seeking to recover from its losses, the Japanese Imperial Navy staged a major offensive by attacking the island of Midway, some 1,100 miles northwest of Hawaii. If the Japanese could knock out this U.S. outpost, all American hope for regaining control of the Pacific would be lost.

In one of the most momentous battles of the war, beginning on June 3, 1942, U.S. aircraft launched from the *Hornet, Yorktown,* and *Enterprise* sank four Japanese carriers and inflicted other losses. Reeling from this blow, the Imperial Navy withdrew its fleet, which was pursued by American forces that sank or disabled two heavy cruisers and three destroyers and shot down 322 Japanese planes. The U.S. Navy also took heavy losses—the carrier *Yorktown* and a destroyer were sunk, and 147 aircraft lost—but not only did Midway Island remain under U.S. control, the Japanese suffered losses from which they would never recover, and they were unable to resume the offensive in the Pacific. If any single engagement can be called the turning point of the war in the Pacific, Midway was it.

Battles of Guadalcanal and the Bismarck Sea

Having been defeated at Midway, the Japanese prepared to invade Australia and, as a stepping-off place for the invasion, began building an airstrip on Guadalcanal in the southern Solomon Islands. To stop this, on August 7, 1942, U.S. Marines landed at Guadalcanal and began a six-month battle, ultimately defeating the Japanese contingent.

Guadalcanal was the first step in an American strategy of "island hopping," a plan to take Japanese-held islands selectively, gradually closing in on the Japanese mainland itself, while isolating and cutting off certain Japanese outpost islands.

After Guadalcanal came Rabaul, on the eastern tip of New Britain Island, just east of New Guinea. It was the largest of the Japanese naval and air bases. General Douglas MacArthur led U.S. and Australian troops in a campaign through the Solomons and into New Guinea. When the Japanese rushed to reinforce their position on the islands of Lae and Salamaua, on March 3–4, 1943, American bombers attacked Japanese troop transports and their naval escorts with devastating results. This Battle of the Bismarck Sea cost the Japanese 3,500 men, while the Allies lost only five planes, and by the end of 1943, Rabaul was neutralized, cutting off some 100,000 Japanese troops from any hope of supply, support, or reinforcement.

1943

Action in the Central Pacific

Simultaneously with the Battles of Guadalcanal and the Bismarck Sea in the south Pacific was a massive offensive in the central Pacific, beginning with U.S. assaults against Tarawa and Makin islands. While Makin fell quickly, the Tarawa battle, begun on November 20, 1943, did not end until November 26. Of the 5,000 Japanese troops defending the island, only 17 were taken prisoner at battle's end.

Invasion of Italy

argely at the behest of Britain's prime minister Winston Churchill, the Allies adopted a strategy of invading Europe via what Churchill called its "soft underbelly." After defeating the Italians and Germans in North Africa, Anglo–American forces invaded Sicily, landing there on July 9–10, 1943. The Italian army crumbled before them, but German resistance was much stiffer. Nevertheless, the invasion of Sicily culminated in the fall of Messina to the Allies on August 17, 1943. The month before, Italy's fascist dictator, Benito Mussolini, had been overthrown, and the new Italian government, under Marshal Pietro Badoglio, made secret peace overtures to the Allies. The Germans, however, were determined to defend the Italian peninsula at whatever cost.

At first, the invasion of the Italian mainland went well. British and U.S. forces left Messina on September 3, 1943, and, within a month, southern Italy had fallen to the Allies, but the Allied progress northward was heartbreakingly slow and costly. On January 22, 1944, 50,000 U.S. troops landed at Anzio, just thirty-three miles south of Rome, but were pinned down by German forces, and Rome did not yield until June 4. From this point on, the Germans steadily retreated northward, fighting a bloody campaign in that retreat.

1944

D-Day

From Europe's "soft underbelly," the British and Americans advanced northward through Italy, while the Soviets, who had turned the tide against the Nazis with the monumental Battle of Stalingrad (present-day Volgograd), fought from July 17 to November 18, 1942, pressed from the east. The decision was at last taken to begin the major Allied invasion from the west, and on June 6, 1944—"D-Day"—approximately 5,000 Allied ships, 11,000 Allied aircraft, and more than 150,000 troops assaulted what Adolf Hitler liked to call Fortress Europe. Under the overall command of General Dwight David Eisenhower, the greatest invasion force ever assembled anytime, anywhere landed on the beaches of Normandy.

At some landing points, German resistance was surprisingly light—the Germans having been deceived into expecting the invasion at Pas de Calais—but at others, most notably the sector code named Omaha Beach, the defense was brutal. Still, the invasion was an overwhelming success. Beachheads were established, and, over the next weeks and months, Allied troops and supplies poured into Europe.

1944

The G.I. Bill

As victory began to appear on the horizon during World War II, Congress looked forward to the return of millions of soldiers and began to think about their reintegration into society. At the urging of President Roosevelt, legislators passed the Servicemen's Readjustment Act, more popularly known as the "G.I. Bill of Rights" or, simply, the "G.I. Bill." This unprecedented piece of legislation established veterans' hospitals, made low-interest mortgages available, and provided financing for vocational and college education. In these ways, the legislation did not merely reintegrate returning troops into American society, it reshaped that society, creating a postwar generation that was better educated, better trained, and better housed than any other in history.

Victory in Europe

From the beaches of Normandy and other, secondary landing areas, Allied troops poured into Europe. On August 25, 1944, Paris was returned to Allied hands, and the Allies continued to sweep through France. By early September, British forces liberated Brussels, and American troops crossed the German frontier at Eupen. On October 21, the U.S. First Army captured Aachen, the first German city to fall to the Allies.

It was clear to all rational leaders that Germany had lost the war, but Adolf Hitler was hardly rational and ordered a fight to the last man. On December 16, 1944, General Gerd von Rundstedt mounted a desperate surprise counteroffensive that drove a wedge into Allied lines through the Ardennes on the Franco–Belgian frontier. Because German forces distended the Allied line westward, the contest that followed was called the Battle of the Bulge. Despite heavy losses, the U.S. First and Third armies—the latter led brilliantly by Lieutenant General George S. Patton—pushed back the "bulge" and crushed the last great German offensive. In February 1945, Patton led his armored units to the Rhine River and, on March 7, captured the bridge at Remagen, near Cologne. Allied armies streamed across this bridge and other points along the Rhine.

Although Anglo–American forces were now poised to take Berlin, General Eisenhower, believing Hitler would make his last stand in the German south, chose to head for Leipzig instead and to leave the German capital to the Soviet Red Army. On April 16, 1945, Soviet marshal Georgy Zhukov entered the city, fought for it street by street, and finally took Hitler's underground bunker headquarters, only to discover that the Führer had committed suicide. On May 7, 1945, senior representatives of Germany's armed forces surrendered to the Allies at General Eisenhower's headquarters in Reims. An unconditional surrender was concluded the next day. This left the war in the Pacific still to be won.

Death of Franklin Roosevelt

The terrible news broke over the nation's radios at 5:47 P.M., Eastern War Time, on April 12, 1945. Less than an hour earlier, Franklin Delano Roosevelt, haggard, exhausted, but ever gallant, had died of a cerebral hemorrhage at the "Little White House" in Warm Springs, Georgia.

Not since the assassination of another war president, Abraham Lincoln, had the nation felt the sudden loss of its leader so keenly. FDR had served an unprecedented three full terms and was embarked on his fourth. He had guided the nation through the Great Depression and had led it to the verge of victory in World War II. His vice president, Harry S. Truman, took the oath of office two hours twenty-four minutes after the president's death. What he said the next day to a group of reporters expressed his frank understanding of the burden that had become his: "Boys, if you ever pray, pray for me now. I don't know whether you fellows ever had a load of hay fall on you, but when they told me yesterday what had happened, I felt like the moon, the stars, and all the planets had fallen on me."

Atomic Bombings of Hiroshima and Nagasaki

On April 25, 1945, less than two weeks after the death of Franklin Roosevelt, Secretary of War Henry L. Stimson handed the new president, Harry Truman, a typewritten memorandum: "Within four months," it began, "we shall in all probability have completed the most terrible weapon ever known in human history, one bomb of which could destroy a whole city."

President Roosevelt had confided very little in his vice president. Stimson's note was the first time Truman heard about the "Manhattan Project," code name for one of the biggest scientific and technological projects ever undertaken by any nation at any time in history. Begun in 1941, the entire project had one objective and one purpose. The objective was to liberate the enormous energy that holds together atomic nuclei, to liberate that energy in a split second as an explosion more terrible than any humankind had ever before created. The purpose was to use this explosion to win World War II.

Overall direction of the Manhattan Project was assigned to Brigadier General Leslie R. Groves, an army engineer. While Groves commanded the logistics of the Manhattan Project, the charismatic American physicist J. Robert Oppenheimer directed the science, brilliantly coordinating the efforts of a civilian army of the most prominent physicists, chemists, and mathematicians in the world. As vast a scientific undertaking as it was, the Manhattan Project was also a tremendous manufacturing enterprise. Two radioactive isotopes, uranium 235 and plutonium 239, undergo fission most readily—if present in sufficient quantity to constitute critical mass. Enormous processing facilities are required to produce enough of these isotopes to build bombs. Groves oversaw construction of giant, but completely secret, plants at Oak Ridge, Tennessee, for the separation of uranium 235 from its natural companion isotope, uranium 238, and at Hanford, Washington, for the production of plutonium 239, while Oppenheimer supervised creation of a laboratory on a remote mesa at Los Alamos, New Mexico. Here is where theoretical physics had to be transformed into a bomb. Methods had to be found to reduce the fissionable products produced at Oak Ridge and Hanford to pure metal, to fabricate that metal into shapes suitable for bringing the chain reaction to an explosive level, and to instantly bring together sufficient amounts of the fissionable material to achieve a supercritical mass—an explosion.

In a remarkably short time, all of the problems were solved, and the first test of the bomb, code named Trinity, took place in the Alamogordo desert at Los Alamos at 0529:45 on July 16, 1945. Everyone who witnessed the detonation said it was like the creation of a sun on Earth.

On August 6, 1945, a lone B-29 Superfortress took off from an airfield on Tinian Island. The pilot, Colonel Paul Tibbets, named it after his mother, Enola Gay. At 8:15 in the morning, local time, the uranium-235 bomb, nicknamed "Little Man," was released from *Enola Gay*'s bomb bay. It detonated 1,900 feet above the city of Hiroshima, instantly destroying two-thirds of the city and killing, wherever they stood or sat or lay, 78,000 of Hiroshima's

> "**We waited until** the blast had passed, walked out of the shelter and then it was extremely solemn. We knew the world would not be the same. A few people laughed, a few people cried. Most people were silent. I remembered the line from the Hindu scripture, the *Bhagavad Gita:* Vishnu is trying to persuade the Prince that he should do his duty . . . and says, 'Now I am become death, destroyer of worlds.' I suppose we all thought that one way or another." —J. Robert Oppenheimer in 1965, recalling the 1945 Trinity test

350,000 residents. By the end of 1945, about 62,000 more succumbed to injuries or radiation sickness.

On August 9, a plutonium-239 bomb, called "Fat Man," was loaded aboard another B-29, *Bock's Car*, bound for Kokura. Dense cloud cover over that target sent the crew to Nagasaki, and, at 11:02 A.M. local time, Fat Man detonated at 1,650 feet. Half the city was flattened by the blast. Of 270,000 people there, about 70,000 would be dead before the end of the year.

Now, at last, Japan's emperor, Hirohito, overruled the military dictatorship that had long wielded the real power in Japan. At noon on August 15, 1945, he broadcast his first-ever radio message to his people, announcing his acceptance of the Allied surrender terms and citing as his reason the explosion of a "cruel new bomb." World War II was over, and the Atomic Age, in two terrible flashes of universal death, had been born.

1947

The Marshall Plan

World War II devastated Europe more thoroughly than had any previous calamity, natural or human made. In a commencement address delivered at Harvard University on June 5, 1947, Secretary of State George C. Marshall, army chief of staff during World War II, proposed a plan by which the United States would finance much of the rebuilding of Europe, giving aid to allies and former enemies alike.

The Marshall Plan was a bold humanitarian step—as Winston Churchill said of it, the "most unsordid political act in history"—and a means of countering the spread of communism. For Marshall and the other diplomats had learned the lessons of the Treaty of Versailles, which punished Germany after World War I, creating the desperate economic and social conditions in which disastrous dictatorship took root and flourished. By supplying economic assistance, the United States sought to foster the development of democracy in Europe.

1947

Branch Rickey and Jackie Robinson Cross the "Color Line"

Nineteenth- and twentieth-century American history is punctuated by a number of momentous laws—from the Emancipation Proclamation and the Thirteenth, Fourteenth, and Fifteenth Amendments to the Civil Rights Act of 1964 and the Voting Rights Act of 1965, among others—all intended to bring an end to racial inequality in the republic. Ultimately, however, it has been the people—individuals, one by one—who have created the most meaningful changes.

One of these changes came in 1947 when Branch Rickey, president and general manager of the Brooklyn Dodgers, boldly crossed the "color line" by hiring the great African-American athlete Jackie Robinson for his team. Robinson was the first black player in major league baseball, and America's "national pastime" was now integrated.

Long excluded from the white professional leagues, African Americans formed their own teams, which, during the 1920s, were loosely organized as the Negro League. It soon became obvious to anyone who watched a Negro League game that segregation was depriving white baseball of some great talent, but it wasn't until the post–World War II era, a time of social ferment, that Branch Rickey, influenced by advanced social thought on race and looking for the best players he could find, felt emboldened to recruit Robinson.

Robinson was unusual for a black man and for a baseball player of the period. He had gone to college and had been a star player on the UCLA team. He was serious about being an athlete, but he was also serious about being a black man in America. In the army, he faced a court-martial for having challenged the illegal segregation to which he was subjected on an army bus. In hiring Robinson, Rickey did not quite jump in with both feet. He relegated Robinson to a year on the farm team before moving him up to the Dodgers, and then Rickey extracted from Robinson a pledge to endure, silently and without protest, any abuse he might receive from fans. That abuse came in the form of jeers, insults, hate mail, and a series of death threats. Through it all, for two years, Robinson honored his pledge, even refusing comment to the press. During this time, under great stress, he played magnificently and soon became a household name. At last, in 1949, he began to speak out against racial discrimination, Jim Crow laws, and the slow pace with which professional baseball moved forward with integration. By this time, Rickey and most fans were more than willing to hear Robinson speak out.

Jackie Robinson retired from baseball in 1957. While it is true that the National Football League had been integrated the year before Robinson became a Dodger, it was the combination of Robinson's talent as a ball player, his personality, his decency, and his dignity that captured the imagination of the nation and heightened the social consciousness of many ordinary Americans, of all races and origins.

1948

The Berlin Airlift

Throughout World War II, the United States and Britain were allied with the Soviet Union against Nazi aggression. Immediately following the end of the war, this alliance between the democracies and the Soviets disintegrated, as occupied Germany was divided into sectors controlled by the United States, France, England, and the Soviet Union. By the end of March 1948, the Soviets had become wary of the strong alliances being formed among the Western democracies to combine the German sectors they controlled into a separate, independent, capitalist state: West Germany. In an effort to block the creation of this state, Soviet forces began detaining troop trains bound for West Berlin, the U.S.–French–British sector of the divided German capital, which lay deep within Soviet-controlled eastern Germany. Unintimidated by Soviet harassment, on June 7, 1948, the western nations publicly announced their intention to create West Germany. Slightly more than two weeks after this announcement, on June 24, Soviet forces blockaded West Berlin. The Soviets protested that West Berlin, a mere enclave within the Soviet sector of Germany, could not serve as the capital of West Germany.

United States president Harry S Truman declared his belief that to yield West Berlin to Soviet threats would mean ultimately relinquishing all of Germany to the Soviets. His administration was guided by a policy newly developed by the State Department. "Containment" it was called, and its object was to counter Soviet expansion wherever it occurred in the world. The blockade of Berlin was the first test of the new policy.

Truman ordered the U.S. Air Force, itself newly independent

from the U.S. Army, to organize a massive emergency airlift to keep West Berlin supplied with food and, equally important, fuel (mostly coal for heating and generating purposes) for as long as necessary. Truman did not want to start a war with the Soviets, but he was determined to defy and defeat the Soviet blockade. Responding to the president's orders, on June 25, 1948, U.S. Army general Lucius D. Clay telephoned Lieutenant General Curtis E. LeMay, commander of United States Air Forces–Europe (USAFE), and asked: "Curt, can you transport coal by air?" LeMay did not hesitate: "Sir, the Air Force can deliver anything."

On the very next day, June 26, LeMay called in all available transport aircraft, and on June 27 "Operation Vittles" began. Through September 30, 1949, the USAF made 189,963 flights over Soviet-held territory into West Berlin, and cooperating British forces made 87,606 flights. The Air Force flew in a total of 1,783,572.7 tons of food, coal, and other cargo; the Brits, an additional 541,936.9 tons. In addition, some 25,263 inbound and 37,486 outbound passengers were flown (British pilots flew in 34,815 and flew out 164,906). The pilots flew twenty-four hours of every day in all kinds of weather. Extremely hazardous, the Berlin Airlift was a logistical and political triumph for the West. Recognizing that the blockade had failed, the Soviets lifted it on May 12, 1949. The separate nations of East and West Germany were formally created later that month.

The United States and Great Britain had taken a key stand against Soviet aggression and had won the first battle in what would be more than four decades of "Cold War" between the "free world" and the Soviet-dominated communist bloc. In more immediate terms, the Berlin Airlift became the basis for NATO (North Atlantic Treaty Organization), the West's principal alliance against the Soviet Union and its satellite states.

1948

A Powerful New Medium Emerges

A practical television system had been developed by 1933, but the conservatism of radio broadcasters and the demands of World War II put the commercial development of the medium on hold. While it was true that, in 1944, regularly scheduled programs were broadcast a few hours out of the week to a handful of New York–area subscribers (mostly electrical engineers), television was caught in the chicken-or-egg dilemma. Television receivers were costly and very temperamental. Few people could afford to buy a set, and even fewer wanted to buy one when there was almost nothing to watch. The early programming that developed immediately after the war included one or two lame variety shows, a couple of quiz shows, and, soon, professional boxing. What TV desperately needed was compelling programming, but the radio-broadcast networks were in no hurry to invest the necessary money in a medium for which an audience barely existed. But, without programming, there would never be such an audience. A jump-start was needed, and it was administered by a most unlikely individual.

Mendel Berlinger, the son of immigrants, was born on July 12, 1908, in New York City and, after changing his name to Milton Berle, struggled to eke out a living as a dime-a-dozen stage comic in the waning days of vaudeville. He was the kind of low-rent talent early television producers could afford, and, in 1948, when NBC approached Berle to emcee a show called the "Texaco Star Theater," almost no major star would be caught dead on this gimmick called television.

From the moment Berle debuted on September 21, 1948,

something clicked. Berle was outlandish, silly, inventive, and yet ordinary—the classic Everyman figure (albeit often dressed in very homely drag, sporting enormous falsies, a dyed rag mop for hair, and a frumpy housedress). "Uncle Miltie," he called himself, but he was soon far more accurately dubbed "Mr. Television." His presence rapidly came to dominate the new medium. All over the nation, people dropped whatever they were doing every Tuesday evening at eight o'clock to watch the hour-long program.

At first as the "Texaco Star Theater" and then as the "Milton Berle Show," the program was broadcast from 1948 to 1956, was resurrected from 1958 to 1959, and again from 1966 to 1967. In its early days, viewers hurriedly assembled in the parlor of whatever neighbor happened to be doing well enough to be able to afford a TV set. The weekly presence of Berle motivated many of these people to buy sets of their own, and as more sets were purchased, broadcasters programmed more shows, which drove sales of more sets. The price of TV sets began to drift lower, pushing more people toward a purchase. By and by, many families bought more than one set, so that each family member could watch whatever interested him or her. On American roofs, TV antennas sprouted like some spidery forest, and by the mid-1950s, television was more influential than books, movies, and radio—combined.

> **The seven days** of a week consist of 168 hours, of which at least 40 are consumed by earning one's daily bread and another 56 are devoted to sleep. Of the 72 hours that remain, according to the ACNielsen company, the leading compiler of TV statistics, Americans currently dedicate an average of 28 hours to television viewing.

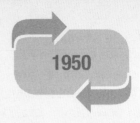

U.S. Responds to a Communist Invasion of South Korea

The world took little notice when Japan annexed Korea in 1910. But immediately after the Japanese attack on Pearl Harbor, December 7, 1941, American politicians and diplomats acknowledged, among many other things, that Japan had made Korea one of its first victims of imperialist aggression, and that was enough to connect the Korean cause with that of the United States and its western allies. After World War II came to an abrupt end with the atomic bombings of Hiroshima and Nagasaki, the United States proposed that the Soviets receive Japan's surrender in Korea north of the thirty-eighth parallel while the United States accept surrender south of this line. Thus, a partition of Korea was created, but only as a strictly temporary administrative expedient until Korea could be fully restored to peace and independence was introduced. The Soviets, however, seized on the "temporary" division to bring northern Korea into the communist fold. Red Army troops erected fortifications along the thirty-eighth parallel and refused to cooperate with the United States on the establishment of a Korean provisional government. America appealed to the United Nations, which, over Soviet objections, decided that a unified government should be established for Korea after a general election and that the UN would provide a security force to protect Korean independence.

Yet the country was hardly unified. The north was dominated by communists, the south by capitalists with democratic leanings. Egged on by the Soviets, the North Korean communists prevented the UN commission from holding elections north of the thirty-eighth parallel. South of the parallel, the elections proceeded on May 10, 1948, creating the Republic of Korea (ROK) under President Syngman Rhee. Twice the UN affirmed the ROK as the only lawful government of Korea. The Soviets responded by setting up a rival government in North Korea under the leadership of Kim Il Sung, a Soviet-trained Korean communist. The UN refused to recognize the northern government as legitimate, but Korea was now effectively divided into two countries, each driven by an ideology hostile to the other. The United States, determined to block the postwar spread of communism wherever it could, resolved to train and equip a security force for the South and to provide economic aid while also pressing through the UN for reunification.

The situation was extremely delicate. America wanted to arm South Korea for defense, yet it did not want to give the appearance that it was sponsoring South Korean aggression, which might lead to full-scale war involving the North Koreans as well as the Soviets. But, on June 25, 1950, units of the North Korean People's Army crossed the thirty-eighth parallel, brushed aside inferior South Korean forces, and marched on Seoul, the South Korean capital, about thirty-five miles below the thirty-eighth parallel. Smaller communist forces simultaneously moved down the center of the Korean peninsula and along the east coast. Seoul quickly fell, and President Truman was caught between the objectives of containing communist aggression yet avoiding a major war. He ordered the U.S. 7th Fleet to proceed toward Korea, but then sent most of it to Taiwan, to prevent the Chinese Communists on the mainland from attacking the Chinese Nationalists' Taiwanese stronghold. In the meantime, Truman gave General Douglas MacArthur the desperate assignment of using the modest U.S. air and land forces immediately available to strike at North Korean positions below the thirty-eighth parallel.

With the situation critical in Korea, there came the terrifying news that the Soviets had entered into a treaty of alliance with Communist China. However, the USSR also announced that it would boycott all UN organizations and committees on which Nationalist—noncommunist—China participated. The Soviet boycott meant that it was not present to veto the UN Security Council resolution authorizing military action against North Korea. Backed, then, by UN sanctions, President Truman named MacArthur commander of U.S. and UN forces, and America and other nations girded for another war, just five years after World War II had ended.

The McCarthy "Witch Hunt"

As 1950 began, the colorless, thoroughly undistinguished, hard-drinking Republican senator from Wisconsin, Joseph R. McCarthy, found his popularity flagging. He needed to make a bold play on a vital issue, and at the February 9, 1950, meeting of the Women's Republican Club of Wheeling, West Virginia, he seized his chance. Addressing this audience, he suddenly held aloft a piece of paper on which—he said—was a list of 205 known communists currently employed in the United States Department of State.

The audience was electrified. The United States was caught in the grip of a Cold War against communism. From the Soviet Union, the anticapitalist, antidemocratic ideology spread in a red stain across eastern Europe, while, in Asia, all China went red, and communism pushed at the borders of such nations as Korea and Vietnam. Americans were thoroughly prepared to take McCarthy at his word. Indeed, no one even bothered to examine the list McCarthy exhibited to the women Republicans of Wheeling. Had anyone done so, they would have made the disquieting discovery that it was blank, a mere prop—though in the climate of the nation at the time, even such a discovery probably would not have prevented what happened next.

McCarthy's Wheeling speech was reported nationally, and the junior senator from Wisconsin suddenly became famous. Over the next four years, he spearheaded a legislative crusade to "root out" communists in government and in other positions of influence and power. Many Americans believed McCarthy was leading a great *crusade,* whereas others—a minority at first—called it what it ultimately was: a *witch hunt,* reckless and destructive, destructive of reputations, of careers, and even of lives.

McCarthy gained chairmanship of the powerful Senate Subcommittee on Governmental Operations and, from this post, launched investigations into the Voice of America broadcasting service and the U.S. Army Signal Corps. His method of operation was merely to point fingers, make accusations, and raise suspicions. The constitutional guarantees of due process of law, the rules of evidence, and the presumption that a person is innocent until *proven* guilty were discarded in what he deemed a war against internal subversion. In the prevailing climate of fear and disillusionment, however, a pointed finger was more than sufficient to ruin a reputation or destroy a career. McCarthy and his followers hauled before the committee suspects who, to exonerate themselves, were asked to "name names," to expose other individuals with communist affiliations. Those who refused, typically resorting to the Fifth Amendment guarantee against self-incrimination, were charged with contempt of Congress and, often, imprisoned.

McCarthy spawned a legion of followers, some earnest—at least at first—but most, like McCarthy himself, opportunistic seekers after power and influence. The most prominent of McCarthy's acolytes was an oily young attorney named Roy Cohn, who was the prime mover of perhaps the most sensational phase of the witch hunt, an inquisition into "communist influence" in the Hollywood film industry. Paraded before the Senate committee was a succession of movie executives, producers, directors, and stars, some of whom eagerly "named names," while others refused. Cohn rarely bothered to charge these "noncooperative witnesses" with contempt of Congress. He had a much more powerful weapon at hand. Those who did not name names or who simply stood accused were blacklisted. This was not an official procedure, let alone a legal one. It was simply a way of letting the studios and other powers that be know that to hire a certain actor or writer or director invited the wrath of the United States government and, more particularly, Joseph McCarthy. The blacklist proved highly effective. Studios dutifully refused to hire "tainted" individuals, and a host of careers were crippled or killed.

"Containing" Communism in Korea

The objectives of World War II had been clear-cut: Do or die, a commitment to total victory. But, in fighting the Korean War, an all-out effort could bring on World War III and the end of civilization. Of course, an overly cautious approach would produce nothing more than defeat. Not that the United States was even immediately capable of an all-out effort. Demobilization after World War II had been swift and deep, so that the once mighty U.S. military was now both undermanned and underequipped.

With objectives unclear and prospects dim, American ground forces began arriving in Korea just six days after the June 25 Communist invasion. The news was consistently bad. By July 13, the North Koreans had pushed South Korean and U.S. forces to Taejon, in south central South Korea. That city fell on July 20. As disheartening as the defeats were, General MacArthur understood that the rapid advance of the North Koreans had stretched their lines of communication and supply to the breaking point. While U.S. ground troops were badly outnumbered, the U.S. Air Force quickly mastered the air and began hitting communist supply lines. Bidding for time to bring in more forces, MacArthur ordered the U.S. 8th Army to hold a line north of Pusan, the 140-mile-long "Pusan perimeter," extending in an arc from the Korea Strait to the Sea of Japan. While this desperate defense was being fought, MacArthur decided on a high-stakes, high-risk move. He would land major forces at Inchon, an ideal point for launching a surprise assault against the tenuously supplied communist invaders, but also an inlet with highly variable tides, creating terrible hazards for landing craft. Moreover, assuming the landing craft successfully negotiated the treacherous Inchon channel, the troops, once ashore, would immediately have to scale a high seawall, then fight through an extensively built-up, thickly settled area. MacArthur rolled the dice, leaving nothing in reserve. Should the landing fail, there would be no reinforcements available to rescue the troops.

As it happened, everything went right on September 15, 1950. Planners had predicted the treacherous tides accurately, the ships steered safely through the perilous straits, and the troops encountered nothing but light resistance—for no one (except MacArthur) had thought a landing possible here. Within two weeks, Seoul had been retaken, and, soon afterward, the North Korean army had been pushed back beyond the thirty-eighth parallel.

Now it was necessary to decide whether or not to cross the thirty-eighth parallel and invade North Korea. The reasons for doing so were ample: Some 30,000 NKPA troops had escaped to the North, which harbored at least another 30,000, making for an effective military force of 60,000, which posed a continuing threat to the South. Furthermore, defeating North Korea on its own territory would greatly advance the cause of reunification. Yet there was also a single compelling reason not to invade: Both Communist China and the Soviet Union had declared their intention to defend against such an invasion. President Truman agonized, then decided to take the risk. On September 27, he ordered MacArthur to pursue the North Korean forces across the thirty-eighth parallel, but to steer well clear of the Yalu River (the Manchurian border) and the Tumen River (the Soviet border). The invasion was swift and highly successful, so that by October 24, 1950, UN forces were close to the Chinese border.

United States and Red China Face Off in Korea

By the fall of 1950, under the brilliant tactical command of Douglas MacArthur, U.S.-dominated United Nations forces had driven the North Korean invaders out of the South and, indeed, had pushed them close to the Yalu River, the border with China. When China threatened to intervene, President Truman conferred with MacArthur on Wake Island. The general declared his certainty that the Chinese threats were empty, but by November, it had become clear that Chinese troops were in the battle. MacArthur insisted that Chinese operations were strictly defensive and that, in fact, few Chinese troops had actually crossed into North Korea. Accordingly, he ordered the UN advance to continue, and, on November 24, U.S. forces reached the Yalu. The next night, massive numbers of Chinese troops attacked the U.S. 8th Army hard on its center and right. Two days later, even more powerful Chinese attacks overran units of X Corps on its left flank. By November 28, UN positions were caving in. On December 15, after suffering severe losses, UN forces had pulled back to the thirty-eighth parallel and were now establishing a defensive line across the breadth of the Korean peninsula.

MacArthur responded to the Chinese entry into the war by lobbying for authorization to expand the war into China. Seeing the specter of World War III, Truman and his advisors said no. In the meantime, a massive Chinese attack on New Year's Eve sent the 8th Army into retreat toward Seoul, which fell on January 4, 1951. Yet the Chinese did not pursue the 8th Army south of Seoul, and within weeks, all Chinese advances had halted. MacArthur continued to demand permission to attack China, but Truman and his advisors ordered 8th Army commander Matthew Ridgway to pound away at the stalled Chinese troops within South Korea, which he did in a methodical and excruciating offensive, dubbed the "meatgrinder" by frontline G.I.s, beginning on January 25, 1951. By the middle of March, Ridgway had regained Seoul, and by March 21, UN troops were back at the thirty-eighth parallel.

1951

Truman Fires MacArthur

After U.S.-dominated UN forces regained their positions at the thirty-eighth parallel dividing North and South Korea, the UN member nations agreed that securing South Korea below the thirty-eighth parallel was an acceptable outcome for the Korean War. But when General MacArthur was informed that President Truman would announce his willingness to commence negotiations with the Chinese and North Koreans on the basis of current positions, he made an unauthorized announcement of his own, declaring that, if the UN would expand the conflict to North Korea's coastal areas and interior strongholds, the Chinese would back down. Worse, on April 5, 1951, Representative Joseph W. Martin read into the *Congressional Record* a letter from MacArthur stating the necessity of opening up a second front against China itself, using Nationalist Chinese troops. MacArthur wrote that he could not stomach a war without victory.

For Truman, this was the last straw. In a showdown between the civilian commander in chief and a five-star general, Truman was determined that the president must prevail. In an act of great courage, on April 11, 1951, President Truman removed MacArthur, one of the most venerated and popular heroes of World War II, and replaced him as supreme commander of UN forces in Korea with General Matthew Ridgway. This occasioned from MacArthur a sentimental and stirring farewell speech to a joint session of Congress, in which the general quoted an "old barrack ballad": "Old soldiers never die, they just fade away." Many—mistakenly, it turned out—wrote off Harry Truman as a political dead man.

1953

An Ambiguous End to the Korean War

Truman relieved MacArthur of command in Korea because the general was insubordinate and because the president feared that his actions would expand a limited, if brutal, war into a thermonuclear World War III. Peace talks between the Chinese and North Koreans on one side and the UN, U.S., and South Koreans on the other side began at the end of June 1951 and dragged on, with frequent breakdowns and impasses, for the next two years. During this period, the war ground on, mostly along the thirty-eighth parallel. At last, in April 1953, it was agreed that the war would end with a cease-fire along that parallel.

The only individual who remained adamant in his dissatisfaction with this arrangement was Syngman Rhee, the president of South Korea. He would settle for nothing less than Korean unification under his leadership, and when the armistice was signed on July 27, 1953, it did not formally include South Korea. Still, the shooting war was over, and, since July 27, 1953, North and South Korea have existed in a kind of limbo, suspended between war and peace, a coexistence neither peaceful nor overtly hostile, but at all times threatening, as evidenced by North Korea's apparent reactivation of a nuclear weapons program in 2003.

It is not known how many Chinese and North Korean troops were killed in the Korean War, but guesses range from between 1.5 and 2 million, in addition to at least a million civilians. The UN command lost 88,000 killed, of whom 23,300 were American.

1953

The Rosenberg Case

Early in 1950, federal investigators arrested David Greenglass, who had served in the U.S. Army in World War II and had been stationed near the atomic laboratory at Los Alamos, New Mexico. By this time, British agents had already picked up Klaus Fuchs, a German-born British atomic scientist and communist sympathizer, who confessed to having transmitted to the Soviets not only atomic secrets but also secrets relating to the far more powerful hydrogen bomb, a device that uses nuclear fission to trigger a much more energetic nuclear fusion explosion. Fuchs implicated as his accomplice Harry Gold, an American chemist whom Greenglass had supplied with information pilfered from Los Alamos. Greenglass told investigators that his brother-in-law, a New York machine-shop owner named Julius Rosenberg, acted as a go-between in his exchanges with Gold. Based on this information, which was extracted, in part, on a promise not to ask for the death penalty against Greenglass, federal agents arrested Rosenberg and his wife, Ethel, on July 17, 1950.

There is no doubt that the Rosenbergs had a history of communist affiliation. They did not deny this, but they pleaded not guilty to the charges of having conspired to obtain national defense information for the Soviet Union. The subsequent trial riveted the attention of the nation, which became deeply divided over the question of the Rosenbergs' guilt or innocence. The proceedings were made more poignant by the fact that the couple had two young children, who defense lawyers liberally paraded before newsreel and press cameras. Today, historians continue to debate the degree of the couples' involvement in espionage. Although most scholars now believe that Julius Rosenberg at least dabbled in passing information, some also point to the fact that the major item he was accused of passing, Greenglass's sketches of a bomb component, were too crude and vague to be of any practical use. Others, however, point out that memoirs written by several Soviet leaders after the collapse of the USSR specifically mention the great value of atomic information that came via Julius Rosenberg.

What is clear is that the Rosenbergs' liberal intellectual leanings, their connection with socialism and communism, and, perhaps most of all, their being Jews hurt them at least as much as any evidence prosecutors presented against them. Disturbing even to those who believed the Rosenbergs were guilty was the self-serving nature of Greenglass's testimony against them. Although he was certainly more deeply involved than the Rosenbergs in passing atomic secrets, he was sentenced only to a fifteen-year prison term, of which he served ten. The Rosenbergs, in contrast, found guilty, were sentenced to death.

The Rosenberg trial, verdict, and sentence deeply divided America. Many regarded the proceedings as symptoms of an anti-Semitism that lay under the surface of democratic America. Others saw it as the product of the Cold War and McCarthyism. Still others thought the couple had reaped what they had sown. The Rosenberg lawyers unsuccessfully appealed the sentence to the Supreme Court, and, on June 19, 1953, Julius and Ethel Rosenberg were put to death in the electric chair.

The Army–McCarthy Hearings

The dangerous Cold War era did produce an army of spies, including insiders in the American military, government, and technology industries. It was bona fide American traitors who communicated U.S. atomic secrets to the Soviets, which enabled the USSR to develop an atomic bomb in 1949 and a hydrogen bomb in 1954. Yet the "witch hunts" of Senator Joseph McCarthy did not turn up such spies, and McCarthy made no serious, sustained effort to separate fact from fantasy in his accusations. He thrived on the creation of national hysteria and was, in fact, little interested in the nuts and bolts of actual espionage. Just how irrational McCarthyism was became apparent when the senator stepped up his investigation even *after* his own Republican party had captured the White House in 1952. He brought the proceedings to a crescendo in 1954, when he accused the entire United States Army of being not just infiltrated, but positively riddled with communists. This reckless accusation was enough to provoke President Dwight D. Eisenhower, a career army officer and former supreme commander of all Allied military forces in Europe during World War II, to encourage Congress to form a new committee, one focused on investigating McCarthy himself.

The committee looked into the senator's illegal and self-serving attempts to coerce army brass into granting preferential treatment for a former McCarthy aide, Private G. David Schine. The "Army–McCarthy Hearings" were conducted from April to June 1954, and, perhaps most important of all, were broadcast on the still-infant medium of television. On camera, before the nation, Joseph McCarthy was exposed for the heedless demagogue he

On June 9, 1954, the Army–McCarthy hearings reached a dramatic high point in an exchange between McCarthy and Joseph N. Welch, special counsel for the U.S. Army. In an effort to interrupt Welch's persistent cross-examination of his chief counsel, Roy M. Cohn, McCarthy suddenly injected into the hearings a charge that one of Mr. Welch's Boston law firm associates, Frederick G. Fisher, Jr., had been a member of the National Lawyers Guild, "long after it had been exposed as the legal arm of the Communist Party."

MR. WELCH: . . . Until this moment, Senator, I think I never really gauged your cruelty or your recklessness. Fred Fisher is a young man who went to the Harvard Law School and came into my firm and is starting what looks to be a brilliant career with us. When I decided to work for this committee, I asked Jim St. Clair, who sits on my right, to be my first assistant. I said to Jim: "Pick somebody in the firm to work under you that you would like." He chose Fred Fisher and they came down on an afternoon plane. . . . I . . . said to these two young men: "Boys, I don't know anything about you except I've always liked you, but if there's anything funny in the life of either one of you that would hurt anybody in this case, you speak up quick." And Fred Fisher said: "Mr. Welch, when I was in the law school and for a period of months after I belonged to the Lawyer's Guild," as you have suggested, Senator. . . . And I said, "Fred, I just don't think I'm going to ask you to work on the case. If I do, one of these days that will come out and go over national television and it will hurt like the dickens." So, Senator, I asked him to go back to Boston. Little did I dream you could be so reckless and so cruel as to do an injury to that lad. . . . If it were in my power to forgive you for your reckless cruelty, I would do so. I like to think I'm a gentle man, but your forgiveness will have to come from someone other than me. . . . Senator, may we not drop this? We know he belonged to the Lawyer's Guild. . . . Let us not assassinate this lad further, Senator. You've done enough. Have you no sense of decency, sir? At long last, have you left no sense of decency?

was. The hearings ended the witch hunt and McCarthy's career. Censured by action of the Senate later in 1954, he lost all power and influence. A chronically heavy drinker, he retreated further into the bottle and died, in 1957, at the age of forty-nine. Few mourned his passing. Perhaps worse still, few noted it.

The "Domino Theory"

World War II interrupted France's colonial hold on Vietnam, at the time called French Indochina. After the surrender of Japan, the United States, seeking to block the spread of communism in Asia—it would soon engulf China and divide Korea—supported French attempts to reassert control of Vietnam and to fight against guerrillas led by Ho Chi Minh, a Soviet-trained nationalist. On August 3, 1950, the first contingent of U.S. military "advisors" arrived to aid the French, and by 1953, the United States was funding 80 percent of the cost of France's war effort. The French attempted to strike a decisive blow against Ho's forces on the strategically situated plain of Dien Bien Phu, near Laos. But, in a stunning development, Dien Bien Phu fell to the forces of Ho Chi Minh on May 7, 1954. The military disaster completely demoralized French forces, which suffered a string of defeats that prompted France to seek peace. At a July 1954 conference, the French and Ho's provisional government, the Viet Minh, agreed for the time being to divide Vietnam along the seventeenth parallel. A cease-fire was declared.

While the French were still struggling in the Dien Bien Phu campaign, on April 7, 1954, U.S. president Dwight D. Eisenhower explained to reporters why he thought it important to aid France, a foreign power, to fight against communism in another foreign country, Vietnam. "You have a row of dominoes set up," he explained, "you knock over the first one, and what will happen to the last one is the certainty it will go over very quickly." It was an offhanded figure of speech, but the press took it up and dubbed it the "domino theory." It would become the leading rationale for escalating America's involvement in the Vietnam War.

1954

Brown Versus the Board of Education

During the Depression and World War II, increasing numbers of African Americans left the rural South to settle in cities, both in the North and South, in search of employment. More and more, the issue of racial integration came to the fore in American society. In the North, no laws enforced segregation, but all-black and all-white neighborhoods were nevertheless the norm in northern cities. In the South, segregation was typically enforced by law. In the early 1950s, while racial segregation in public schools was common in the North, it was universal in the South and protected by law. Authorities defended its legality by referring to the "separate but equal" doctrine, which had been annunciated in a late-nineteenth-century Supreme Court decision in the case of *Plessy v. Ferguson.* The legal theory was this: Maintaining separate schools for blacks and whites was constitutional, provided that, in any given district, the schools were equal in quality and resources offered. For years, bolstered by *Plessy v. Ferguson,* the "separate but equal" doctrine endured, southern schools remained segregated, and segregation in this arena was used to justify segregation in other public accommodations, such as restaurants, hotels, bus and train stations and waiting rooms, public restrooms, and so on.

At the start of the 1950s, African-American legal activists mounted a determined challenge against *Plessy v. Ferguson* and the segregation doctrine it upheld. In Topeka, Kansas, an African-American third-grader named Linda Brown had to walk a full mile—and through a hazardous railroad switchyard—to get to her segregated, all-black elementary school. A white elementary school was a safe seven-block walk from her house. When the principal of the white school refused to enroll Brown, the girl's father, Oliver Brown, approached the Topeka branch of the NAACP (National Association for the Advancement of Colored People). Other African-American parents indicated their willingness to join Brown in forcing the integration of the Topeka schools. In June 1951, the NAACP filed for an injunction to accomplish exactly this. The U.S. District Court for the District of Kansas listened to the argument of the NAACP, which was, in essence, that segregated schools sent the message to black children that they were inferior to whites; therefore, the schools were inherently unequal, regardless of whatever physical facilities or teaching faculty they might offer. In defense of its segregation policy, the Topeka Board of Education argued that because segregation in Topeka and elsewhere in the United States was pervasive—the norm—segregated schools realistically prepared black children for the segregation they would experience as adults. Therefore, the argument went, a segregated education was actually a valuable developmental service!

The district court concurred with the NAACP position that segregation "has a detrimental effect upon the colored children," instilling in them a "sense of inferiority" that negatively "affects the motivation of a child to learn"; however, the court decided that the firmly established legal precedent of *Plessy* v. *Ferguson* allowed separate but equal school systems for blacks and whites. Without a ruling from the Supreme Court overturning *Plessy*, the district court believed its hands were tied and, in the court's language, it was "compelled" to rule in favor of the Board of Education. Although ostensibly a legal defeat, the district court decision conspicuously threw open the door to a Supreme Court appeal, which Brown and the NAACP made on October 1, 1951. Their case was combined with other cases that challenged school segregation in South Carolina, Virginia, and Delaware. On May 17, 1954, the high court handed down a decision declaring segregated public schools unconstitutional because they were inherently unequal as a result of intangible social factors. Two years later, the court issued detailed guidelines to be used in a nationwide program of desegregation of America's schools.

Brown v. *Board of Education* not only achieved integration of public schools, it also encouraged African Americans—and socially conscious white Americans—to challenge all laws and traditions that segregated society and that violated civil rights. Indeed, if we wish to fix the birth date of the modern civil rights movement, no date is more significant than May 17, 1954—with the possible exception of December 1, 1955.

Montgomery Bus Boycott

On December 1, 1955, in Montgomery, Alabama, an African-American department-store tailor did what any other person would do at the end of a long workday. She settled into a bus seat, intending to ride home. It was an ordinary act by an ordinary woman—but it was performed in what seems today the extraordinary context of legally sanctioned racial segregation. When the bus driver, James F. Blake, ordered Mrs. Rosa Parks to give up her seat in the white-only front of the segregated city bus and relinquish it to a white man who had boarded, she refused. Blake called the police, who arrested Parks for violating the city's segregation ordinance.

Leaders of Montgomery's black community seized the incident as an opportunity for launching a high-profile protest against the city's segregation laws. During the weekend of December 3–4, Rev. Ralph Abernathy and Rev. Martin Luther King, Jr., prominent Montgomery pastors, met with Jo Ann Robinson, head of the Women's Political Council, and E. D. Nixon, of the local chapter of the National Association for the Advancement of Colored People (NAACP), to plan a nonviolent response to Mrs. Parks's arrest: a boycott against the Montgomery city bus lines. Forty thousand handbills were quickly printed and circulated throughout Montgomery's black neighborhoods, and, on December 4, African-American ministers included the boycott in their Sunday sermons.

The message and the movement electrified the black community. On Monday, December 5, as revealed by bus company receipts, some 90 percent of the blacks who routinely rode the buses found other means of transportation. That evening, black leaders created the MIA (Montgomery Improvement Association), with Martin Luther King, Jr., as president. The MIA directed the boycott day after day, week after week, month after month, well into 1956. Police frequently harassed black carpoolers. Bombs were set off at the houses of both King and Nixon, and King was arrested on an inconsequential traffic offense. Unintimidated, the leaders continued to lead, and the community continued the boycott, even as the nation began to pay attention and watch. Using an Alabama statute against boycotts, conspiracy charges were brought against King as well as the other leaders of the MIA. This only served to accelerate the U.S. Supreme Court decision, in November of 1956, declaring that segregation on public buses was unconstitutional.

The boycott, sparked by the refusal of a forty-two-year-old seamstress to move to the back of the bus, changed American law and launched the modern civil rights movement, propelling Martin Luther King, Jr., to its forefront. The boycott also set the pattern of nonviolence, which would dominate the civil rights movement under King, giving to that movement the full measure of moral force.

1961

Bay of Pigs

In 1959, Fidel Castro, a charismatic leftist guerrilla leader, successfully led a revolution in Cuba, overthrowing the government of Fulgencio Batista, corrupt but friendly to the United States. Over the succeeding two years, Castro, the new dictator, allied his nation more and more closely to the Soviet Union. Communism was coming perilously close to American shores, so, toward the end of the administration of Dwight David Eisenhower, the U.S. Central Intelligence Agency (CIA) devised a plan to overthrow Castro. Incoming president John F. Kennedy bought into the scheme, which was to assemble a force of anti-Castro Cuban exiles now living in the United States and land them in Cuba, at a place called the Bay of Pigs, from which they would invade the island. The CIA was confident that this would be sufficient to spark a great popular uprising against Castro.

As it turned out, the CIA couldn't have been more wrong. It was a disaster from the moment the operation stepped off on April 17, 1961. Not only did the Cuban people fail to rally to the invaders, the United States failed to provide promised air support, and, within three days, the invasion had been crushed by Castro's small army and even smaller air force. This was a major disaster for the brand-new Kennedy administration, and it served only to heighten tension between Cuba and the United States. Convinced that another invasion attempt would come, Castro agreed to allow the Soviets to build nuclear missile bases on the island. A crisis of potentially doomsday proportions was in the making.

Into the Vietnam Quagmire

L ike Korea before it, Vietnam was divided into a communist-controlled north and noncommunist south after the defeat of French colonial forces in 1954. A key condition of the armistice agreement between France and the Viet Minh nationalists was that the divided Vietnam would hold popular elections with the object of reunifying under whatever regime the people chose. Because South Vietnam's president, Ngo Dinh Diem, was well aware that the charismatic Ho Chi Minh would win any popular election, he abrogated the peace agreement and refused to hold the promised elections. More concerned to stem the communist tide than to uphold the principles of democracy, the United States backed Diem's refusal, and John F. Kennedy, who succeeded Dwight Eisenhower in 1961, progressively increased the number of military "advisors" sent to Vietnam.

Throughout the Kennedy years, American policy makers did their best to overlook the profound unpopularity and corruption of the Diem regime. Not only did Diem's cronies control top government positions, but Diem, a Catholic, was unstinting in his support of the nation's Catholic minority at the expense of its Buddhist majority. The world was shocked by newsreel images of protest demonstrations in which Buddhist monks soaked themselves in gasoline and set themselves ablaze in the streets of Saigon. Deciding at long last that the Diem regime was a liability, President Kennedy secretly allowed the CIA to arrange the assassination of Diem in a U.S.-backed military coup of November 1, 1963. This led only to more coups, as South Vietnam became increasingly unstable, a situation that encouraged the communists, now drawing aid from the Soviets and Chinese, to escalate the war.

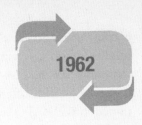

1962

Cuban Missile Crisis

In October 1962, a United States U-2 spy plane, on one of the surveillance flyovers that had become routine over Cuba, photographed Soviet nuclear missile bases under construction. President Kennedy presented the photographic evidence to the American people in a televised broadcast on October 22, and he demanded of Soviet premier Nikita Khrushchev the immediate withdrawal of the missiles. Still reeling from the Bay of Pigs debacle, the Kennedy administration was faced with a crisis of unprecedented gravity. Do nothing, and the Soviet Union would have nuclear missiles in America's backyard, capable of hitting virtually any United States city. Act rashly, and a confrontation could be triggered in that other Cold War flashpoint, Berlin, which might well engulf Europe in a thermonuclear World War III. Delay or act ineffectively, and a nuclear strike could be launched directly at the United States.

Before addressing the nation and after brainstorming with the finest minds in his administration, Kennedy decided on his course of action: to order a naval "quarantine" of Cuba—he avoided the word "blockade," since a blockade is technically an act of war—on October 24. All incoming ships were to be stopped, boarded, and inspected. Any carrying nondefensive military hardware would be turned back. With each day that the quarantine was in place, an armed confrontation between American and Soviet vessels seemed more likely. Thermonuclear Armageddon was an intensely real possibility.

Yet the quarantine never developed into a shooting war, and the standoff in the waters surrounding Cuba was ended on October 28, when Soviet premier Nikita Khrushchev, approached by Kennedy indirectly via quasi-diplomatic back channels, proposed to remove the missiles under United Nations supervision. Quietly, in exchange, JFK offered to remove obsolescent U.S. missiles stationed in the NATO nation of Turkey and, even more important, made a pledge never to attempt an invasion of Cuba.

On October 29, President Kennedy suspended the quarantine, and by November 2 the missile bases were being dismantled. The showdown was a triumph for American diplomacy, but the Cuban missile crisis also demonstrated just how dangerous the thermonuclear world had become.

1963

Assassination of John Kennedy

Partisans and historians will long continue to argue the merits of the Kennedy presidency. There was plenty that went wrong with it. There were the tragically bungled Bay of Pigs invasion and the early escalation of American involvement in Vietnam. While JFK was popular with youth and intellectuals, he was never able to put together much support in Congress, especially where his efforts to improve civil rights and to provide a program of medical care for the elderly were concerned. Yet there was an undeniable magic about the Kennedy years. He introduced important, forward-looking programs, such as the Peace Corps, an American space program targeting the moon, and the Alliance for Progress with Latin American countries, and, of course, there was his masterful handling of the Cuban Missile Crisis. Perhaps most magical of all was the general tone of the Kennedy White House, as a gathering place for the very best in American art and culture and thought, presided over not only by JFK, but also by his incomparable wife, the elegant Jacqueline Bouvier.

However one evaluates the Kennedy years, his assassination, during a visit to Dallas, Texas, on November 22, 1963, seemed to rob America, at gunpoint, of youth, of idealism, of hope, and it underscored the essential fragility that underlay the vigor of democracy. In more immediate terms, Kennedy's death came as a kind of martyrdom. His successor, Lyndon B. Johnson, used the Kennedy aura to usher through Congress all of the great social legislation Kennedy had been unable to pass—and then some. Civil Rights and Medicare became the cornerstones of LBJ's "Great Society" program of social reforms. More enduringly, the Kennedy legend—the melancholy romance of a youthful, courageous, vigorous man cut down in his prime—made it impossible for many to believe that he could have been shot by a lone malcontent, the misfit Lee Harvey Oswald, whose own story we never heard, because he himself was gunned down, in the garage of Dallas police headquarters, by a local mob-connected nightclub owner, Jack Ruby.

Hoping to lay to rest a welter of conspiracy theories, President Johnson named a commission, headed by Chief Justice Earl Warren, to investigate the assassination. After a ten-month investigation, the Warren Commission concluded that Oswald was, in fact, the lone assassin. But the conspiracy theories continued to survive and to proliferate, and in 1976, no less a body than the United States Congress issued startling new revelations concerning the activities of the CIA and the FBI, and a special committee concluded that, the Warren Commission notwithstanding, an assassination conspiracy was likely. The speculation has never stopped.

1964

The Civil Rights Act of 1964

The years following World War II saw a slow but inevitable march toward making racial equality the law of the land in the United States. In 1947, Harry S. Truman ordered the integration of the U.S. armed services, a step that gave many whites and blacks their first opportunity to live and work together. In 1954, the U.S. Supreme Court ruled that segregated public schools were unconstitutional, and in 1956 that same court declared segregated public transport unconstitutional as well. For many, the culminating event of the first great phase of the modern civil rights movement was the August 1963 March on Washington, when more than 200,000 converged on the capital—peacefully—to demand racial equality. In this atmosphere, President John F. Kennedy hoped to gain passage of a civil rights act, which would give desegregation the full force of federal law. Discrimination on the basis of race would be banned in employment, in unions, and in all enterprises that drew federal funding of any kind. All public places—hotels, theaters, restaurants, and the like—would be, by law, integrated. Yet Kennedy was never able to get the legislation past a strong southern congressional bloc, and it fell to his successor, Lyndon Johnson, to invoke the memory of the "martyred" JFK, the idealist and fighter for social justice, cut down in his prime, to gain passage of the momentous Civil Rights Act of 1964.

Although it gave equality the full measure of federal law, the act did not immediately or miraculously provide true social equality to the nation's African Americans and other minorities. Many state and local governments defied the federal government and continued to act from motives of racism and racial segregation.

Even some federal institutions, most notoriously the FBI, retained racist policies; FBI director J. Edgar Hoover, who looked upon Martin Luther King, Jr., as a menace to the stability of the nation, covertly ordered illegal wiretaps and other surveillance aimed at embarrassing and discrediting him. Violence within the black community became especially heated during the 1960s, a period in which America's urban ghettoes routinely flamed into riot during a series of "long, hot summers." Violence against black activists descended to its most tragic depths with the assassinations of Malcolm X in 1965 and Martin Luther King, Jr., in 1968.

The changes wrought by the Civil Rights Act of 1964 were profound and have left a lasting mark on American culture and society. Certainly, the most blatant and overt forms of racial discrimination have greatly diminished. The social acceptance of expressed bigotry is no longer the norm. And all officially sanctioned segregation of public establishments, schools, and facilities has come to an end. Black politicians occupy many top offices throughout the United States. Yet no one looking at American society today can honestly say that the mass of black Americans and the mass of white Americans enjoy equally all of the benefits our society offers. If *de jure* (law-based) segregation has disappeared, *de facto* (actual) segregation remains strong in many places, and true racial harmony is still enough of a rarity to merit feature stories on TV news programs or in the magazine section of the Sunday paper. The struggle continues.

1964

The Gulf of Tonkin Resolution

The American destroyer *Maddox,* conducting electronic surveillance in international waters, was attacked by North Vietnamese torpedo boats on August 2, 1964. Undamaged, it was joined by a second destroyer, the *C. Turner Joy.* On August 4, it was reported that both ships had been attacked. Evidence of the second attack was thin (later, it was discovered that the second attack had not even occurred), but President Lyndon B. Johnson ordered retaliatory air strikes, and he asked Congress for support. That support came, on August 7, when the Senate passed the so-called Gulf of Tonkin Resolution, which gave the president virtually unlimited authority to expand United States involvement in what was a long-standing war in a part of the world few Americans knew, much less cared, about. The Vietnam War would devastate Vietnam, and it would nearly tear apart the United States.

The Gulf of Tonkin Resolution:

Joint Resolution of Congress H.J. RES 1145 August 7, 1964
Resolved by the Senate and House of Representatives of the United States of America in Congress assembled,

That the Congress approves and supports the determination of the President, as Commander in Chief, to take all necessary measures to repel any armed attack against the forces of the United States and to prevent further aggression. . . .

1965

Vietnam War—LBJ Commits the Nation to Combat

In February 1965, Lyndon Johnson sent his personal advisor, Mc-George Bundy, on a fact-finding mission to Saigon in an effort to decide whether or not to commit more troops to defend an unpopular and corrupt South Vietnamese regime. At this very time, on February 7, the Viet Cong—the popular military front of the communist North—attacked U.S. advisory forces and the headquarters of the U.S. Army 52d Aviation Battalion near Pleiku, killing 9 Americans and wounding 108. U.S. forces retaliated against North Vietnam, which made a counterstrike on February 10 against a barracks at Qui Nhon. On the next day, U.S. forces struck back with a long program of air strikes deep into the North, a campaign dubbed Rolling Thunder. The operation formally began on March 2, 1965, and marked the first great U.S. escalation in Vietnam, as 50,000 new ground troops were sent into the country, ostensibly to "protect" U.S. air bases.

LBJ had sent Bundy to find facts, but the facts found the president. Pleiku and its aftermath prompted escalation of the war and the commitment of U.S. forces for the long haul.

The Tet Offensive and the Antiwar Movement

President Johnson's aim in prosecuting the Vietnam War was to fight a war of gradual escalation, wearing down the North Vietnamese without provoking overt intervention from China or the Soviets. It was, in fact, a no-win strategy, for the North Vietnamese were willing to make tremendous sacrifices and were not about to be worn down. As the North's apparently inexhaustible will to fight became increasingly apparent, LBJ embraced a strategy of "Vietnamization," giving the South Vietnamese ARVN (Army of the Republic of Vietnam) the tools and training to take over more and more of the fighting, so that American forces could ultimately disengage. Despite this, the numbers of Americans "in country" continued to rise. In 1965, 75,000 Americans were fighting in Vietnam. In 1966, the number jumped to 375,000, and, by 1968, more than half a million American troops were at war there.

By 1968, the war had become intensely unpopular with a growing majority of Americans, and a full-blown antiwar movement developed, first on college campuses (after all, it was the nation's college-age men who were subject to the draft), and then throughout all sectors of American activity. Increasingly, Americans became divided into pro-war supporters of the administration and antiwar detractors, who had lost trust and faith in the administration. Demonstrations and "confrontations," sometimes escalating into riots, became commonplace.

On January 30, 1968, the communists unleashed a series of massive offensives, first along the border with South Vietnam, attacking the U.S. base at Khe Sanh, and then against South Vietnamese provincial capitals and principal cities. The offensives coincided with Tet, a Vietnamese lunar holiday, and while they were costly to U.S. and ARVN forces, they were far more costly to the Viet Cong. Yet, psychologically, it was an unalloyed victory for the communists. It was the Tet Offensive that finally persuaded many Americans, including politicians and policy makers, that the Vietnam War was unwinnable.

On March 31, President Johnson made two surprise television announcements. He declared that he would restrict bombing above the twentieth parallel, a gesture that opened the door to a negotiated settlement of the war, and he announced that he would not seek another term as president. He recognized that his advocacy of the war was tearing the nation apart.

1968

Assassination of Martin Luther King, Jr.

The year 1968 saw more internal turmoil in the United States than at any other time since the Civil War. The Tet Offensive, a massive communist military campaign throughout South Vietnam, began the year and, in the United States, triggered new waves of antiwar protests. These tended to merge with growing racial unrest in the country. For one thing, a disproportionate number of African-American draftees served in Vietnam, and, for another thing, it was quite justifiably believed that the economic demands of the war had drained the funding for LBJ's vaunted "Great Society" social programs. On February 29, the large, black ghetto neighborhood of Watts in Los Angeles erupted into riot, the most destructive since the Draft Riots of the Civil War era.

Against this background of national upheaval, Martin Luther King, Jr.—the most prominent of the nation's civil rights leaders, winner of the Nobel Peace Prize, the champion and master of nonviolent protest—continued to do what he did best: work at the grassroots of the movement for social justice. He went to Memphis, Tennessee, not to launch some great public initiative or address some august group of philosophers and political leaders, but to talk to the city's striking sanitation workers and to encourage them in their cause. In a show of solidarity with the African-American community of Memphis, King chose accommodations at the black-owned Lorraine Motel. At 6:01 on the evening of April 4, Dr. King prepared to get dinner. He stepped out of his room and onto a balcony. As he leaned over the railing to speak to his driver, a single shot rang out from a high-powered rifle. It found its mark, and Martin Luther King, Jr., lay dying of a wound to the head. He was thirty-nine years old.

Arrested for the assassination was a small-time thief named James Earl Ray, who allegedly shot King from the bathroom of a flophouse across from the Lorraine Motel. No witness saw Ray shoot, but a bag found in front of a store near the flophouse contained a rifle, which bore Ray's fingerprints. Although he subsequently confessed to the crime, was convicted (without public trial), and was sentenced to life imprisonment, Ray retracted his confession. Many, including the family of Dr. King, continue to doubt that Ray was the murderer and suspect that King had been the target of a broader conspiracy, perhaps even involving the federal government. (In 1998, Ray died, in prison, of cancer, still professing his innocence.)

Grief and outrage came in the immediate aftermath of the assassination, and many inner cities erupted into riot. Even after these outbreaks had been quelled, there remained the depressing, anxious sense that all hope for racial equality and harmony in the nation had been extinguished. However, it soon became apparent that Dr. King's example had not been in vain. The struggle for Civil Rights continued, and, beginning in 1986, King's birthday was commemorated as a national holiday.

1968

Assassination of Robert Kennedy

The Tet Offensive in Vietnam at the beginning of 1968 raised the antiwar movement in America to a new pitch. Senator Eugene McCarthy, most eloquent and popular of Congressional "doves" (as legislators who opposed the war were called), very nearly defeated incumbent Lyndon B. Johnson in the crucial New Hampshire Democratic primary, a fact that encouraged the charismatic brother of the slain JFK, Robert Kennedy, to declare, on March 16, his candidacy for the Democratic nomination. Less than two weeks later, on March 31, President Johnson announced in a televised address to the nation that he would not run for re-election. Change was in the air, some violent, some hopeful, all unsettling.

Appointed attorney general in the administration of his brother, Robert F. Kennedy had continued to serve in that post briefly under Johnson, but soon left the LBJ administration and embraced the antiwar movement. RFK proved an effective vote-getter by winning primaries in Indiana and Nebraska. After this, Lyndon Johnson withdrew, and Kennedy went on to the all-important California primary. A win here would show that an antiwar candidate had a strong chance of becoming president and, indeed, ending the war in Vietnam. For if the election pitted a "dove" against a "hawk," it would be nothing less than a national referendum on the war.

Just before midnight on June 5, 1968, the California results were in. Kennedy had won. Shortly after midnight, on June 6, Kennedy made an informal speech to campaign workers, then, at a quarter past twelve, he left the ballroom of the Ambassador Hotel in Los Angeles to give a press conference. By prearrangement, his route cut through a food service pantry. As he passed through, a Palestinian immigrant, Sirhan Sirhan, stepped forward and fired a .22 revolver. In the close quarters of the passageway, Sirhan was quickly subdued, but Kennedy and five others lay wounded. Kennedy, shot in the head, died shortly afterward. Arrested at the scene, Sirhan was charged and convicted of first-degree murder. He continues to serve a life sentence.

As with the assassination of Martin Luther King, Jr., and, for that matter, the 1963 assassination of John F. Kennedy, many believed and many continue to believe that Robert Kennedy was not the victim of a lone, twisted gunman, but the target of a conspiracy. We may never learn the full truth, or, perhaps, we already know all there is to know. What cannot be known is what would have happened had Robert Kennedy lived to oppose Richard M. Nixon in the 1968 race. Would he have won? And would the Vietnam War have ended in 1969, perhaps, or very soon afterward? We cannot know the answers to these questions. What is certain is that the assassination of Robert Kennedy robbed mainstream, middle-class America of a chance in 1968 to embrace the movement against an unwinnable war.

1968

The Democratic National Convention

By August 26–29, 1968, when the Democratic Party held its national convention in Chicago, Americans had lived through the aftershock of the Tet Offensive, which turned increasing numbers against the war in Vietnam; they had also lived through the Watts Riots in Los Angeles and the assassinations of Martin Luther King, Jr., and Robert F. Kennedy. The nation became more profoundly divided politically and racially. Many liberals and young people, including young voters, turned their backs on "the system," and the 1968 Democratic National Convention nominated Hubert H. Humphrey, who was not opposed to the Vietnam War and who, in fact, offered no real alternative to Republican candidate Richard M. Nixon.

The convention had become the focal point of a massive youth, leftist, and antiwar protest that turned violent and led to what witnesses described as a "police riot" as Chicago officers unleashed their rage indiscriminately against protesters and residents of African-American neighborhoods south and west of Grant Park, the lakefront site of the protesters' makeshift tent camps.

It was not Chicago police officers who were tried in the aftermath of the convention and riot, but, instead, the so-called "Chicago Seven"—seven of the most visible leaders of the antiwar movement. During a five-month proceeding, David Dellinger (National Mobilization Against the War), Tom Hayden and Rennie Davis (Students for a Democratic Society, SDS), Abbie Hoffman and Jerry Rubin (Youth International Party, YIPPIEs), John Froines and Lee Weiner (local Chicago protest leaders), and Bobby Seale (Black Panther Party) were tried on charges of conspiracy to incite rioting. Five were found guilty in a trial presided over by the grotesquely biased Judge Julius Hoffman—who, at one point, ordered Seale bound and gagged—although their convictions were subsequently overturned on appeal.

The entire sequence of events—protest, police overreaction, the trial, the appeal—epitomized a decade of protest and suggested to many that the United States was on the verge of revolution if not dissolution. Some found this prospect enormously liberating. Others found it terrifying. Most were simply bewildered and demoralized.

1969

Americans Land on the Moon

The year 1968 had been harrowing and dispiriting, a year of assassination, riot, and escalation in war. There was little to suggest that 1969 would be much better. Then, on July 20, 1969, at 4:17 P.M. (EDT), the nation—and much of the world— suddenly united in a moment of supreme achievement for the human race: Two men, Neil Armstrong and Buzz Aldrin, visitors from the planet Earth, walked on the surface of the moon.

As many saw it, the lunar landing was the culmination of the "space race" that had begun on October 4, 1957, when the Soviet Union successfully launched and orbited a thirty-eight-pound metal sphere containing nothing more than a simple radio transmitter. *Sputnik I* was the first human-made object to orbit the Earth, and it sent America into a frenzied game of catch-up with the communist dictatorship. It wasn't until January 1958 that America successfully orbited *Explorer I,* but, on April 12, 1961, the Soviets sprinted far into the lead by orbiting the first man in space, cosmonaut Yuri Gagarin. About three weeks later, on May 5, 1961, U.S. Navy commander Alan B. Shepard was sent on a fifteen-minute *suborbital* flight, a great day for Americans, but a distant second to the Russians' orbital achievement. Nevertheless, just twenty days later, with the American manned space program very much in its infancy, President John F. Kennedy addressed Congress: "I believe this nation should commit itself to achieving the goal, before the decade is out, of landing a man on the moon and returning him safely to earth. No single space project in this period will be more impressive to mankind, or more important for the long-range exploration of space, and none will be so difficult or expensive to accomplish."

Throughout the 1960s, the Soviets and the Americans continued to send men (and, in the case of the Soviets, a woman as well) into space. The United States did so with the goal of creating the technology and techniques for the eventual lunar mission: the *Apollo* program, nothing less than the biggest, most daring scientific and technological venture in the history of humankind. A giant *Saturn V* multistage booster would start the three-man *Apollo* spacecraft on a two-and-a-half-day voyage to the moon. The craft would assume lunar orbit, then the Lunar Excursion Module, with two men aboard, would separate from the orbiting Command Module and land on the moon. After a period of exploration on the lunar surface, the astronauts would climb back into the Lunar Excursion Module, lift off, and dock with the orbiting Command Module, which would blast out of lunar orbit and carry the three astronauts back to Earth.

The technological choreography involved in so complex a set of procedures was daunting, and the entire program got off to a tragic beginning when a fire broke out inside the *Apollo 1* spacecraft during a routine launchpad test on January 27, 1967. Astronauts Virgil I. "Gus" Grissom, Edward H. White, and Roger B. Chaffee were killed, and there was serious talk of scrapping or, at least, greatly delaying the entire lunar program. Yet NASA (the National Aeronautics and Space Administration) was able to persuade a wary Congress to proceed, and, after a series of Earth- and moon-orbital flights, *Apollo 11* was launched on July 16, 1969, manned by Neil A. Armstrong, Edwin E. "Buzz" Aldrin, Jr., and Michael Collins. As planned, Armstrong and Aldrin left the Command Module and entered the Lunar Excursion Module while the spacecraft was in lunar orbit. The Lunar Excursion Module, called *Eagle,* separated from the Command Module and took the pair to the surface. Touchdown came at 4:17 Eastern Daylight Time (8:17 P.M. Greenwich Mean Time) on July 20.

Leaping off the module's ladder into the unreality of one-sixth

Earth gravity, Armstrong declared: "That's one small step for [a] man, one giant leap for mankind."

For the next twenty-one hours thirty-six minutes, Armstrong and Aldrin explored the moon, collecting lunar soil and "moon rocks" and setting up various scientific experiments. All of this was important, to be sure, but it was the fact itself—the realization of human imagination and national will in aiming at, flying toward, and landing on the moon—that reached far beyond science to speak eloquently of and to the human spirit. That landing and the televised images of two men, no longer earthbound, walking, leaping, and skipping across the face of an alien world brought our own nation and our own world together in a joyous passage of human triumph during a time marked so deeply by bitterness, doubt, and despair.

> "Here men from the planet Earth first set foot on the moon, July 1969 A.D. We came in peace for all mankind."
> —plaque left on the moon to mark the site of the first lunar landing

Nixon's Vietnam Policy

I n the wake of President Johnson's announcement that he would not seek reelection, cease-fire negotiations with the North Vietnamese began in May 1968, but broke down repeatedly. Republican Richard Milhous Nixon won election to the presidency in 1968 on a platform that promised a plan to end the war. However, he began his administration by expanding the war into neighboring Laos and Cambodia, pursuant to a grand strategy he had worked out with his foreign policy advisor (and, later, secretary of state), former Harvard political science professor Henry Kissinger. This called for improving relations with the Soviets (through trade and an arms-limitation agreement) in order to disengage Moscow from Hanoi, and for normalizing relations with China. Once the USSR and China had cut the North Vietnamese loose, Kissinger believed, the United States could negotiate what Nixon called "peace with honor" in Vietnam.

As this strategy proved ineffective, however, Nixon decided to accelerate the "Vietnamization process," only to find that, as U.S. troops were withdrawn, the South Vietnamese were unable to take up the slack. The war was being lost, and Nixon turned from diplomacy to force, by striking at Communist supply and staging areas in Cambodia. This incursion into an ostensibly neutral Buddhist nation brought angry protests at home, including a demonstration at Kent State University in Ohio on May 4, 1970, which resulted in the killing of four unarmed students and the wounding of nine more when inexperienced National Guardsmen opened fire on them. After Kent State, 100,000 demonstrators descended on Washington, and Congress registered its own protest by rescinding the Gulf of Tonkin Resolution. Under pressure, Nixon withdrew ground troops from Cambodia, but stepped up bombing raids.

Yet the Nixon administration also continued to withdraw U.S. ground forces from Vietnam. While this eased dissension on the home front, it destroyed military frontline morale. Drug and alcohol abuse assumed epidemic proportions among troops, some of whom were openly rebellious and even mutinous. When peace talks faltered, President Nixon, freshly reelected to "four more years," ordered massive B-52 bombing raids north of the twentieth parallel, which forced the North Vietnamese back to the conference table. On January 31, 1973, the United States and North Vietnam signed the Paris Accords, which finalized U.S. withdrawal and the return of prisoners of war, some of whom had been languishing in North Vietnamese prisons for nearly a decade.

The Nixon administration continued to send massive amounts of aid to South Vietnam, and it even resumed bombing Cambodia to intimidate the North Vietnamese into observing the cease-fire. Congress, however, was war weary and had turned against President Nixon, whose administration was now deeply mired in the Watergate Scandal. In November 1973, the War Powers Act was passed, precisely to prevent another Gulf of Tonkin Resolution. The act required the president to inform Congress within forty-eight hours of deployment of U.S. military forces abroad and mandated troop withdrawal within sixty days if Congress did not approve. Congress also ruthlessly slashed aid to South Vietnam. Whatever hopes South Vietnam's President Nguyen Van Thieu held out for support from the Nixon administration were extinguished when Nixon, facing impeachment, resigned in August 1974.

The Pentagon Papers

I n 1967, Lyndon Johnson's Secretary of Defense, Robert Mc-Namara, commissioned a top-secret study by members of the Rand Corporation, an ultra-high-level political and policy "think tank." Officially titled *The History of the U.S. Decision Making Process in Vietnam,* the forty-seven-volume study traced the history of America's involvement in and conduct of the Vietnam War. The fully documented, excruciatingly detailed story was one of deliberate deceit, illegal covert action, and simple confusion, extending from the administration of Harry S. Truman to that of Lyndon Johnson and hopelessly miring the United States in a tragic war.

Daniel Ellsberg, an MIT professor who had collaborated on the study, leaked the massive work to the *New York Times,* which, on June 13, 1971, began publishing a series of articles based on it. Popularly dubbed *The Pentagon Papers,* it created a national sensation. At the behest of the Nixon White House, the U.S. Department of Justice obtained a court injunction against further publication on national security grounds, but, on June 30, the Supreme Court ruled that constitutional guarantees of a free press overrode other considerations, and allowed further publication. The government indicted Daniel Ellsberg in 1971 and a colleague, Anthony J. Russo, on charges of espionage, theft, and conspiracy, but, in 1973, a federal judge dismissed all charges against them due to improper government conduct.

The vindication of the *New York Times,* Ellsberg, and Russo were all triumphs of the U.S. Constitution and, therefore, heartening. But the revelations of *The Pentagon Papers* were profoundly disturbing, creating a picture of what had been, in effect, a shadow government operating outside of the Constitution virtually since the end of World War II.

1972

The Watergate Break-in

June 17, 1972, should have been like any other day in the re-election campaign of Richard M. Nixon—upbeat, since the president's victory seemed a sure thing. But that night, Washington, D.C., police officers were summoned by a security guard to the prestigious Watergate apartment and office complex to stop a burglary in progress. The target was the headquarters of the Democratic National Committee.

At first, the story was buried in the local news—until it was revealed that the five burglars were employees of the Nixon campaign's Committee to Re-elect the President, an organization better known by its remarkable acronym: CREEP. As burglars, they were amateurs, but as espionage agents they were, in varying degrees, pros, members of an unofficial White House unit dubbed the "Plumbers," because they had been formed in 1971, at the behest of Richard Nixon himself, to plug "leaks"—not the kind of leaks that might pose a national security risk, but the kind that might be embarrassing to the president and his administration. The Plumbers' first mission, in 1971, had been to burglarize the office of Daniel Ellsberg's psychiatrist. Ellsberg was the man who had leaked *The Pentagon Papers* to the *New York Times,* and the Nixon White House was desperate to obtain material that might discredit him. The following year, at the Watergate, the Plumbers attempted to tap the telephones of Democratic leaders and to obtain documents outlining the Democratic campaign strategy.

The five Watergate burglars included three anti-Castro Cuban refugees, all veterans of the ill-fated Bay of Pigs invasion, and James McCord, Jr., a former CIA agent and now "security" officer for CREEP, who reported directly to CREEP's director, John Mitchell, who had resigned as attorney general to become Nixon's campaign manager. In a lapse of security, one of the burglars carried in his pocket an address book with the name of E. Howard Hunt. A former CIA agent, Hunt had planned the Bay of Pigs operation and, by 1972, was a writer of pulpy spy novels as well as an assistant to Charles Colson, special counsel to President Nixon. What address did the burglar's little black book give for E. Howard Hunt? "The White House."

As the Watergate story gained national exposure, Mitchell declared that the "White House has had no involvement whatever in this particular incident," and President Nixon himself would later try to dismiss the episode as a "third-rate burglary." All through the summer and fall of 1972, elements of an ominous scandal broke in the press, mainly in the *Washington Post,* through the efforts of two dogged reporters, Bob Woodward and Carl Bernstein. Each revelation pointed more sharply to a conspiracy at the very highest levels of government. At last, in September, the burglars and two co-plotters—Hunt and former FBI agent G. Gordon Liddy (another CREEP operative, known for his almost flamboyant right-wing extremism)—were indicted on charges of burglary, conspiracy, and wiretapping. As each Nixon associate was convicted, each (except for Liddy) began to talk, and each word led investigators higher up the ladder of the executive branch of government.

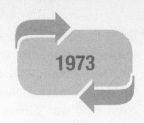

The Watergate Year

Despite the arrests and early revelations surrounding the Watergate burglary, Richard Nixon won election to a second term. No sooner had that term begun, however, than the unraveling of the Watergate conspiracy accelerated. In February 1973, the Senate created an investigative committee headed by North Carolina Senator Sam Ervin, Jr., and, as the Army–McCarthy Hearings had done two decades earlier, the televised Watergate Hearings commanded the rapt attention of the nation. A bizarre routine set in: After each shattering disclosure the committee produced, the president announced the resignation of another key aide. John Ehrlichman and H. R. Haldeman, his closest advisors, fell. The White House counsel, John W. Dean III, was dismissed. In the end, Senator Ervin, going about his questioning with the drawling, cunning persistence of a "country" lawyer educated at Harvard, elicited testimony uncovering malfeasance and crimes that reached far beyond a "third-rate burglary" at the Watergate. It was revealed that John Mitchell, while still attorney general, controlled secret monies used to finance a campaign of forged letters and false news items intended to damage the Democratic party. These were known as "dirty tricks," and the Nixon campaign used them extensively. The nation learned that major U.S. corporations had made illegal campaign contributions amounting to millions of dollars, that Hunt and Liddy were the burglars who had looted the office of Daniel Ellsberg's psychiatrist in order to discredit the *Pentagon Papers* whistle-blower and that they had plotted to assault Ellsberg physically. It was revealed that President Nixon had promised the Watergate burglars clemency and even bribes in return for their silence, and that L. Patrick Gray, Nixon's nominee to replace the recently deceased J. Edgar Hoover as head of the FBI, illegally surrendered FBI records on Watergate to White House counsel John Dean. The Ervin committee discovered that two Nixon cabinet members, Mitchell and Maurice Stans, took bribes from John Vesco, a shady financier with ties to organized crime. Witnesses testified that illegal wiretap tapes were in the White House safe of Nixon advisor John Ehrlichman, that Nixon had directed the CIA to instruct the FBI not to investigate Watergate, that Nixon used $10 million in government funds to improve his personal residences, and—not least of all—that during 1969–1970, the United States had secretly bombed Cambodia without the knowledge, let alone the consent, of Congress.

As if Watergate weren't debacle enough, in the midst of it all, Vice President Spiro T. Agnew was indicted for bribes he had taken as Maryland governor. He resigned as vice president in October 1973 and was replaced by Congressman Gerald Ford of Michigan. Then came the final blows. When it was revealed that President Nixon not only had wiretap tapes, but also covert tapes of White House conversations, the committee subpoenaed them. The president sought to evade the subpoena by asserting "executive privilege" and withheld the tapes. He then ordered Attorney General Elliot L. Richardson to dismiss special Watergate prosecutor Archibald Cox. Richardson refused and resigned in protest. When his deputy, William Ruckelshaus, also refused to fire Cox, he, too, was dismissed. Nixon's solicitor general, Robert H. Bork, did not share the scruples of Richardson and Ruckelshaus. Bork discharged Cox. All of this—the resignation of Richardson, the firing of Ruckelshaus, and the dismissal of Cox—took place on the evening of October 20, 1973, and was dubbed by the press the "Saturday night massacre." It spoke volumes about a man who had much to hide.

1974

President Nixon Resigns

By the summer of 1974, President Richard Nixon had run out of legal options for blocking the release to Congress of secret audiotapes made in the White House. He released transcripts of some of the tapes—except for a suspicious eighteen and a half minutes—and, after reviewing the material during July 27–30, the House Judiciary Committee delivered its recommendation that the president be impeached on three charges: obstruction of justice, abuse of presidential powers, and attempting to impede the impeachment process by defying committee subpoenas.

Nixon released the remaining tapes on August 5, 1974, which revealed unequivocally that he had taken steps to block the FBI's inquiry into the Watergate burglary. Four days later, on August 9, 1974, in a televised announcement, Richard Milhous Nixon became the first president in American history to resign from office.

In the end, all of the Watergate conspirators, save Nixon, were convicted, and all of them, save Nixon, went to jail. Nixon's successor, President Gerald Ford, presented the former chief executive with a preemptive pardon, for all crimes committed or that "may have been" committed.

In the decades following the scandal, Richard Nixon persisted in attempts to minimize the gravity of Watergate, protesting that he had neither planned nor ordered the "third-rate burglary," and that his political enemies had used it as a pretext for hounding him out of the White House. Indeed, to a remarkable degree, the Nixon of later years did rehabilitate his image and was viewed by many as an elder statesman. Even those who deplored Watergate and the White House policies that had spawned it, were inclined

From President Nixon's national television address,
August 9, 1974:

". . . I have never been a quitter. To leave office before my term is completed is abhorrent to every instinct in my body. But as President, I must put the interests of America first. America needs a full-time President and a full-time Congress, particularly at this time with problems we face at home and abroad. . . .

"Therefore, I shall resign the Presidency effective at noon tomorrow. Vice President Ford will be sworn in as President at that hour in this office. . . .

"I regret deeply any injuries that may have been done in the course of the events that led to this decision. I would say only that if some of my judgments were wrong—and some were wrong—they were made in what I believed at the time to be the best interest of the Nation. . . ."

to remind their fellow Americans that, whatever else he may have done, it was Nixon who started down the road to détente with the Soviets, who inaugurated nearly cordial relations with Communist China, and who led the United States to the conclusion of the war in Vietnam. Yet it is impossible to overlook the Richard Nixon whose imperious contempt for the Constitution and solemn oath to uphold it drove him to corrupt the legitimate electoral process, to seek the expansion of executive power far beyond constitutional limits, and to subvert nothing less than the American legal system.

Evacuation of Saigon

The year 1975 brought one South Vietnamese defeat after another. President Thieu resigned, leaving the presidency to Duong Van Minh, whose single official act was unconditional surrender to the North on April 30, 1975. This was followed by a frenzied evacuation of remaining U.S. personnel, and the American television audience was stunned by the spectacle of hundreds being airlifted by helicopter from the roof of the U.S. embassy in Saigon. It was a humiliating and heartbreaking end to a war that had cost the nation more than $150 billion and 58,000 American lives, not to mention a degree of faith in the righteous might of the United States. By any tactical measure, the Vietnam War was actually a victory for United States forces. If almost 60,000 Americans had been killed, millions of North Vietnamese, Viet Cong, and other hostile troops had died. Yet, strategically and—even worse, as many Americans saw it—morally, Vietnam stood as the only major military defeat in the history of the United States.

1979

Three Mile Island

T he close of the 1970s was a time of discontent throughout America. The nation was suffering a prolonged recession aggravated by inflation—an economically distressing situation dubbed "stagflation"—and there was a growing, dispiriting sense that the nation's best days were behind it. The infrastructure of America, especially in the cities, seemed to be crumbling—roads in poor repair, bridges abandoned as unsafe—crime was on the rise, and even that great symbol of American industrial know-how and American personal freedom, the automobile, was under attack. The domestic auto industry was rapidly losing ground to Japanese imports, which were better built, more reliable, more efficient, and cheaper than many of their American counterparts.

One of the most frightening events of this period not only forced Americans to question their faith in made-in-the-U.S.A. technology, but seemed symbolic of the decline of American power and competence. On March 28, 1979, a nuclear reactor at the Three Mile Island electric generating plant, near the Pennsylvania capital of Harrisburg, lost coolant water, which initiated a partial "meltdown" of the reactor's radioactive core. A badly shaken Pennsylvania governor Richard Thornburgh appeared on television to warn residents to remain indoors, and he advised pregnant women to evacuate the area, because the partial meltdown had already released some radioactive gases into the atmosphere. For several days, Pennsylvania and the nation watched with great anxiety as efforts to correct the problem slowly succeeded and the danger of a nuclear "meltdown" receded.

In retrospect, there is ample evidence that plant officials improperly delayed notifying public authorities of the accident, and it is clear that a combination of human and mechanical error nearly created a catastrophe of a magnitude unprecedented in the United States. Yet it is also true that backup safety features in the plant functioned as they were supposed to. That, however, was not sufficient to keep Three Mile Island from looking like yet another in a train of dismal failures of American industry, technology, and competence. The accident all but killed the nuclear power industry in the United States, and it deepened the already yawning credibility gap between the officers of big business and ordinary Americans.

Iran Hostage Crisis

T he radical Islamic cleric and political leader Ayatollah Ruhollah Khomeini successfully led a revolution in Iran that ousted longtime U.S. ally Muhammad Reza Shah Pahlavi, the shah of Iran, who fled into exile in January 1979. In October, critically ill with cancer, the shah was invited to travel to the United States to receive specialized medical treatment. This invitation inflamed the leading radical element in Iran and, on November 4, some 500 Iranians stormed the U.S. embassy in Tehran. There they took 66 U.S. embassy employees hostage, demanding for their release nothing less than the return of the shah.

The policy of the United States was not to bargain with terrorists, and, besides, President Jimmy Carter was not about to deliver to certain death a leader who had been a faithful ally. The shah left the United States on his own initiative in early December, but this did not end the crisis. Except for thirteen hostages, who were black or female, released on November 19–20, the others remained in captivity. Stalemated, President Carter authorized a U.S. Army Special Forces unit to attempt a rescue. The mission was hurriedly cobbled together and launched on April 24, 1980. After a series of mishaps, culminating in a disastrous collision between a helicopter and a transport plane, the mission was aborted. Fortunately, the failure did not result in reprisals against the hostages, but it seemed just one more humiliating defeat for a superpower unaccountably rendered impotent.

Day after day, week after week, month after month, the hostage crisis dragged on. It was not until November 1980 that the Iranian parliament proposed new conditions for the release of the hostages. These included an American pledge to refrain from meddling in Iranian affairs, the release of Iranian assets frozen in the United States by President Carter, the lifting of all U.S. sanctions against Iran, and the return of the shah's property to Iran. An agreement was concluded early in January 1981, as President Carter, having lost his bid for reelection to the buoyant Ronald Reagan, approached the end of his term. In an act most certainly of personal vengeance and contempt, the Ayatollah Khomeini delayed the actual release of the hostages until January 20, the very day of Ronald Reagan's inauguration. To President Reagan's enduring credit, he bestowed on Carter the honor of traveling to a U.S. air base in West Germany as his special envoy to welcome the returning hostages. They had endured 444 days of captivity, at gunpoint, and always under threat.

The Cold War Ends

On December 25, 1991, Mikhail Gorbachev resigned as president of the Union of Soviet Socialist Republics. In point of fact, by this time, Gorbachev was a president with neither a party (the Communist Party had effectively dissolved) nor a nation (many of the "republics" that had formed the Soviet Union had declared independence, and those that remained re-formed themselves into the Commonwealth of Independent States). On that momentous day in Russian history, a long chapter of American history also closed. Since the end of World War II, much of our history had been defined by the "Cold War" against communism, which, most of the time, meant a Cold War against the Soviet Union. Now, suddenly, that opposition ideology and force against which the United States had for so long defined itself was gone.

The collapse of the Soviet Union was sudden, but the Soviet system bore within itself the seeds of its own destruction. It may well be impossible for any state to forcibly hold and sustain its people in a demand economy when the nature of human society embraces free-market capitalism. Certainly, Gorbachev did not set out to hasten the end of Soviet communism. Quite the contrary, he sought to preserve it by reforming it. When he succeeded Konstantin Chernenko as general secretary of the Communist Party of the Soviet Union after Chernenko's death in 1985 (in the USSR, leadership of the party entailed de facto leadership of the government), Gorbachev was, at fifty-four, the youngest party head ever. In contrast to his much older predecessors, he was willing to confront the reality that the Soviet economy was stagnant and therefore doomed. He called for a crash program of technological innovation and increased productivity from a workforce that, guaranteed an income, had become apathetic. He moved aggressively to streamline the doddering complexity of the Soviet bureaucracy. Yet even as he carried out his reforms, Gorbachev realized that they were insufficient, and so, during 1987–1988, he instituted two vast initiatives: *glasnost* ("openness") and *perestroika* ("restructuring"). Under traditional communism, culture and government had been paranoically closed and secretive. All news was stringently filtered through party channels, paramountly *Pravda* ("Truth"), the party newspaper. Now, in a single stroke, the press was given vastly expanded access to information and was encouraged to report the news fully and with candor. Equally significant was the opening of at least certain elections to multiple candidates, not just the individuals handpicked by the party. New laws began to open the Soviet economy to private enterprise and free-market mechanisms. This last reform was the principal thrust of *perestroika*.

While the Soviet Union was experiencing the tremors that heralded its demise, Germany, ever since the end of World War II divided into a communist East and a democratic West, moved toward reunification. East Germany had come into being as a puppet of Moscow, and Erich Honecker, the communist functionary who assumed leadership of East Germany in 1971, was content to keep things that way—at first. But when the western democracies—including, ultimately, West Germany—extended to East Germany long-withheld recognition as a sovereign nation, Honecker started to navigate a more liberal course, hesitantly, clumsily, and grudgingly opening up East Germany to the West. Spiritually and politically, the Berlin Wall—that brick, mortar, and barbed-wire symbol of the division between Free World and Communist World—was coming down.

The actual wall had stood since 1961. It was built because, since 1949, when East Germany was created, some 2.5 million East Germans had fled to the West. After erection of the wall, about 5,000 East Germans managed somehow to overcome the

barrier and reach West Berlin, but at least 5,000 more were captured and 191 killed. By the 1970s, increased contact between
East and West heightened the discontent of East Germans, who
saw how meanly they lived, compared to those on the other side of
the wall. Honecker sought to reverse his own liberal reforms, but
as the volume of protest increased, he executed a new about-face
in the 1980s, this time even allowing East Germans to visit the
West. In October 1989, the East German politburo replaced Honecker with Egon Krenz. Although he was a hard-line communist,
Krenz yielded to the impossibility of controlling the flow of
refugees, and so opened East Germany's borders. On either side of
the Berlin Wall, East and West Germans began physically tearing
it down, brick by brick.

The symbolic dismantling of communism was counterpointed
to its collapse throughout eastern Europe, and the fall of the Berlin
Wall was the death blow for the Soviet Union. Mikhail Gorbachev
repudiated the so-called "Brezhnev Doctrine," promulgated by
Leonid Brezhnev (president of the Soviet Union from 1977 to
1982), asserting the right of the USSR to crush any uprisings
within Soviet satellite nations. As soon as Gorbachev put an end to
this policy, many of the Soviet republics declared themselves sovereign or independent.

Gorbachev scrambled to renegotiate relations with the fifteen Soviet republics, nine of which agreed to a new union treaty, but hard-line Soviet Communists organized a coup d'etat on August 19, 1991, and attempted to take back the government from Gorbachev. In Moscow, Boris Yeltsin, president of the Russian republic, led the resistance against the coup, which collapsed within days of its beginning. On December 25, 1991, what had been the Soviet Union and what was now a smaller Commonwealth of Independent States was in the hands of Boris Yeltsin. America's Cold War enemy had not surrendered. It had crumbled, evaporated, vanished, and the United States stood as the one great superpower of the post–Cold War world.

Impeachment of Bill Clinton

On September 11, 1998, the Republican-controlled U.S. Congress published on the Internet the full text of a report written under the direction of Kenneth Starr, an "independent counsel" appointed to investigate allegations of possibly impeachable offenses committed by President Bill Clinton. Millions of Americans were free to read laboriously detailed accounts of the president's sexual liaison with a twenty-one-year-old White House intern, Monica Lewinsky.

The "Starr Report" was the culmination of a four-year, $40-million-plus investigation into a number of questionable aspects of Clinton's conduct. It had begun as an inquiry into the involvement of the president and first lady in a shady real estate undertaking known as Whitewater (a name that coincidentally echoed the culminating scandal of the Nixon presidency, Watergate) and other possible financial improprieties. When Starr failed to find evidence of wrongdoing in these areas, he focused instead on the President's sexual behavior, creating a luridly documented account of Clinton's affair with Lewinsky. The details notwithstanding, Starr and the other investigators insisted that sex was not the issue in question. The issue, they claimed, was that the president had violated his oath of office by lying about the affair in a sworn deposition he had given in a sexual harassment civil lawsuit brought against him by a former Arkansas state employee, Paula Jones. It was alleged that the president had also lied about the affair to a grand jury.

Based on the Starr Report, Congress voted, along strict party lines, to impeach President Clinton, and, for the first time since

Andrew Johnson was impeached in 1868, the U.S. Senate was the scene of an impeachment trial.

Although Republicans held a simple majority of Senate seats, removal of a president from office requires more: a two-thirds Senate vote. Because no one believed that such a vote would be forthcoming, the months of congressional proceedings that followed made for engrossing television, but also struck many Americans as a time-wasting exercise in partisan vindictiveness. True, the American people generally deplored President Clinton's unbecoming behavior and were often vocal in their criticism of his character, yet they also overwhelmingly approved of his performance as a chief executive presiding over a booming economy. Most people believed that, even if true, the charges against the president did not "rise to the level" of removal from office, and even in the midst of the impeachment proceedings, public-opinion polls gave Clinton his highest approval ratings ever.

Heedless of popular sentiment, the Republican-controlled Congress pressed on with what members solemnly called their "constitutional duty." Nevertheless, on February 12, 1999, to no one's surprise, the Senate acquitted the president, and a potentially momentous national event receded into the media circus that had all along surrounded it, only to fade from the airwaves and the printed page—and, apparently, the consciousness of the American public.

2000

The Supreme Court "Elects" a President

The lackluster presidential campaign of the year 2000 pitted Democrat Al Gore against Republican George W. Bush, the son of President Bill Clinton's predecessor, George H. W. Bush. Few were enthusiastic in their support of either candidate, who differed so little from one another that third-party spoiler Ralph Nader referred to them as Tweedle-Dee and Tweedle-Dum, and the election ended as too close to call. The first complete returns gave Gore 50,996,116 votes against Bush's 50,456,169. Gore led by a margin of more than half a million votes, but it is the electoral college that puts a president into office, and it was soon apparent that the election hinged on who would capture the twenty-five electoral votes of Florida.

In that state, which happened to be governed by candidate Bush's younger brother, Jeb, the vote was stupefyingly close. The tally on the day after the election gave Bush a lead of 1,784 votes over Gore, but Florida law required an automatic recount of votes when the difference between totals was less than half a percent. The result of the automatic recount, reported on November 9, two days after the election, cut the Bush lead to 327 votes. Three hundred twenty-seven votes would determine who would next occupy the White House and who would hold the reins of the most powerful government on the planet.

In an automatic recount, the ballots were simply run through the vote-counting machines a second time. (It was later revealed that, in some counties, the actual rerun of votes never took place; officials just rechecked tally-sheet totals.) Deeming the automatic recount insufficient, Democrats demanded a recount by hand in four counties: Palm Beach, Miami-Dade, Broward, and Volusia—all counties in which the Gore camp expected that a manual recount would net the vice president more votes. Why make such an assumption? After all, in the twenty-first century, in the most technologically sophisticated nation in the world, how could one fail to trust that the machines would do an accurate job of such a simple task as counting votes?

In Palm Beach County, a long list of candidates for local office had prompted election officials to design a ballot with enough space to accommodate all the names. The result was a punch-hole ballot consisting of two facing pages, a so-called butterfly ballot. The trouble with this design was that while the punch hole for Bush appeared directly to the right of his name, the punch hole below belonged to right-wing extremist Patrick J. Buchanan. In third place was the punch hole for Gore. Immediately following the election, officials were flooded with calls, mostly from elderly Jewish voters, who, confused by the butterfly ballot, claimed to have realized (*after* voting) that they had mistakenly punched the hole for Buchanan—widely believed to be an anti-Semite—when they had meant to vote for Gore. Democrats wanted this investigated.

In Palm Beach and the other three counties, Democrats were also concerned that many of the punch-card ballots were faulty, that votes were not counted simply because voters had not pushed the stylus all the way through the card. If a punch-out wasn't clean, the resulting hole could be blocked by a tiny rectangular fragment of cardboard—called a "chad"—and the vote would not be counted. Florida law required election officials to evaluate disputed ballots in a way that attempts to "determine the intention" of the voter. Democrats wanted each ballot inspected for "hanging chad." Where this was found, a vote should be counted. Some Democrats called for even more: an inspection for what was called (incredibly enough) "pregnant chad," chad that had not been punched out on *any* of its four sides, but bulged—evidence that some stylus pressure had been applied. Now it seemed as if the fate of the nation and the free world rested on a few infinitesimally small pieces of scrap cardboard.

On November 11, candidate Bush filed a federal lawsuit to stop the manual recounts. The court rejected the suit, even as Katherine Harris, Florida's secretary of state, declared that she intended to certify the election—with Bush as winner—on the legal deadline for certification, November 14, and that, in her official opinion, manual recounts should not be permitted. Gore supporters in Florida and across the nation were not a little concerned that Harris, the state's top election official, was not only a Republican, but had served as a Bush delegate to the Republican National Convention and was one of eight cochairs of the Bush campaign in Florida.

Over the next several days, manual counts started and stopped in the disputed counties, and a battle raged in the Florida courts, with one legal decision countering another. At last, Secretary of State Harris denied a request from Palm Beach County for more time to complete its recount, and, on Sunday, November 26, certified George W. Bush as the winner in Florida by 537 votes.

The certification of the Florida vote did not end the battle, however. On December 1, the U.S. Supreme Court began hearing arguments in Bush's appeal of a Florida Supreme Court decision to extend the deadline for certification, and on December 9, voting

Associate Justice Stephen Breyer was one of four U.S. Supreme Court justices who dissented from the majority decision overturning the order of the Florida Supreme Court to resume the manual recount of disputed ballots. This is from the conclusion of Breyer's dissenting opinion:

"... Although we may never know with complete certainty the identity of the winner of this year's Presidential election, the identity of the loser is perfectly clear. It is the Nation's confidence in the judge as an impartial guardian of the rule of law. ..."

five to four, the justices of the U.S. Supreme Court ordered the manual recount to stop. On December 12, the high court overturned the Florida Supreme Court, again by a five-to-four decision, thereby rejecting all further manual recounts. Al Gore conceded the election to George W. Bush on December 13.

Even for supporters of the winning candidate, the election of 2000 was largely a dispiriting and unnerving business. It spoke of voter apathy, it made many ask why candidates for the highest office in the land should be so uniformly unimpressive, and it suggested just how fragile the mechanics of democracy are. On the other hand, the nation swore in a president, the forty-third since 1789, and it did so without violence and without serious political protest.

2001

Terrorist Attacks on New York and Washington, D.C.

At 8:45 (EDT) on the morning of September 11, 2001, a Boeing 757 passenger jetliner (later identified as American Airlines Flight 11 out of Boston) exploded into the north tower of the 110-story World Trade Center in lower Manhattan. Live television pictures of the disaster were beamed across the nation and the world almost immediately, and millions stared in disbelief at the great gash in the gleaming steel skin of the building, evil black smoke roiling out of it. The news camera video was rolling when, at 9:03, a second 757, United Airlines Flight 175, also out of Boston, hit the as-yet-undamaged south tower.

Emergency workers, firefighters, and police officers rushed to the site. At 9:30, President George W. Bush, attending an education-related function in Sarasota, Florida, announced that the nation had suffered "an apparent terrorist attack."

But that attack was far from over.

At 9:40, for the first time in American history, the Federal Aviation Administration (FAA) shut down all United States airports. Three minutes later, American Airlines Flight 77 burrowed into the Pentagon, America's military headquarters. Two minutes after this, the White House was evacuated, and, back in New York, at 10:05, the south tower of the World Trade Center collapsed: 110 stories of steel, concrete, glass, and humanity suddenly folded in on itself amid a death-dealing cloud of billowing smoke and debris. Just five minutes later, in Arlington, Virginia, a section of the wounded Pentagon also fell in, and, at almost exactly that moment, United Airlines Flight 93 tore into the soil of rural Somerset

County, Pennsylvania, not far from Pittsburgh. At 10:28, the north tower of the World Trade Center collapsed, ejecting a monumental plume, as if it had been swallowed into a volcano.

How many lives were lost in the space of less than two hours? No one knew. Asked to speculate, New York mayor Rudolph Giuliani replied quietly, "More than any of us can bear." (Ultimately, the death toll would approach 3,000—devastating, but, miraculously, far lower than had been feared.)

President Bush was flown from Florida, not to the White House, but to a "secure location" at Barksdale Air Force Base, Louisiana, and, later, to Offutt Air Force Base, outside of Omaha, Nebraska, a facility built to withstand thermonuclear attack. He finally returned to the White House shortly before 7 P.M. By that time, another part of the World Trade Center, the forty-seven-story Building 7, had collapsed, and the media was reporting that the airplane downed in Pennsylvania had been headed for the White House or the United States Capitol.

Although no organization claimed responsibility for the attacks, it was soon discovered that all four aircraft had been hijacked by terrorists executing carefully planned suicide missions. Later, the nation learned that cellphone calls made by crew members and passengers on the doomed aircraft—calls made to airline supervisors, to 911 operators, and to family members—described how the terrorists had operated. Handguns are difficult to smuggle on board an airplane, so the hijackers used small knives and box cutters to take over the aircraft, break into the cockpit, kill or disable the pilots, and commandeer the controls. The first three planes hit their targets in rapid succession: the south tower of the World Trade Center, the north tower, the Pentagon. But by the time the fourth plane was being taken over, passengers who made cellphone calls were told of the attack on the World Trade Center. A group of passengers on that fourth plane decided to attempt to seize control. The result was a terrible crash—but a crash in Shanksville, Pennsylvania, and not at the White House or the Capitol.

"The First War of the Twenty-First Century"

As early as 4 P.M. on September 11, the day terrorism struck at the United States, CNN correspondent David Ensor reported that U.S. government officials had "good indications" that Osama bin Laden was involved in the attacks. Forty years old, heir to a great fortune, Yemenite by birth, Saudi by nationality, and now living in Afghanistan, bin Laden routinely financed and sponsored terrorist acts while enjoying the protection of Afghanistan's radical Islamic Taliban government. Osama bin Laden was the suspected mastermind behind the bombings of two U.S. embassies in 1998 and the attack on the U.S. guided missile destroyer *Cole,* in port at Yemen, on October 12, 2000. At least since the early 1990s, bin Laden had led al-Qaeda (Arabic for "The Base"), a center for training, coordinating, and financing Muslim terrorists in a jihad (holy war) directed against Israel, the West, and, above all, the United States. President Bush, addressing the nation at 8:30 in the evening, vowed to "make no distinction between the terrorists who committed these acts and those who harbor them." It was, in effect, a declaration of war, and the very next day the president remarked that "We have just seen the first war of the twenty-first century."

Following the September 11 attacks, American military forces were deployed to strategic positions from which they could readily attack Afghanistan. The Bush government launched an intense diplomatic effort to secure the support—and in some cases, the direct aid—of many nations in fighting what was frankly described as a *war* against terrorism. Even Islamic nations voiced their opposition to terrorism; several, including Afghanistan's neighbor, Pakistan, promised support for American action.

Without a formal declaration of war, the first air attack against the Taliban government was launched at 16:38 Greenwich Mean Time, October 7—nighttime in Afghanistan. Over the next several weeks, U.S. and some British aircraft bombed Taliban military targets. Small groups of U.S. and British ground forces worked with indigenous opposition to the Taliban and, by the end of the year, had almost completely taken control of the country. While many al-Qaeda and Taliban troops and leaders were killed or captured, Osama bin Laden remained at large.

Most Americans knew little about Afghanistan and were far more anxious over the fact that terrorism had penetrated the American homeland. FBI and other investigators quickly discovered that the suicide hijackers of the four September 11 flights, all of Middle Eastern origin, had trained in small American flight schools and had lived not in secret safe houses but in ordinary American motels and apartment complexes while hardening their bodies in neighborhood gyms. How many more terrorists were among us? American and international law enforcement agencies made many arrests and detained more than a thousand suspects on immigration violation.

In the meantime, on October 4, even before the war got under way in distant Afghanistan, U.S. health officials reported that a Florida man, a photo editor for a supermarket tabloid, had contracted anthrax—the only case in the United States since the 1970s. At first, authorities discounted any link between the infection and terrorism, but after the Florida man succumbed to the disease on October 5, a second instance of exposure was discovered on October 8, and a third on October 10. More followed, including the cutaneous anthrax infection of a personal assistant to the popular NBC news anchor Tom Brokaw. The infections were traced to letters laced with dry anthrax spores—clearly a "weaponized" form of the anthrax bacillus—and in the course of October, at least forty persons were found to have been exposed to anthrax. A minority of these became ill, either with the highly treatable cutaneous form of the disease or the far more lethal inhalation anthrax. One anthrax-laced letter reached the office of Senate minority leader Tom Daschle, and on October 17, thirty-one members of Daschle's staff tested positive for anthrax exposure. The Capitol and several Senate and House office buildings were temporarily shut down, but, by this time, the tainted letter (or perhaps other tainted mail) had contaminated a Washington, D.C., postal facility, fatally infecting two postal employees. Two additional fatal cases followed, and as of April 2003, the perpetrator or perpetrators remained at large.

It was not determined what relation, if any, the anthrax attacks bore to the terrorism of September 11, 2001.

As for the war against terrorism, it seemed to go well, both in Afghanistan and elsewhere, although, as of April 2003, Osama bin Laden remains at large. By late 2002, it became apparent that President Bush was targeting Iraq as the next theater of the war. Although no direct link was demonstrated between the repressive regime of Saddam Hussein and the events of 9/11, the Bush Administration argued that Saddam's possession of weapons of mass destruction required action. Key UN Security Council members opposed U.S. military intervention and favored a lengthy program of UN-led weapons inspections. Despite widespread opposition at home and abroad, U.S. and British forces invaded Iraq, beginning on March 20, 2003, with the avowed objective of removing Saddam Hussein and his two sons from leadership in Iraq.